A SPECIAL MESSAGE FROM THE AUTHORS

This workbook contains over 150 Learning Activities which we have used successfully with both elementary and secondary school teacher trainees in the courses we offer. Learning By Doing: Developing Teaching Skills is intended to be a supplementary textbook for use in courses in Educational Psychology, Methods, Guidance, and Human Relations where there is some focus on learning basic teaching skills. This workbook promotes these skills by presenting Learning Activities and by presenting a theoretical and/or research based Rationale for doing each Learning Activity.

Thus, this workbook is more than a compendium of Learning Activities and a specially designed set of worksheets for doing them--it is also a textbook in which important information is presented, not to "survey" the whole field of Educational Psychology and Methodology, but to provide students with a "knowledge base" for the Learning Activities they are doing to develop basic teacher skills.

This is not a competency-based (mastery learning) textbook, although some of the Learning Activities in it could be adapted to that purpose.

The Learning Activities in this textbook are not "games" but are meaningful learning experiences that promote the development of basic teaching skills in: communication, motivating students to learn, classroom discipline, learning and cognitive development, socialization, and curriculum.

TABLE OF CONTENTS

CHAPTERS OF LEARNING ACTIVITIES

CHAPTER 1

WHAT THIS BOOK IS ALL ABOUT

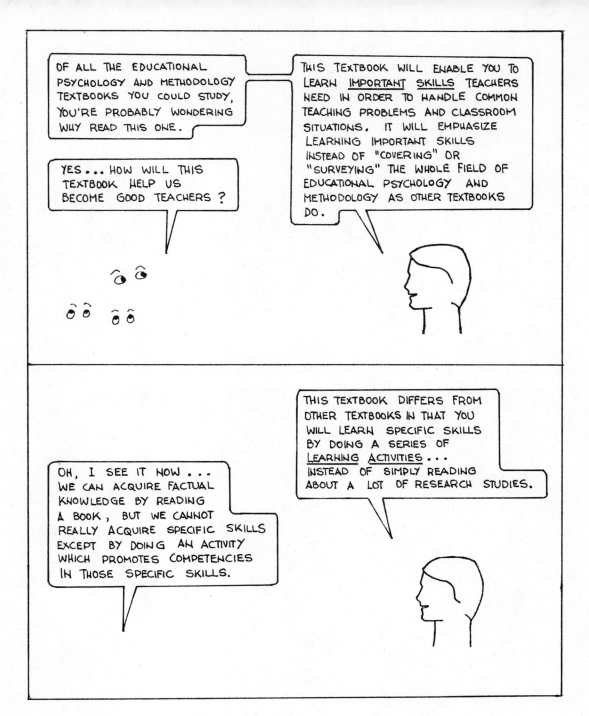

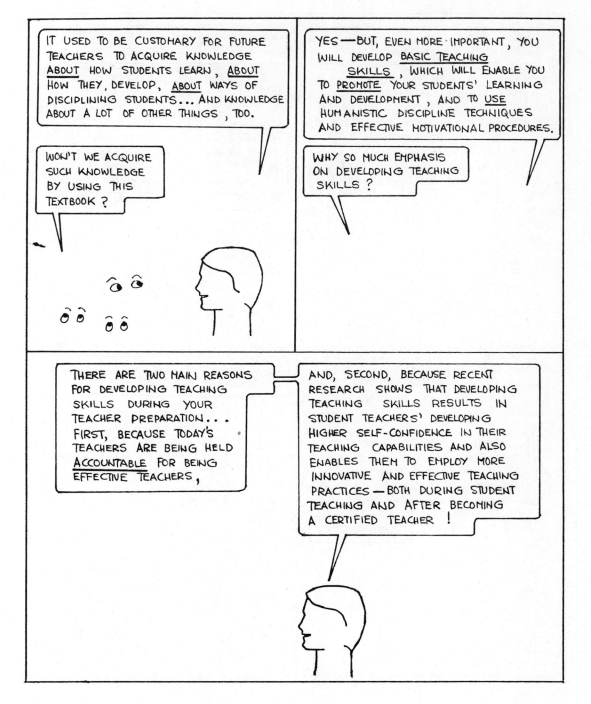

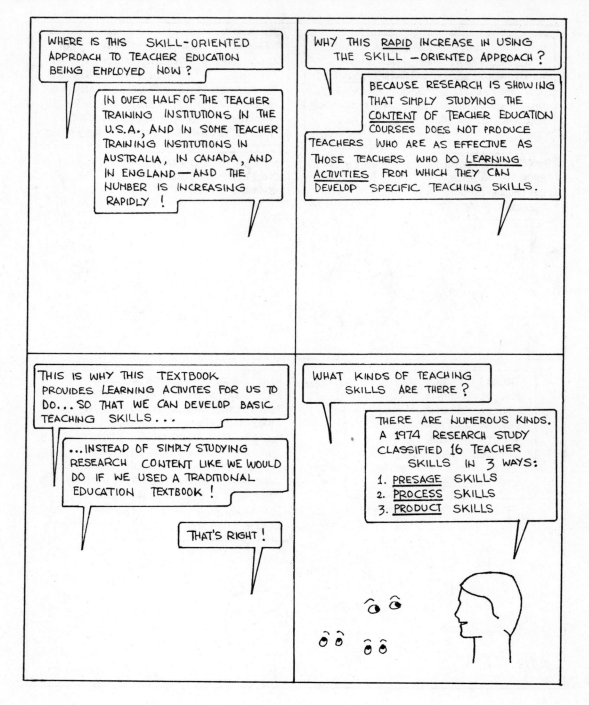

4

PRESAGE SKILLS REFER TO WHAT A TEACHER BRINGS TO THE TEACHING SITUATION — SUCH AS PERSONALITY OR INTELLECTUAL CHARACTERISTICS, KNOWLEDE OR PERFORMANCE ACHIEVED DURING TRAINING, AND INSERVICE CHARACTERISTICS SUCH AS YEARS OF TEACHING EXPERIENCE.

PROCESS SKILLS REFER TO WHAT HAPPENS IN THE CLASS DURING THE PROCESS OF TEACHING —SUCH AS TEACHERS' AND STUDENTS' BEHAVIORS, TEACHING METHODS, MATERIALS USED FOR LEARNING, AND CLASSROOM CONTROL TECHNIQUES.

PRODUCT SKILLS REFER TO THOSE EFFECTS A TEACHER PRODUCES ON STUDENTS —SUCH AS CHANGES IN STUDENTS' THINKING SKILLS, KNOWLEDGE OF SUBJECT MATTER, OR ATTITUDES TOWARDS LEARNING, SCHOOL, THEMSELVES, AND THEIR TEACHERS.

IT SOUNDS LOGICAL THAT THE EFFECTIVE TEACHER IS THE ONE WHO HAS PRODUCT SKILLS — i.e., CAN PRODUCE AN INCREASE IN STUDENTS' LEARNING OF SKILLS, KNOWLEDGE, AND ATTITUDES.

MOST PEOPLE DO THINK OF THIS CRITERION WHEN MEASURING THE EFFECTIVENESS OF TEACHERS...

BUT, A SURVEY OF 264 TEACHERS AND ADMINISTRATORS RATED THE "AMOUNT STUDENTS LEARN" AS ONLY THE ELEVENTH MOST IMPORTANT CRITERIA FOR JUDGING TEACHER EFFECTIVENESS OUT OF 16 CRITERIA PRESENTED.

WHAT WERE THE CRITERIA WHICH WERE RATED HIGHER?

MEAN RATINGS (OUT OF 9 POINTS) OF 16 TEACHING SKILLS
WHICH TEACHERS WOULD USE IN JUDGING A TEACHER'S EFFECTIVENESS

TEACHING COMPETENCIES	TYPE OF COMPETENCY	MEAN RATING
1. Relationship with class (good rapport)	Process	8.31
2. Willingness to be flexible, to be direct or indirect as situation demands	Presage	8.17
3. Effectiveness in controlling his class	Process	7.88
4. Capacity to perceive the world from the student's point of view	Process	7.79
5. Personal adjustment and character	Presage	7.71
6. Influence on student's behavior	Product	7.65
7. Knowledge of subject matter and related areas	Presage	7.64
8. Ability to personalize his teaching	Process	7.63
9. Extent to which his verbal behavior in classroom is student-centered	Process	7.27
10. Extent to which he uses inductive (discovery) methods	Process	6.95
11. Amount his students learn	Product	6.86
12. General knowledge and understanding of educational facts	Presage	6.43
13. Civic responsibility (patriotism)	Presage	6.25
14. Performance in student teaching	Presage	5.66
15. Participation in community and professional activites	Presage	4.88
16. Years of teaching experience	Presage	3.89

TYPE OF COMPETENCY	COMBINED MEAN RATING
Process Competency	7.64
Product Competency	7.26
Presage Competency	6.43

By permission of Jenkins, J.R. and Bausell, R.B. How Teachers View The Effective Teacher: Student Learning Is Not The Top Criterion. Phi Delta Kappan, Vol. LV, No. 8, April 1974, 572-573.

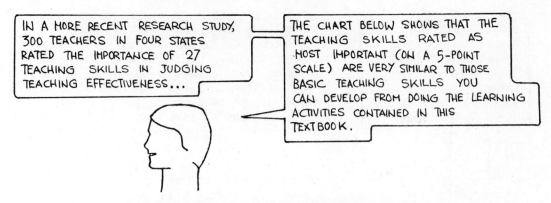

IN A MORE RECENT RESEARCH STUDY, 300 TEACHERS IN FOUR STATES RATED THE IMPORTANCE OF 27 TEACHING SKILLS IN JUDGING TEACHING EFFECTIVENESS...

THE CHART BELOW SHOWS THAT THE TEACHING SKILLS RATED AS MOST IMPORTANT (ON A 5-POINT SCALE) ARE VERY SIMILAR TO THOSE BASIC TEACHING SKILLS YOU CAN DEVELOP FROM DOING THE LEARNING ACTIVITIES CONTAINED IN THIS TEXTBOOK.

MEAN RATINGS (OUT OF 5 POINTS MAXIMUM) FOR 27 TEACHER
COMPETENCIES AS RATED BY 300 TEACHERS

TEACHER COMPETENCIES	MEAN RATING
1. Ability to develop learners who are self-motivated and capable of taking a major responsibility for directing their own learning.	4.70
2. Ability to arouse student interest in subject material.	4.69
3. Ability to promote positive student attitudes toward school and education.	4.66
4. Ability to diagnose individual learning difficulites.	4.59
5. Ability to organize material to promote student learning.	4.57
6. Ability to create awareness of and respect for fellow students.	4.51
7. Ability to organize classroom to promote student learning.	4.48
8. Ability to control disruptive situations effectively.	4.47
9. Ability to self-diagnose the instructional effectiveness of a lesson.	4.43
10. Ability to make the classroom an enjoyable place to spend time.	4.41
11. Ability to communicate facts and information to students.	4.38
12. Ability to help students develop their creativity.	4.33
13. Ability to be perceived by students as warm and concerned.	4.27
14. Ability to construct valid teacher-made tests to assess student learning.	4.20
15. Ability to use a variety of instructional aids in class activity.	4.19
16. Ability to cooperate with fellow teachers.	4.16
17. Ability to cooperate with school administrative staff.	4.12
18. Ability to aid in the social adjustment of students.	4.12
19. Ability to plan remediation activities.	4.08
20. Ability to communicate general facts and information to parents.	4.00
21. Ability to counsel students who are having personal problems.	3.97
22. Neatness and personal appearance of teacher.	3.83
23. Ability to explain a child's test score to his parents.	3.73
24. Ability to improve pupil performance on teacher-constructed tests.	3.59
25. Ability to carry out programs initiated by the principal.	3.58
26. Ability to contribute to committee work.	3.20
27. Ability to improve pupil performance on standardized tests.	2.84

By permission of Good, T.L., Coop, R., Dembo, M., Denton, J., and Limbacher, P.
How Teachers View Accountability. Phi Delta Kappan, Vol. LVI,
No. 5, January 1975, 367-368.

BOTH OF THESE RESEARCH STUDIES INDICATE THAT PRACTICISING TEACHERS WOULD EMPHASIZE <u>WHAT</u> TEACHERS AND STUDENTS <u>DO</u> IN THE CLASSROOM WHEN JUDGING TEACHER EFFECTIVENESS.

RIGHT! AND THAT'S WHY THIS TEXTBOOK EMPHASIZES DEVELOPING SKILLS WHICH WILL ENABLE TEACHERS TO <u>COMMUNICATE</u>, <u>INTERACT</u>, <u>MOTIVATE</u>, AND GENERALLY <u>RELATE</u> BETTER WITH THEIR STUDENTS... THIS EMPHASIS IS FURTHER SUPPORTED BY THE RESEARCH FINDINGS CITED BELOW AND ON THE NEXT PAGE.

RESEARCH FINDINGS ON THE IMPORTANCE OF DEVELOPING INTERPERSONAL
COMMUNICATION SKILLS

1. Teachers who displayed <u>high</u> levels of such interpersonal skills as empathy, genuineness, and positive regard for their students influenced their students to gain about 2½ <u>years</u> in academic achievement over the course of a year teaching them. In contrast, teachers who displayed a <u>low</u> level of such interpersonal competencies influenced their students to gain only six <u>months</u> in academic achievement.

2. The teachers displaying high interpersonal competencies influenced their students to gain 9 I.Q. points, an increase which was found to be statistically significant.

3. Teachers who displayed a high level of interpersonal warmth towards their students, significantly increased their students' achievement in vocabulary and mathematics, stimulated their interest in science and their creativity in writing poetry, and influenced them to produce a higher quality of art work.

4. The 1969 Coleman Report on the <u>Equality of Educational Opportunity</u> in the U.S.A. produced research findings which indicate that students' achievement is highly related to their <u>self-concept</u> (especially for whites and Oriental Americans), and to their <u>sense of control</u> over their environment (especially for blacks and other minority groups). These two student variables are optimally developed by teachers who show high levels of such interpersonal skills as empathy and respect for their students.

Continued

5. Teachers and student teachers can be systematically trained to develop their interpersonal communication competencies. A group of student teachers, who had been so trained, were rated by their classroom supervisors as significantly higher in total competency, in classroom management, in understanding children, in understanding the learning process, in using a democratic approach to motivation and discipline, and in using positive reinforcement in relating to their students. Overall, this group of student teachers evidenced superiority on 31 indices of teacher competency and student learning when compared to student teacher groups using an authoritarian, didactic approach to their students.

References:
1. Gazda, G.M., Asbury, F.R., Balzer, F.J., Childers, W.C., Deselle, E.R., and Walters, R.P. Human Relations Development: A Manual For Educators. Boston: Allyn and Bacon, 1973, pp. 13-16.

2. Gazda, George M. Systematic Human Relations Training in Teacher Preparation And Inservice Education. In H. Altman (Ed.), Readings In Human Relationships. Berkeley, California: McCutchan Publishing Company, 1972, pp. 117-122.

9

IT IS TRUE THAT MOST OF YOU HAVE BEEN TAUGHT BY A LECTURE METHOD OR HAVE LEARNED PRIMARILY FROM WHAT YOU HAVE READ IN A BOOK — BUT THIS KIND OF DIDACTIC (ONE-WAY) TRANSMISSION OF INFORMATION BY MEANS OF SPOKEN AND WRITTEN WORDS IS ONLY ONE WAY OF LEARNING.

WELL, TELL US WHAT KIND OF LEARNING WE WILL BE DOING.

IT IS CALLED "EXPERIENTIAL LEARNING" BECAUSE WHAT YOU LEARN COMES FROM WHAT YOU EXPERIENCE FIRST-HAND FOR YOURSELF RATHER THAN FROM WHAT SOMEONE ELSE TRANSMITS TO YOU IN SPOKEN OR WRITTEN WORDS...

IT IS ALSO CALLED "ACTIVE LEARNING" BECAUSE YOU WILL LEARN AS AN ACTIVE PARTICIPANT IN AN ACTIVITY OR EXPERIENCE RATHER THAN AS A "PASSIVE RECIPIENT" OF WHAT SOMEONE ELSE TELLS YOU IN SPOKEN OR WRITTEN WORDS.

IT SOUNDS LIKE THIS "EXPERIENTIAL LEARNING" GETS THE LEARNER ACTIVELY INVOLVED IN HIS OWN LEARNING.

THAT'S RIGHT! A RECENT SEVEN-YEAR RESEARCH STUDY HAS SHOWN THAT "ACTIVE LEARNING" IS NOT ONLY ENJOYABLE BUT CAN ALSO IMPROVE PEOPLE'S ATTITUDES, AND ENABLE THEM TO LEARN SPECIFIC SKILLS...

10

11

IT SOUNDS LIKE MRS. SMITH PROVIDED AN ACTIVE, CONCRETE LEARNING EXPERIENCE FOR YOU BY HAVING YOU USE COLORED RODS IN ORDER TO LEARN THE SKILLS AND CONCEPTS INVOLVED IN ADDING AND SUBTRACTING.

YEAH, I GUESS SHE DID... AND I REMEMBER REALLY ENJOYING IT BECAUSE I COULD UNDERSTAND WHAT SHE WAS TRYING TO TEACH ME.

MY GRADE 1 TEACHER DIDN'T HAVE US USE COLORED RODS — I RECALL HER STANDING AT THE CHALKBOARD TELLING US HOW TO ADD AND SUBTRACT .... BUT THAT'S ABOUT ALL.

THIS DISCUSSION HAS ILLUSTRATED MANY OF THE IMPORTANT DIFFERENCES BETWEEN CONVENTIONAL DIDACTIC LEARNING AND EXPERIENTIAL LEARNING... OTHER DIFFERENCES ARE PRESENTED ON THE NEXT PAGE.

THIS DISCUSSION HAS ALSO PROVIDED THREE MAIN REASONS FOR USING THIS TEXTBOOK...

FIRST, BECAUSE IT WILL GET US ACTIVELY INVOLVED...

SECOND, BECAUSE IT WILL ENABLE US TO DO SPECIFIC LEARNING ACTIVITIES WHICH WILL, IN TURN, ENABLE US TO EXPERIENTIALLY LEARN SPECIFIC SKILLS, SENSITIVITIES, AND KNOWLEDGE...

... AND, THIRD, BECAUSE THESE LEARNING EXPERIENCES WILL HELP US TO REMEMBER BETTER WHAT WE LEARN.

IT SOUNDS LIKE WE WILL LEARN SOME VERY USEFUL TEACHING SKILLS AS WE DO THE VARIOUS LEARNING ACTIVITIES IN THIS TEXTBOOK.

WHAT WILL A TYPICAL LEARNING ACTIVITY BE LIKE?

EACH LEARNING ACTIVITY STARTS WITH A STATEMENT OF "BEHAVIORAL AIMS" WHICH THAT ACTIVITY WILL PROMOTE.

<u>A COMPARISON OF TYPICAL SCHOOL LEARNING OF TRANSMITTED INFORMATION</u>

AND

<u>EXPERIENTIAL LEARNING THAT RESULTS FROM DOING LEARNING ACTIVITIES</u>

STEPS IN TYPICAL SCHOOL LEARNING OF TRANSMITTED INFORMATION	STEPS IN EXPERIENTIAL LEARNING ACTIVITIES FROM DOING LEARNING ACTIVITIES
STEP 1. RECEPTION OF TRANSMITTED INFORMATION requires the learner to understand the symbolic medium (e.g. words) through which the information is transmitted.	STEP 1. ACTING IN A SITUATION OR ACTIVITY so that the learner can observe the effects of his action in that situation (e.g. learning how to obtain his goals in that situation).
STEP 2. UNDERSTANDING THE GENERAL PRINCIPLE - i.e., taking in the information and interpreting its meaning so that a general principal is learned.	STEP 2. UNDERSTANDING THE PARTICULAR SITUATION - i.e., understanding the effects of one's actions, so that if a similar situation reappeared, one would know how to act in order to obtain one's goals.
STEP 3. UNDERSTANDING A PARTICULAR APPLICATION by seeing how a general principle applies in a particular situation.	STEP 3. UNDERSTANDING THE GENERAL PRINCIPLE under which the particular situation falls so that the learner will know how to act over a range of situations. (This is transfer of learning at its best).
STEP 4. ACTING or applying the general principle to a particular situation (i.e., using the information received in Step 1.)	STEP 4. ACTING IN A NEW SITUATION in such a way as to anticipate the effects of one's actions in a new situation when the general principle applies.

Continued

13

DISTINGUISHING CHARACTERISTICS OF INFORMATION LEARNING	DISTINGUISHING CHARACTERISTICS OF EXPERIENTIAL LEARNING
A. "Known knowledge" can be transmitted and learned more efficiently because a symbolic medium is used. However, some students experience a hurdle in translating the symbolic information to understandable action patterns.	A. Experiential learning is time-consuming because it requires repeated actions in a number of similar situations in order for the learner to "discover" the general principle.
B. General principles can be transmitted in "logical sequences" to assure logical understanding.	B. A discussion of Steps 1 and 2 is necessary for some students to be able to understand and articulate the general principle.
C. Step 4 - application of knowledge-is often not reached, thus the learner "has knowledge", but has not learned an application for it.	C. Application of knowledge begins in Step 1 and continues through Step 4.
D. External sources of motivation (e.g. grades, gold stars), are used to keep the learner learning symbolic information, which likely will not be used in school.	D. The learner is internally motivated to learn because he is actively doing something and learning useful knowledge.

(This chart is based on the following research study: J. S. Coleman,
S. A. Livingston, G. M. Fannersey, K. J. Edwards, and S. J. Kidder.
The Hopkins Games Program: Conclusions From Seven Years of Research.
Educational Researcher, Vol. 2, No. 8, August 1973, 3 - 7.)

15

CHAPTER 2

DEVELOPING SKILLS FOR COMMUNICATING MORE EFFECTIVELY

AIMS: 1.   To give class members a chance to know each other better in a non-threatening way.

            2.   To build trust between class members.

RATIONALE FOR DOING THIS ACTIVITY:

EVERYONE SEEMS SO UNFRIENDLY. NO-ONE HAS SPOKEN TO ME ONCE.
I DON'T KNOW ANYONE HERE, I WISH THIS CLASS WERE OVER.
WHAT'S THIS TEACHER GOING TO DO WITH US? SAME OLD BORING CHALK-TALK, I BET.
THERE'S NO WAY I'M GOING TO SPEAK OUT IN FRONT OF A BUNCH OF STRANGERS.
THIS CLASS SEEMS SO TENSE AND NERVOUS! I WISH THERE WAS SOMETHING I COULD DO TO HELP THEM LOOSEN UP AND FEEL MORE RELAXED ABOUT WORKING WITH EACH OTHER.
GOOD MORNING CLASS, MY NAME IS BOB AND I'M YOUR NEW TEACHER.
I INTRODUCED MYSELF TO THE CLASS AND TRIED TO ACT FRIENDLY, BUT EVERYONE SEEMED SO COLD AND STIFF — LIKE THEY WERE ALL SITTING IN A DENTIST'S OFFICE.

20

EXERCISES IN SECTION "A"	WORKSHEETS
1. Going Around The Circle	————
2. Paired Encounter	————
3. Personal Introductions	————
4. Twenty Questions	Twenty Questions Worksheet

TWENTY QUESTIONS WORKSHEET

<u>INSTRUCTIONS</u>: Place a sheet of paper over this page so that only one item
at a time is revealed. Take turns initiating responses to
items. Both participants should respond to the same items.

1. My name is ...

2. My nicknames are ...

3. I come from ...

4. Most of my life I lived in ...

5. My family consists of ...

6. I have travelled to ...

7. My favorite leisure activities are ...

8. My favorite T.V. programs are ...

9. What I like best about university is ...

10. What I like least about university is ...

11. When I join a new group I feel ...

12. If I had all the money I needed I would ...

13. What makes me really angry is ...

14. What makes me really happy is ...

15. The best thing about being a teacher is ...

16. The worst thing about being a teacher is ...

17. My most important values are ...

18. When I think of the future I see myself ...

19. Something unpleasant that happened to me recently was ...

20. Something pleasant that happened to me recently was ...

UNDERSTANDING THE IMPORTANCE OF FEEDBACK IN COMMUNICATION

AIMS: 1. To identify problems in understanding a one-way communication.

2. To identify the advantages of employing a two-way communication.

3. To identify school situations in which two-way communication is especially important.

RATIONALE FOR DOING THIS ACTIVITY :

24

BOB HAS DISCOVERED A BASIC PRINCIPLE OF EFFECTIVE COMMUNICATION——NAMELY, THAT WHEN A COMMUNICATION IS ONLY <u>ONE-WAY</u>, THE RECEIVER OF THE MESSAGE DOES NOT HAVE AN OPPORTUNITY TO FIND OUT IF HE OR SHE REALLY UNDERSTANDS WHAT BOB SAID, AND BOB (AS THE SENDER OF THE MESSAGE) CANNOT FIND OUT IF THE RECEIVER REALLY UNDERSTOOD THE MESSAGE HE SENT OR TRANSMITTED . . .

BOB HAS ALSO DISCOVERED THAT WHEN THE RECEIVER OF HIS MESSAGE IS GIVEN AN OPPORTUNITY TO <u>REPHRASE</u> WHAT HE OR SHE UNDERSTOOD BOB TO SAY, THE RECEIVER CAN CHECK WITH BOB TO FIND OUT IF HE OR SHE REALLY UNDERSTOOD BOB'S MESSAGE . . . AND BOB OBTAINS <u>FEEDBACK</u> FROM THE REPHRASING TO ENABLE HIM TO SEND A CLEARER MESSAGE IF NECESSARY... THIS IS CALLED A <u>TWO-WAY COMMUNICATION</u> BECAUSE BOTH THE SENDER AND RECEIVER OF A MESSAGE COMMUNICATE WITH EACH OTHER TO MAKE CERTAIN THAT "THE MESSAGE SENT IS THE MESSAGE HEARD".

NOW YOU WILL DO TWO EXERCISES TO FIND OUT FOR YOURSELF
(1) THE PROBLEMS IN UNDERSTANDING A ONE-WAY COMMUNICATION, AND
(2) THE ADVANTAGES IN EMPLOYING A TWO-WAY COMMUNICATION.

A ONE-WAY COMMUNICATION

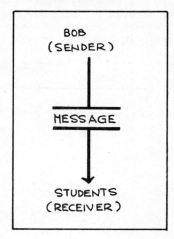

A TWO-WAY COMMUNICATION

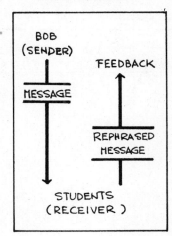

25

ONE-WAY/TWO-WAY COMMUNICATION WORKSHEET

INSTRUCTIONS:

Students working in pairs, will list on his/her own Worksheet: (A) the Problems Experienced In Doing The One-Way Communication Task, and (B) the Advantages of Receiving Feedback In Doing The Two-Way Communication Task.
Time: 10 minutes

A. PROBLEMS EXPERIENCED IN DOING THE ONE-WAY COMMUNICATION TASK

1.

2.

3.

4.

5.

6.

B. ADVANTAGES OF RECEIVING FEEDBACK IN DOING THE TWO-WAY COMMUNICATION TASK

1.

2.

3.

4.

5.

SITUATIONS FOR USING TWO-WAY COMMUNICATION WORKSHEET

INSTRUCTIONS:

    Students, working in pairs, list on their own Worksheet, all of the situations in which they (as teachers) need to employ two-way verbal communication with their students in order to prevent misunderstandings.

Time: 10 minutes

A. TEACHING SITUATIONS

B. DISCIPLINE SITUATIONS

C. SITUATIONS WITH CERTAIN TYPES OF STUDENTS

D. OUT-OF-CLASS SITUATIONS

QUESTIONS FOR CONSIDERATION:

A two-way verbal communication is especially required:

1. When teaching which subject areas?

2. When handling what type of discipline problem?

3. When communicating with what type of student?

4. In what out-of-class situation?

C IDENTIFYING INTERPERSONAL COMMUNICATION SKILLS

AIMS: 1. To discover your strongest and weakest interpersonal skills.

2. To develop skills in recognizing the 8 basic interpersonal skills.

RATIONALE FOR DOING THIS ACTIVITY:

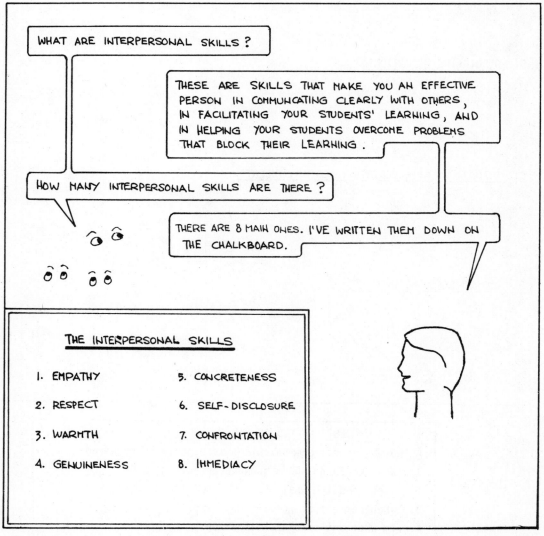

WHAT ARE INTERPERSONAL SKILLS ?

THESE ARE SKILLS THAT MAKE YOU AN EFFECTIVE PERSON IN COMMUNICATING CLEARLY WITH OTHERS, IN FACILITATING YOUR STUDENTS' LEARNING, AND IN HELPING YOUR STUDENTS OVERCOME PROBLEMS THAT BLOCK THEIR LEARNING.

HOW MANY INTERPERSONAL SKILLS ARE THERE ?

THERE ARE 8 MAIN ONES. I'VE WRITTEN THEM DOWN ON THE CHALKBOARD.

THE INTERPERSONAL SKILLS

1. EMPATHY
2. RESPECT
3. WARMTH
4. GENUINENESS
5. CONCRETENESS
6. SELF-DISCLOSURE
7. CONFRONTATION
8. IMMEDIACY

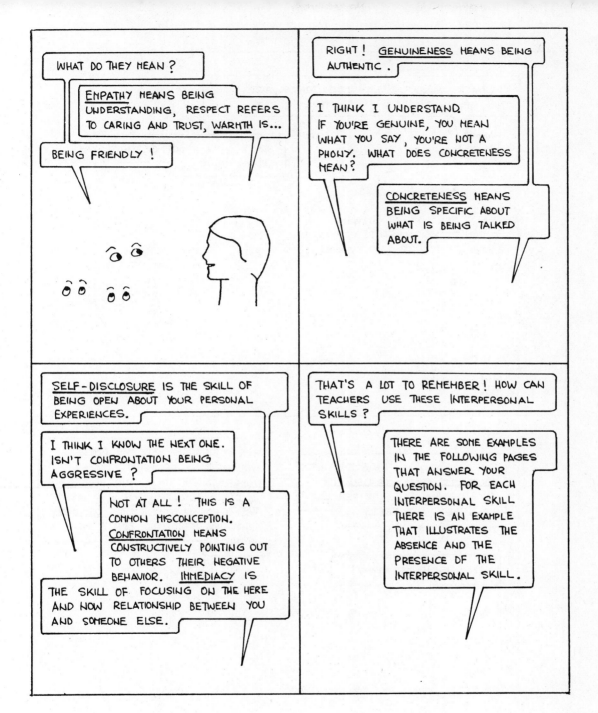

WHAT DO THEY MEAN?

EMPATHY MEANS BEING UNDERSTANDING, RESPECT REFERS TO CARING AND TRUST, WARMTH IS...

BEING FRIENDLY!

RIGHT! GENUINENESS MEANS BEING AUTHENTIC.

I THINK I UNDERSTAND. IF YOU'RE GENUINE, YOU MEAN WHAT YOU SAY, YOU'RE NOT A PHONY. WHAT DOES CONCRETENESS MEAN?

CONCRETENESS MEANS BEING SPECIFIC ABOUT WHAT IS BEING TALKED ABOUT.

SELF-DISCLOSURE IS THE SKILL OF BEING OPEN ABOUT YOUR PERSONAL EXPERIENCES.

I THINK I KNOW THE NEXT ONE. ISN'T CONFRONTATION BEING AGGRESSIVE?

NOT AT ALL! THIS IS A COMMON MISCONCEPTION. CONFRONTATION MEANS CONSTRUCTIVELY POINTING OUT TO OTHERS THEIR NEGATIVE BEHAVIOR. IMMEDIACY IS THE SKILL OF FOCUSING ON THE HERE AND NOW RELATIONSHIP BETWEEN YOU AND SOMEONE ELSE.

THAT'S A LOT TO REMEMBER! HOW CAN TEACHERS USE THESE INTERPERSONAL SKILLS?

THERE ARE SOME EXAMPLES IN THE FOLLOWING PAGES THAT ANSWER YOUR QUESTION. FOR EACH INTERPERSONAL SKILL THERE IS AN EXAMPLE THAT ILLUSTRATES THE ABSENCE AND THE PRESENCE OF THE INTERPERSONAL SKILL.

OH NO! I LOST MY TEXT BOOK AND ALL MY NOTES. AND THERE'S A TEST COMING UP. WHAT AM I GOING TO DO?

AM I EVER!

YOU'RE WORRIED THAT YOU'LL FAIL THE TEST IF YOU DON'T HAVE YOUR BOOKS TO STUDY FROM.

WELL, IF YOU CAN'T FIND YOUR TEXT, I HAVE A SPARE ONE YOU CAN BORROW. BUT FIRST, WHY DON'T WE PUT OUR HEADS TOGETHER AND SEE IF WE CAN FIGURE OUT WHERE YOU MIGHT HAVE LEFT YOUR BOOKS, MAYBE WE CAN FIND THEM.

HERE THE TEACHER SHOWS RESPECT FOR THE STUDENT'S PROBLEM BY TREATING IT AS SERIOUS AND WORTHY OF CONSIDERATION.

THAT LAST POINT IS A GOOD ONE. THE RESPECTFUL TEACHER NEVER ROBS HIS STUDENTS OF THEIR INDEPENDENCE BY JUST LAYING HIS SOLUTION ON THEM. THE TEACHER ALSO SHOWED RESPECT FOR THE STUDENT'S ABILITY TO SOLVE HER PROBLEM BY SUGGESTING THEY DISCUSS TOGETHER WHERE THE BOOKS MIGHT HAVE BEEN LOST.

I LIKED HIS RESPONSE: HE SHOWED HIS CARING FOR THE STUDENT BY BOTH ACTIVE LISTENING TO THE STUDENT'S FEELINGS AND SUGGESTING A WAY TO FIND THE LOST BOOKS.

THE RESPECTFUL TEACHER BELIEVES IN HIS STUDENT'S ABILITY TO SOLVE HIS OWN PROBLEMS. AND THIS FOSTERS RESPONSIBILITY, INDEPENDENCE, AND CONSTRUCTIVE PROBLEM SOLVING IN STUDENTS.

THIS HAS BEEN REALLY BOTHERING ME. MAYBE I CAN TALK IT OVER WITH BOB.

WHEN I GOT IN FRONT OF THAT CLASS FOR THE FIRST TIME, I WAS SO NERVOUS MY KNEES WERE SHAKING. I REALLY FELT BAD ABOUT IT. HAVE YOU EVER EXPERIENCED ANYTHING LIKE THAT?

THAT FIRST TIME I TAUGHT I WAS TERRIBLE. I FEEL SO INADEQUATE WHEN I THINK ABOUT IT. I'D DIE IF ANYONE KNEW ABOUT IT.

UH...ER...NO, NOT REALLY.

I BETTER SHUT UP. HE PROBABLY THINKS I'M A NUT!

THE AVOIDER NEVER SHARES REALLY PERSONAL EXPERIENCES WITH OTHERS.

HE AVOIDS GETTING PERSONAL.

YES. HE'S AFRAID HE'LL GET HURT IF HE REVEALS "WEAKNESSES" SO HE CLAMS UP. HE MISSES OUT ON A REAL CHANCE TO SHARE HIS EXPERIENCE AND HELP HIS FRIEND BY SHOWING THAT HE'S NOT ALONE IN HAVING THIS KIND OF EXPERIENCE. THE AVOIDER OFTEN FEELS VERY ALONE HIMSELF.

40

41

43

THE DEFLECTOR AVOIDS TALKING ABOUT WHAT IS GOING ON IN THE "HERE AND NOW" BETWEEN HIM AND THE PERSON HE IS TALKING WITH. HE "DEFLECTS" THE TOPIC AWAY FROM HIMSELF.

BECAUSE THE TEACHER AVOIDS DISCUSSING THE REAL IMMEDIATE CONCERNS THIS STUDENT HAS, THE STUDENT IS LEFT WITH HIS PROBLEM: THE FEELING THIS TEACHER IS UNFAIR. THE TEACHER MISSED A CHANCE TO HELP ALLAN RESOLVE HIS FEELINGS.

IN THIS EXAMPLE, THE STUDENT IS APPARENTLY TALKING ABOUT TEACHERS IN GENERAL, BUT HE'S REALLY SAYING SOMETHING ABOUT HIS FEELINGS TOWARDS HIS TEACHER.

IN THIS EXAMPLE, THE TEACHER RESPONDS WITH IMMEDIACY. HE ZEROS IN ON THE IMMEDIATE PROBLEM WHICH IS THE RELATIONSHIP BETWEEN HIM AND THE STUDENT AND NOT "TEACHERS IN GENERAL".

THE TEACHER DEMONSTRATED OPENNESS BY NOT DEFLECTING THE STUDENT'S CRITICISM AWAY FROM HIMSELF. NOW THAT THE REAL PROBLEM IS OUT IN THE OPEN, IT HAS A GOOD CHANCE OF BEING SOLVED.

I LIKED THE WAY THE TEACHER REFLECTED THE STUDENT'S FEELINGS AND THEN INVITED HIM TO TALK ABOUT THE TEACHER'S BEHAVIOR.

IN THE FOLLOWING EXERCISES YOU WILL FIND OUT WHAT YOUR OWN INTERPERSONAL SKILLS ARE AND LEARN TO IDENTIFY THESE SKILLS IN OTHERS.

INSTRUCTIONS:

1. For each of the statements below, place a check (✔) in the appropriate column to the right to indicate the extent to which you currently behave in the way described in the statement.

2. Next, go through the inventory again, this time placing an "x" in the appropriate column to the right of each of the statements below to indicate the extent to which you would ideally like to behave.

	ALWAYS	FREQUENTLY	OCCASIONALLY	SELDOM	NEVER
1. I accept others for who they are.					
2. When someone isn't being honest with me, I let him know how I feel about it.					
3. When I don't understand something someone is saying, I ask questions for clarification.					
4. When I am talking with someone and he seems annoyed with me, I will talk about it with him then and there.					
5. I am able to zero in on exactly what someone else is feeling.					
6. I confront people with the truth, even though it may be unpleasant for them to hear it.					
7. I don't like to be bothered with other people's problems.					
8. When someone is vague about what he is saying, I try to get him to be specific.					
9. I talk to others about the things that make me feel inadequate.					
10. I pretend to be happy, even though I'm upset.					
11. When someone is vague about what he is saying, I don't mind.					
12. I give others my advice, even though they may not want it.					
13. When someone I know is upset, I don't realize it.					
14. I am warm and friendly towards others.					
15. When talking with others, I tend to dominate the conversation.					

Continued

	ALWAYS	FREQUENTLY	OCCASIONALLY	SELDOM	NEVER
16. Rather than tell it like it is, I keep quiet.					
17. If someone feels angry with me, I get it "out in the open" and talk about it with him.					
18. I find it hard to open up and talk about myself.					
19. I encourage the person I am talking with to talk about what's happening between us "right now".					
20. I act like a phony, I put on a false front.					
21. I am affectionate towards others.					
22. When other people talk about their feelings, I sometimes feel a little uncomfortable listening to them.					
23. I tend to be cold and impersonal in my dealings with others.					
24. I can really "tune in" to what another person is feeling.					
25. I am cautious in revealing personal things about myself to others.					
26. When someone is "beating around the bush", I try and get them to come "right to the point".					
27. I like people.					
28. When someone I know is upset, I let him know that I know how he is feeling.					
29. I make others feel that I understand them.					
30. I give others immediate feedback on what I think is happening between us.					
31. I manipulate others to get what I want.					
32. When I express an opinion, I do so in a clear and precise way.					
33. When someone reveals an upsetting or embarrassing incident that happened to him, I share with him a similar incident that happened to me.					
34. I am non-assertive--I don't stand up for my rights.					

47

Continued

	ALWAYS	FREQUENTLY	OCCASIONALLY	SELDOM	NEVER
35. I find it hard to figure out what another person is feeling.					
36. I stretch the truth a little to avoid conflict with others.					
37. I get annoyed with people who disagree with me.					
38. I don't express many of my opinions to others because I am unsure how they will take it.					
39. When I am bored with what someone is saying, I pretend to be interested.					
40. If someone puts me down, I let him know how I feel about it.					
41. If someone feels angry with me, I tend to avoid him.					
42. I'm not interested in how other people feel.					
43. I comfort others when they are having problems.					
44. When someone contradicts himself, I point it out to him.					
45. When I disagree strongly with someone, I keep quiet to avoid conflict.					
46. I say to others, things like: "I like you", "I like being with you", "I enjoy your company".					
47. If someone feels upset with something I did, I encourage him to talk to me about it.					
48. If I don't understand something someone is saying, I just wait for him to say something that makes sense.					

SCORING KEY FOR THE INTERPERSONAL SKILLS INVENTORY

1. Transfer the "✓" and the "X" you just gave to each statement in the Interpersonal Skills Inventory onto this Scoring Key for each item below. For example: suppose for the first statement on the Interpersonal Skills Inventory, you placed a "✓" in the "Seldom" column, you will now place a "✓" in the "Seldom" column for item 2 on this Scoring Key. Similarly, if you placed an "X" in the "Always" column on the Inter-personal Skills Inventory, you will now place an "X" in the "Always" column for item 1 on this Scoring Key.

2. Each item below corresponds to one of eight types of Interpersonal Skills. Add up the eight "✓" scores you gave yourself for each type of Interpersonal Skill, and then place this total on the Results Sheet (on the next page) under "Current Skill Level" for that type of Inter-personal Skill. Also, add up the eight "X" scores you gave yourself for each type of Interpersonal Skill, and then place this total on the Results Sheet under the "Ideal Skill Level" for each type of Inter-personal Skill.

SCORING KEY FOR THE INTERPERSONAL SKILLS INVENTORY   EXERCISE #1

ITEM	ALWAYS	FREQUENTLY	OCCASIONALLY	SELDOM	NEVER	INTER-PERSONAL SKILL	ITEM	ALWAYS	FREQUENTLY	OCCASIONALLY	SELDOM	NEVER	INTER-PERSONAL SKILL
1	4	3	2	1	0	Res	25	0	1	2	3	4	S-D
2	4	3	2	1	0	Conf	26	4	3	2	1	0	Gen
3	4	3	2	1	0	Gen	27	4	3	2	1	0	Warm
4	4	3	2	1	0	Imm	28	4	3	2	1	0	Emp
5	4	3	2	1	0	Emp	29	4	3	2	1	0	Emp
6	4	3	2	1	0	Conf	30	4	3	2	1	0	Imm
7	0	1	2	3	4	Res	31	0	1	2	3	4	Cte
8	4	3	2	1	0	Gen	32	4	3	2	1	0	Gen
9	4	3	2	1	0	S-D	33	4	3	2	1	0	S-D
10	0	1	2	3	4	Cte	34	0	1	2	3	4	Conf
11	0	1	2	3	4	Gen	35	0	1	2	3	4	Emp
12	0	1	2	3	4	Res	36	0	1	2	3	4	Cte
13	0	1	2	3	4	Emp	37	0	1	2	3	4	Res
14	4	3	2	1	0	Warm	38	0	1	2	3	4	S-D
15	0	1	2	3	4	Res	39	0	1	2	3	4	Cte
16	0	1	2	3	4	Conf	40	4	3	2	1	0	Conf
17	4	3	2	1	0	Imm	41	0	1	2	3	4	Imm
18	0	1	2	3	4	S-D	42	0	1	2	3	4	Res
19	4	3	2	1	0	Imm	43	4	3	2	1	0	Warm
20	0	1	2	3	4	Cte	44	4	3	2	1	0	Conf
21	4	3	2	1	0	Warm	45	0	1	2	3	4	Cte
22	0	1	2	3	4	S-D	46	4	3	2	1	0	Warm
23	0	1	2	3	4	Warm	46	4	3	2	1	0	Imm
24	4	3	2	1	0	Emp	48	0	1	2	3	4	Gen

FOR THE INTERPERSONAL SKILLS INVENTORY

| Exercise #1 |

After transferring your score totals to this page, subtract scores for Current Skill Level from scores for Ideal Skill Level and place the difference in the last column.

INTERPERSONAL SKILL	IDEAL SKILL LEVEL	CURRENT SKILL LEVEL	IDEAL - CURRENT
EMPATHY (Emp)	24	24	
RESPECT (Res)	24	24	
WARMTH (Warm)	24	24	
GENUINENESS (Gen)	24	24	
CONCRETENESS (Cte)	24	24	
SELF-DISCLOSURE (S-D)	24	24	
CONFRONTATION (Conf)	24	24	
IMMEDIACY (Imm)	24	24	
TOTAL:			

INTERPRETATION OF TOTAL SCORE FOR CURRENT SKILL LEVEL

CURRENT SKILL LEVEL SCORE	INTERPRETATION
169 - 192	WOW! A truly facilitative teacher.
129 - 168	Superior - your students will really appreciate you.
97 - 128	Good - but room for improvement.
65 - 96	So - So.
33 - 64	Philistine.
0 - 32	Shouldn't be allowed near children.

INTERPERSONAL COMMUNICATION SKILLS WORKSHEET A

1. Think of a teacher you really disliked. Describe his/her typical behavior. (Give specific examples).

2. How did you feel towards this teacher? What effect did his/her behavior have on you in the classroom?

3. What interpersonal skills did the teacher lack?

Empathy	_____	Concreteness	_____
Respect	_____	Self-Disclosure	_____
Warmth	_____	Confrontation	_____
Genuineness	_____	Immediacy	_____

INTERPERSONAL COMMUNICATION SKILLS WORKSHEET B

1. Think of a teacher you really liked. Describe his/her typical behavior. (Give specific examples).

2. How did you feel towards this teacher? What effect did his/her behavior have on you in the classroom?

3. What interpersonal skills did the teacher have?

Empathy	_____	Concreteness	_____
Respect	_____	Self-Disclosure	_____
Warmth	_____	Confrontation	_____
Genuineness	_____	Immediacy	_____

ROLE PLAY IN INEFFECTIVE COMMUNICATION

AIMS: 1. To develop skills in recognizing different
         ineffective communication styles.

      2. To facilitate an understanding of how
         students feel when confronted by teachers
         who use ineffective communication styles.

RATIONALE FOR DOING THIS ACTIVITY:

ROLE 3.   THE KNOW-IT-ALL

WHY AREN'T YOU PLAYING? THIS IS RECESS YOU KNOW!

THEY WON'T LET ME. THEY DON'T LIKE ME.

NONSENSE! ALL YOU HAVE TO DO IS SMILE AND BE FRIENDLY.

I WAS FRIENDLY BUT THEY THREW STONES AT ME.

YES, A SMILE WILL WORK WONDERS. EVERYONE LIKES A FRIENDLY PERSON.

THE KNOW-IT-ALL THINKS HE HAS THE ANSWER. HE NEVER CHECKS TO SEE IF IT REALLY FITS THE SITUATION.

ROLE 4.   THE PSYCHOANALYST

DO I HAVE TO GIVE THIS BOOK REPORT IN FRONT OF THE CLASS?

YOU'RE JUST INSECURE — YOU PROBABLY ACT OVERANXIOUS IN FRONT OF THE CLASS.

I HAVE TO SEE A DENTIST ON THE DAY WE DO OUR REPORTS AND I WAS WONDERING...

HOW LONG HAVE YOU HAD THIS PHOBIA AT PUBLIC SPEAKING. MAYBE I CAN HELP.

THE PYSCHOANALYST READS MINDS WITHOUT PERMISSION, OFTEN MAKING WILD PSYCHOLOGICAL ACCUSATIONS.

ROLE 7. THE DETECTIVE

THAT MR. JONES! HE'S SO UNFAIR!

WHO IS MR. JONES?

OUR MATH TEACHER.

WHY IS HE UNFAIR? WHAT DID HE DO?

WELL, EVERYONE GOT UPSET IN OUR LAST CLASS . . .

WHAT DO YOU MEAN BY EVERYONE? WHEN WAS YOUR LAST CLASS? WHAT DO YOU MEAN BY UPSET?

THE DETECTIVE IS SO BUSY COLLECTING FACTS THAT HE FORGETS TO LISTEN TO FEELINGS. HE CONTROLS THE FLOW OF THE CONVERSATION BY BATTERING OTHERS WITH QUESTIONS.

ROLE 8. THE MAGICIAN

OH NO, I FAILED THE TEST AGAIN. MY PARENTS WILL BLOW THEIR TOPS.

DON'T BE SO GLOOMY. HAVE YOU SEEN THE NEW MOVIE DOWNTOWN? IT'S A SCARY ONE ABOUT A SHARK.

DAD SAID HE'LL BELT ME IF I FAILED AGAIN.

OF COURSE HE WON'T!! SAY, SPEAKING OF FISH, HOW'D YOU LIKE TO HELP ME CLEAN THE AQUARIUM?

THE MAGICIAN DENIES THE EXISTENCE OF A PROBLEM AND TRIES TO MAKE IT DISAPPEAR BY CHANGING THE TOPIC.

ROLE 9.   THE GENERALIZER

I'M SORRY I'M LATE, SIR

YOU'RE ALWAYS LATE FOR THIS CLASS.

I COULDN'T HELP IT, I MISSED MY BUS AND...

YOU'VE ALWAYS GOT AN EXCUSE, HAVEN'T YOU, SMITH? YOU NEVER DO ANYTHING RIGHT.

THE GENERALIZER IS DESTRUCTIVE BECAUSE HE'S OFTEN WRONG AND BECAUSE HE DOESN'T ACKNOWLEDGE THAT A PERSON CAN CHANGE HIS BEHAVIOR.

ROLE 10.   THE ACCUSER

I CAN'T STAND THE WAY YOU ACT SOMETIMES. YOU'RE SUCH A PHONY.

WHAT? WHAT DID I DO?

YOU'RE TRYING TO DOMINATE THE CLASS AND BE THE CENTER OF ATTENTION. YOU'RE SO SELFISH I CAN'T BELIEVE IT.

OH YEAH? WHAT MAKES YOU THE JUDGE?

THE ACCUSER ATTRIBUTES UNDESIRABLE MOTIVES TO OTHERS. HIS ACCUSATIONS ARE AN INVITATION TO FIGHT THAT FEW CAN RESIST. HIS REAL GOAL IS TO SLING MUD, NOT TO GIVE OTHERS FEEDBACK ON THEIR BEHAVIOR.

ROLE PLAY DIALOGUE WORKSHEET

<u>INSTRUCTIONS</u>: Use this page to write sample dialogue for a <u>new</u> role play
situation for the ineffective communication role assigned to you.

TEACHER

STUDENT

61

AIMS: 1. To identify the different uses of active listening (empathy).

2. To recognize underlying feelings from written statements.

3. To write active listening responses.

4. To recognize different levels of empathy.

5. To develop skills in practising active listening.

RATIONALE FOR DOING THIS ACTIVITY:

YOU USE THIS FEEDBACK TO CORRECT YOUR GUESSES ABOUT WHAT THEY ARE FEELING AND THEN TRY AGAIN. IT HELPS TO ALWAYS HAVE AT LEAST TWO IDEAS ABOUT WHAT THE OTHER PERSON MIGHT BE FEELING, SO THAT IF YOUR FIRST GUESS IS WRONG, YOU CAN TRY OUT YOUR SECOND ONE.

AS YOU GAIN SKILL IN "ACTIVE LISTENING", YOU'LL FIND YOU CAN ZERO IN ON WHAT THE OTHER PERSON IS REALLY COMMUNICATING IN A SHORT AMOUNT OF TIME.

HERE'S A QUESTION FOR YOU. WHY IS IT SO IMPORTANT THAT I HELP THE OTHER PERSON TO FEEL UNDERSTOOD?

BECAUSE WHEN YOU FEEL UNDERSTOOD, YOU FEEL ACCEPTED. "ACTIVE LISTENING" BUILDS A CLOSE RELATIONSHIP, A CLIMATE OF TRUST. WHERE THERE IS UNDERSTANDING, ACCEPTANCE, AND TRUST, COMMUNICATION IS AT ITS MOST OPEN.

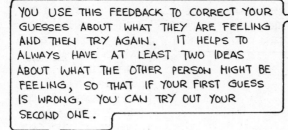

THE PERSON WHO FEELS UNDERSTOOD AND ACCEPTED (ALTHOUGH YOU NEED NOT AGREE WITH WHAT SHE IS SAYING) FEELS FREE TO COMMUNICATE MORE FULLY WHAT SHE DEEPLY FEELS AND THINKS. COMPARE THE KIND OF OPEN COMMUNICATION YOU FIND IN THIS SITUATION WITH THE KIND OF BLOCKED COMMUNICATION YOU GET WHEN YOU FEEL THAT THE OTHER PERSON DOES NOT UNDERSTAND OR WANT TO UNDERSTAND YOU!

FOR EXAMPLE, THE STUDENT MIGHT HAVE HAD TO GO TO THE DENTIST ON THE DAY OF PRESENTATIONS AND THUS BEEN CONCERNED THAT SHE MIGHT MISS AN INTERESTING CLASS. FOR SUCH A SITUATION, THE OFFER OF "ENCOURAGEMENT" WOULD HAVE BEEN INAPPROPRIATE.

"ACTIVE LISTENING" IS PERHAPS THE MOST IMPORTANT COMMUNICATION SKILL A TEACHER CAN POSSESS. THROUGH IT, HE CAN MORE FULLY UNDERSTAND WHAT HIS STUDENTS ARE THINKING AND FEELING. THROUGH "ACTIVE LISTENING" HE CAN HELP THEM TO EFFECTIVELY COMMUNICATE WITH HIM.

HOW CAN WE LEARN TO DO ACTIVE LISTENING?

BY DOING THE FOLLOWING FIVE EXERCISES! IN DOING THESE YOU WILL LEARN TO:

1. IDENTIFY THE DIFFERENT USES OF ACTIVE LISTENING.

2. IDENTIFY FEELINGS IN WRITTEN STATEMENTS

3. WRITE ACTIVE LISTENING RESPONSES

4. RECOGNIZE DIFFERENT LEVELS OF EMPATHY

5. PRACTISE ACTIVE LISTENING WITH YOUR CLASSMATES.

EXERCISES IN SECTION "E"	WORKSHEETS
1. Identifying The Different Uses Of Active Listening	A Classroom Discussion Uses of Active Listening
2. Identifying Feelings	Active Listening Worksheet
3. Active Listening Role Play	Active Listening Worksheet
4. Assessing Empathy Levels	Empathy Levels Chart
5. Active Listening: Casino Style	Empathy Situations Sheet

SITUATION:	Teacher and class of grade 8 students are seated in a circle to discuss a class project.
TEACHER:	Class, we have the opportunity to enter a project in the Science Fair next month. All the grade 8 classes in the city are eligible to enter--so that means us too, if we decide on it! Are you interested?
SEVERAL STUDENTS:	Yes.
JOHN:	What do we have to do to enter?
TEACHER:	We have to work on some kind of Science project--something we can do as a group. During the Science Fair, our project will be on display and if the judges like it, we might win a prize.
SEVERAL STUDENTS:	Hey, great! Let's enter. What can we do?
ALLAN:	What is this bull! We don't hafta do this!
TEACHER:	You feel angry when you think we might decide to enter the fair.
ALLAN:	You bet! Man, that's just a trick to get us all to work hard. I don't need that.
TEACHER:	You don't like the Science Fair because you think its real purpose is to trick students into doing extra work.
ALLAN:	Right.
TEACHER:	How do the rest of you feel?
JOE:	I think it would be a lot of fun to enter the Science Fair. My brother went last year, and it was a gas.
SUE:	Yeah, and think of all the neat prizes we could win!
TEACHER:	I hear some of you saying you'd really enjoy entering the fair. But Allan seems to think we're just being conned.
JULIE:	Allan always says things like that.
TEACHER:	You're saying that Allan often complains about people trying to con him.
MARK:	Last week in Math class, he said the teacher was picking on him.
TEACHER:	Allan thought the teacher was out to get him.
ALLAN:	Everybody picks on me. Nobody ever listens to what I say.
TEACHER:	You're discouraged because people pay no attention to what you say.
ALLAN:	Nobody in this room likes me.
TEACHER:	You think you have no friends here.
ALLAN:	(Silent, looks very sad).
JOE:	We need someone to play second base at recess, Allan. Would you like to?
ALLAN:	Yeah, I'd like to be part of the team.
TEACHER:	Allan is saying he wants to belong and be friends.
MARK:	Hey, Allan, you can use my mitt.
ALLAN:	(Smiles).

TEACHER:	Allan, how do you feel about our entering the Science Fair?
ALLAN:	Oh, I don't care. If Joe and Mark are going to enter, I guess I will too.
TEACHER:	OK class, is anyone strongly opposed to our class entering the Science Fair? It looks like no one is strongly opposed.....so I take this to to mean that all of you want to. Does anyone have any ideas about what project we could enter?
JOAN:	What about something to do with light, and all those neat lenses we used last week. It's got to do with TV and all kinds of things.
TEACHER:	You're excited about the lesson we had on the physics of light and would like to do a project on that.
JIM:	I saw a TV program the other night about how baby ducks get attached to a man and think he's their mother!
TEACHER:	You think it would be interesting to study how baby animals become attached to humans as parents.
TOM:	Well, I don't think I'd make a very good parent to a duck!
CLASS:	(Laughter).
JOE:	My father has some chickens. We could get some baby chicks from him.
MARK:	I have a friend who lives on a farm and he has some geese. They're kinda like ducks, and they had babies recently--could we use them?
ALLAN:	I've got an old hamster cage we could keep them in.
TEACHER:	I hear Joe, Mark and Allan saying that they can get us some animals, and materials to help make a project on Jim's idea. What do the rest of you think about this?

USES OF ACTIVE LISTENING WORKSHEET

INSTRUCTIONS: Indicate three ways in which the teacher in "A Classroom Discussion" used active listening.

1.

2.

3.

ACTIVE LISTENING WORKSHEET

EXERCISES #2 & #3

INSTRUCTIONS:

1. On your own, write down "Possible Feelings Present in The Speaker".
   Time: 20 minutes

2. Reach a group consensus on the most dominant feelings for each of the 12 Situations. Circle these. (This is the end of Exercise #2).

3. For Exercise #3, student pairs will each write an "Active Listening Response" for one of the 12 Situations, and then role play this for the class.
   Time: 20 minutes

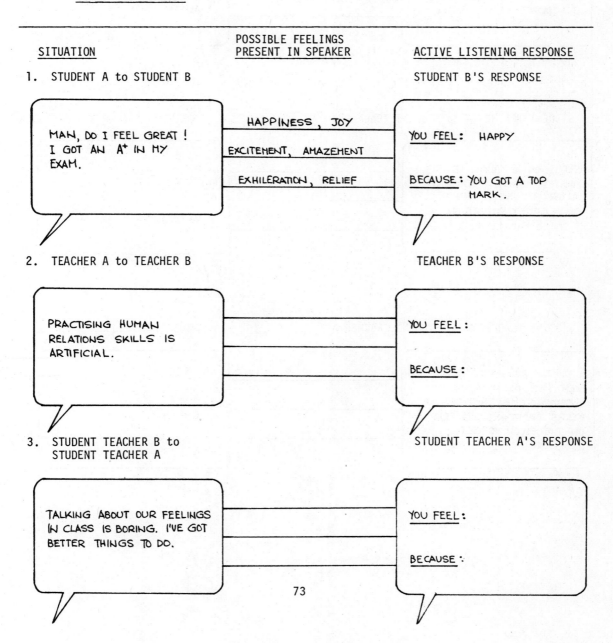

SITUATION	POSSIBLE FEELINGS PRESENT IN SPEAKER	ACTIVE LISTENING RESPONSE
1. STUDENT A to STUDENT B		STUDENT B'S RESPONSE

MAN, DO I FEEL GREAT! I GOT AN A⁺ IN MY EXAM.

HAPPINESS, JOY
EXCITEMENT, AMAZEMENT
EXHILERATION, RELIEF

YOU FEEL: HAPPY

BECAUSE: YOU GOT A TOP MARK.

2. TEACHER A to TEACHER B   TEACHER B'S RESPONSE

PRACTISING HUMAN RELATIONS SKILLS IS ARTIFICIAL.

YOU FEEL:

BECAUSE:

3. STUDENT TEACHER B to STUDENT TEACHER A   STUDENT TEACHER A'S RESPONSE

TALKING ABOUT OUR FEELINGS IN CLASS IS BORING. I'VE GOT BETTER THINGS TO DO.

YOU FEEL:

BECAUSE:

73

| SITUATION | POSSIBLE FEELINGS PRESENT IN SPEAKER | ACTIVE LISTENING RESPONSE |

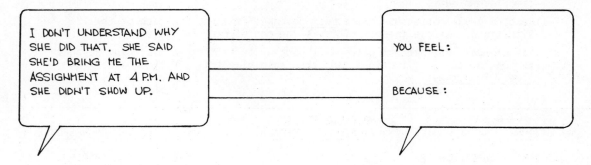

4. TEACHER A to TEACHER B   TEACHER B'S RESPONSE

I DON'T UNDERSTAND WHY SHE DID THAT. SHE SAID SHE'D BRING ME THE ASSIGNMENT AT 4 P.M. AND SHE DIDN'T SHOW UP.

YOU FEEL:

BECAUSE:

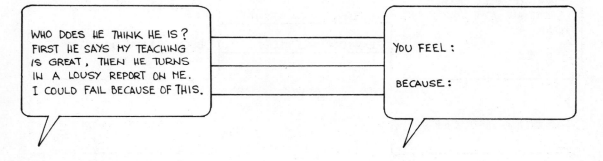

5. STUDENT TEACHER A to STUDENT TEACHER B   STUDENT TEACHER B'S RESPONSE

WHO DOES HE THINK HE IS? FIRST HE SAYS MY TEACHING IS GREAT, THEN HE TURNS IN A LOUSY REPORT ON ME. I COULD FAIL BECAUSE OF THIS.

YOU FEEL:

BECAUSE:

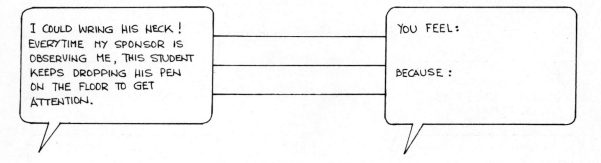

6. STUDENT TEACHER B to STUDENT TEACHER A   STUDENT TEACHER A'S RESPONSE

I COULD WRING HIS NECK! EVERYTIME MY SPONSOR IS OBSERVING ME, THIS STUDENT KEEPS DROPPING HIS PEN ON THE FLOOR TO GET ATTENTION.

YOU FEEL:

BECAUSE:

74

SITUATION	POSSIBLE FEELINGS PRESENT IN SPEAKER	ACTIVE LISTENING RESPONSE

7. TEACHER A to TEACHER B

TEACHER B'S RESPONSE

> I WANTED TO THANK YOU FOR TAKING MY CLASS WHEN I WAS LATE YESTERDAY. THOSE KIDS RUN WILD WHEN NO-ONE IS THERE TO SUPERVISE! IF YOU HADN'T HELPED OUT, I COULD HAVE REALLY CAUGHT IT FROM THE PRINCIPAL.

YOU FEEL:

BECAUSE:

8. STUDENT to TEACHER

TEACHER'S RESPONSE

> THIS IS CRAP. I'M NOT GOING TO DO THIS!

YOU FEEL:

BECAUSE:

9. TEACHER TO STUDENT

STUDENT'S RESPONSE

> I DON'T CARE IF YOU DON'T LIKE WHAT I'M TEACHING. YOU'RE GOING TO DO WHAT YOU'RE TOLD AND THAT'S THAT.

YOU FEEL:

BECAUSE:

10. STUDENT A to STUDENT B   STUDENT B'S RESPONSE

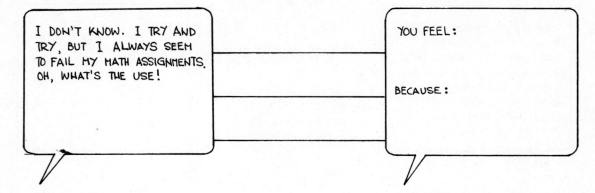

11. PARENT to TEACHER   TEACHER'S RESPONSE

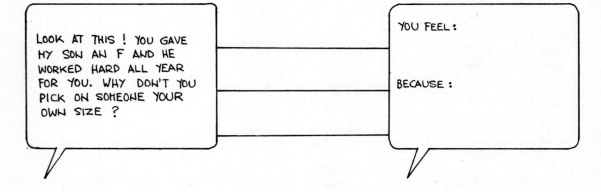

12. STUDENT TEACHER A to   STUDENT TEACHER B'S RESPONSE
     STUDENT TEACHER B

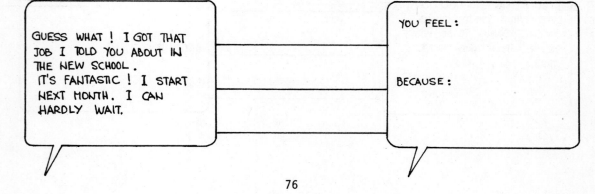

EMPATHY LEVELS CHART

4	Response accurately reflects deeper feelings and concerns experienced by the speaker. Response shows an understanding of underlying feelings not directly expressed by the speaker.
3	Response accurately reflects the surface feeling of the speaker. (Minimum Active Listening Level).
2	Response shows a _partial_ awareness of the speaker's surface feelings.
1	Response shows no empathy whatsoever. A hurtful or destructive response. Ignores or detracts from what the other person has said or is feeling.

EXAMPLE:

SITUATION: STUDENT TO TEACHER:

> MY OLD SCHOOL WAS BETTER. PEOPLE WERE REAL FRIENDLY THERE. NO ONE TALKS TO ME HERE.

FOUR DIFFERENT TEACHER RESPONSES:

Level 1 Response

> NO WONDER! YOU'RE ALWAYS COMPLAINING.

Level 2 Response

> YOU MISS YOUR OLD SCHOOL.

Level 3 Response

> YOU'RE DISAPPOINTED PEOPLE AREN'T AS FRIENDLY HERE AS AT YOUR OLD SCHOOL.

Level 4 Response

> YOU'RE LONELY BECAUSE YOU HAVEN'T MADE ANY FRIENDS HERE YET AND YOU MISS THE FRIENDS YOU HAD AT YOUR OLD SCHOOL.

77

EMPATHY SITUATIONS SHEET

INSTRUCTIONS: For each of the situations shown, imagine that you are the person being spoken to and write:

A. a Destructive response - one that shows no empathy for the speaker.

B. an Active Listening response - one that shows empathy. (Try to write a level 3-4 response).

N.B. Active listening responses for Situations 1, 2 and 3, are written using the structured formula "You feel...... because......". Responses for Situations 4-7, should be written in a more natural, spontaneous, conversational style.

1. STUDENT (WITH TEARS IN HER EYES) TO TEACHER

> EXCUSE ME, SIR. NOBODY WANTS ME IN THEIR GROUP. THEY TOLD ME TO GO AWAY.

A.

B. YOU FEEL :

BECAUSE :

2. UNIVERSITY STUDENT TO UNIVERSITY STUDENT

> THAT PROFESSOR ! WHO DOES HE THINK HE IS? THE WAY HE TALKS DOWN TO ME IN CLASS MAKES MY BLOOD BOIL !!

A.

B. YOU FEEL :

BECAUSE :

3. STUDENT TEACHER TO STUDENT TEACHER

> MY SPONSOR TEACHER IS THE GREATEST. SHE OBSERVED EVERY CLASS I TAUGHT, INTRODUCED ME TO ALL THE STAFF, AND TREATED ME LIKE A REAL PERSON.

A.

B. YOU FEEL :

BECAUSE :

4. TEACHER TO TEACHER

THAT LONG HAIRED LOUT! DO YOU KNOW WHAT HE DID IN MY CLASS TODAY? HE TRIED TO LIGHT A CIGARETTE! LET ME TELL YOU, I HAVE **HAD** IT!!

A.

NATURAL STYLE:

B.

5. STUDENT TO TEACHER

MRS. JONES, I DON'T UNDERSTAND THIS PROBLEM. I TRIED TO DO IT ALL PERIOD. IT'S JUST TOO HARD.

A.

NATURAL STYLE:

B.

6. STUDENT TEACHER TO SPONSOR TEACHER

THOSE KIDS ARE DRIVING ME CRAZY. THEY OUGHT TO BE LOCKED UP. I CAN'T MAKE THEM DO ANYTHING.

A.

NATURAL STYLE:

B.

7. STUDENT TO TEACHER

MAN, WHAT'S THE USE. I BLEW THE TEST AGAIN. ALL MY TEACHERS ARE DOWN ON ME. I MIGHT AS WELL DROP OUT — I'M JUST NOT GONNA MAKE IT.

A.

NATURAL STYLE:

B.

DEVELOPING CONSTRUCTIVE CONFRONTATION SKILLS

AIMS: 1. To develop skills in recognizing the difference between "You" and "I" confrontations.

2. To obtain practice in writing, and in using "I" confrontations.

RATIONALE FOR DOING THIS ACTIVITY:

I CAN SEE THAT "YOU" CONFRONTATIONS ARE INEFFECTIVE, SO WHAT'S THE ALTERNATIVE?

INSTEAD OF MAKING "YOU" CONFRONTATIONS, WE CAN MAKE "I" CONFRONTATIONS. AN "I" CONFRONTATION IS WHERE WE TALK ABOUT HOW WE FEEL ABOUT THE SITUATION, ABOUT HOW IT AFFECTS US.

HOW DO I SEND AN "I" CONFRONTATION?

YOU NEED TO DO THREE THINGS:
1. DESCRIBE THE OTHER PERSON'S BEHAVIOR
2. DESCRIBE THE TANGIBLE EFFECT THEIR BEHAVIOR HAS HAD ON YOU, AND
3. DESCRIBE HOW YOU FEEL

CAN YOU GIVE ME A SPECIFIC EXAMPLE?

WE SAW, ABOVE, HOW SUE GAVE BOB AN INEFFECTIVE "YOU" CONFRONTATION.
IF SHE HAD SAID: "BOB, WHEN YOU DIDN'T ARRIVE ON TIME WITH THE EXAM PAPERS, I WAS WORRIED

AND FRUSTRATED BECAUSE NOW I WILL HAVE TO STAY BACK UNTIL THE EXAM IS COMPLETE AND WILL MISS MY RIDE HOME."
THAT WOULD HAVE BEEN AN "I" CONFRONTATION.

SO, BOB IS STILL BEING CONFRONTED WITH HIS BEHAVIOR BUT THIS TIME INSTEAD OF PUTTING HIM DOWN, SUE CONFRONTS HIM WITH THE EFFECT HIS BEHAVIOR IS HAVING ON HER.

EXACTLY. AND BECAUSE SUE DOESN'T PUT HIM DOWN WITH A BLAMING "YOU" CONFRONTATION, BOB DOESN'T GET DEFENSIVE. HE'S MORE WILLING TO HEAR THE "I" CONFRONTATION AND APPRECIATE THE INCONVENIENCE HE HAS CAUSED. HE'LL TRY HARDER TO BE ON TIME IN THE FUTURE.

IS THIS BEING ASSERTIVE?

YES, "I" MESSAGES ARE ASSERTIVE BECAUSE WE EXPRESS WHAT WE TRULY FEEL WITHOUT PUTTING THE OTHER PERSON DOWN. SENDING "YOU" MESSAGES TENDS TO BE AGGRESSIVE BECAUSE THE SENDER ADOPTS A POSITION OF "I AM O.K., YOU ARE NOT O.K."

HOW CAN I LEARN TO MAKE "I" CONFRONTATIONS?

BY DOING THE ACTIVITY ON THE NEXT PAGE.

CONFRONTATION ROLE PLAY WORKSHEET

SITUATION	"YOU" CONFRONTATION	"I" CONFRONTATION
I. STUDENT TEACHING SITUATIONS		
1. A student keeps whispering loudly to a friend while you are trying to lead an important class discussion.	YOU SHOULD KNOW BETTER THAN TO TALK WHEN I'M TALKING. DON'T _YOU_ HAVE ANY MANNERS ?	WHEN YOU TALK WHILE I'M TALKING TO THE CLASS, _I_ FEEL FRUSTRATED , BECAUSE _I_ GET DISTRACTED FROM WHAT I WANT TO SAY.
2. A student enters your class 10 minutes late for the third time that week.		
3. Your sponsor teacher tells you he thinks you should drop out of teaching, but he's only seen you teach one class.		
4. A student postpones completing a major assignment and you need to turn the marks in to the front office by the end of the week.		
5. Your sponsor teacher is rude to you in front of the class. You go to his office to talk about it.		

Continued

SITUATION:	"YOU" CONFRONTATION	"I" CONFRONTATION
6. At the end of class, one of your students has left Lab materials strewn all over the floor instead of putting them away. You decide to speak to him while the class is leaving.	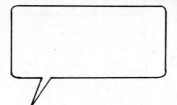	
7. The principal severely reprimands you for sending a student out of your class, but you are innocent: he has you confused with another teacher.		
8. While you are writing on the chalkboard, one of your students throws a paper dart across the room.	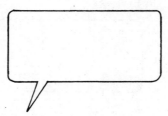	

II. PERSONAL SITUATIONS

9. Your boyfriend/girlfriend is 20 minutes late for a date.	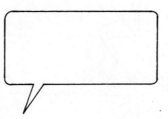	
10. Your boyfriend/girlfriend fails to keep a date. You phone him/her to talk about it.	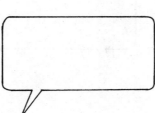	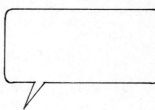

Continued

SITUATION	"YOU" CONFRONTATION	"I" CONFRONTATION
11. Your mother asks you for the fiftieth time when you're going to get married and have kids like "everyone else".	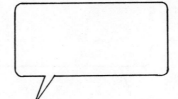	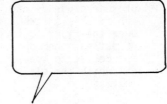
12. You have a large nose. During lunch your friend says: "Hey, is that your nose or are you eating a banana, ha! ha!"	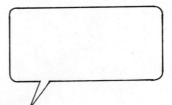	
13. The garage mechanic said your car would cost $20. to fix. When you get the bill, it's $100.	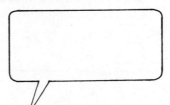	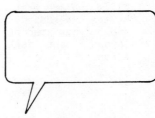
14. You can't get to sleep at night because your roommate keeps bringing friends home late at night and they make a lot of noise.	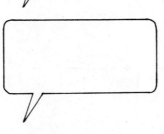	
15. Your closest friend points out your mistakes or negative things about yourself everytime you see him (or her.)		

Continued

SITUATION	"YOU" CONFRONTATION	"I" CONFRONTATION

III. ON CAMPUS SITUATIONS

16. During a university class that you are absent from, another student volunteers your name for an unpleasant job no one else is willing to do.

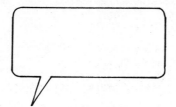 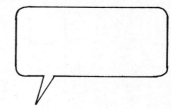

17. Your professor speaks so softly during lectures that you can't hear what he's saying.

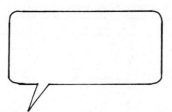 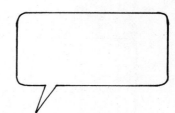

18. When you disagree with your professor, she puts you down in front of the class.

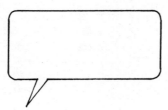 

19. Your professor gives you an F on a course you put an enormous amount of work into. Only two weeks earlier, he told you that you were doing "really well".

20. Whenever you speak out in your small group in class, another student interrupts you.

 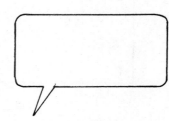

87

AIMS: To develop three basic group communication competencies:

    (a)   group consensus making;

    (b)   promoting maximal participation from all group
          members, and

    (c)   understanding the effect of different group roles.

RATIONALE FOR DOING THIS ACTIVITY:

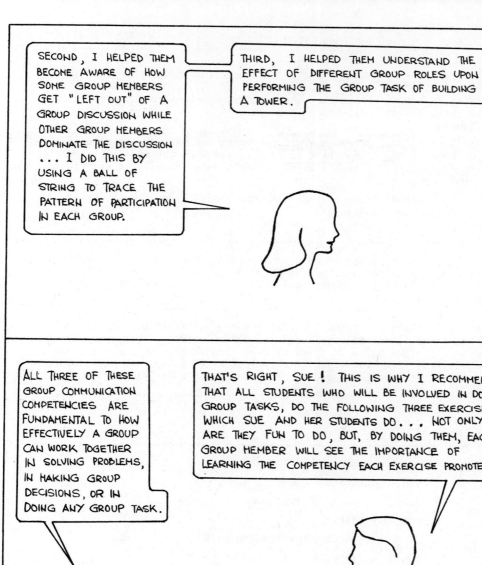

"LOST ON THE MOON EXERCISE" WORKSHEET

INSTRUCTIONS:

1. <u>On your own</u>, read the "Situation" statement below, and then, rank-order the 15 items according to which is <u>most important</u> to your survival on the moon (=1) to which is <u>least important</u> (=15). Let the instructor know when you are finished. Do not start Step 2 until instructed to do so.
   Time: 15 minutes

2. In your designated group, agree on a <u>group ranking</u> for each of the same 15 items according to which is <u>most important</u> to your survival on the moon (=1) to which is <u>least important</u> (=15). When finished, do nothing else until instructed to do so.
   Time: 25 minutes

3. Compute your "Individual Error Scores" and your "Group Error Scores" using the Answer Key provided in the Appendix.
   Time: 10 minutes

THE SITUATION:
Your spaceship has just crash-landed on the "dark side" of the moon. You were supposed to meet the mother ship 200 miles away on the "light side" of the moon, but the crash-landing has ruined your spaceship and destroyed all the equipment on board--except for the 15 items listed below.

YOUR TASK:
Your crew's survival on the moon depends on reaching the mother ship. So, you must choose the <u>most important</u> items still left for the 200-mile trip. Your task, then, is to rank-order the 15 items below in terms of their importance for survival. Under the column below, called, "Your Individual Rank" place a "1" beside the most important, a "2" beside the next most important, and so on through number 15 (=the least important).

YOUR INDIVIDUAL RANK	YOUR GROUP RANK	
_____	_____	Box of matches
_____	_____	Food concentrate
_____	_____	Fifty feet of nylon rope
_____	_____	Parachute silk
_____	_____	Solar-powered portable heating unit
_____	_____	Two .45 caliber pistols
_____	_____	One case of dehydrated milk
_____	_____	Two 100-pound tanks of oxygen
_____	_____	Stellar map (of the moon's constellation)
_____	_____	Self-inflating life raft
_____	_____	Magnetic compass
_____	_____	Five gallons of water
_____	_____	Signal flares
_____	_____	First-aid kit containing injection needles
_____	_____	Solar powered FM receiver-transmitter

<u>NOTE</u>: Do not use the column called "Your Group Rank" until instructed to do so.

90

EXERCISE #1

INSTRUCTIONS:

1. Carefully read the Five Guidelines For Reaching a Group Consensus if you are an Observer/Recorder or are a member of an <u>even-numbered group</u>.

2. The Observer/Recorder for each group will record <u>below</u> what they observe each group doing in following or not following each of the Five Guidelines.

3. After reaching a group consensus on the rank-order for the 15 items in the "Lost On The Moon" Exercise, each group member will record below examples of each Guideline being followed or not followed.

FIVE GUIDELINES FOR REACHING A GROUP CONSENSUS	RECORD SPECIFIC EXAMPLES OF THE FIVE GUIDELINES BEING FOLLOWED OR NOT FOLLOWED AS YOUR GROUP SOUGHT CONSENSUS
1. Seek out differences of opinion and incorporate them into the decision-making process so that the group decision is comprehensively based.	
2. Present your own viewpoints clearly and logically, but do not argue for them. Listen to other viewpoints.	
3. Support someone else's viewpoint if it sounds logical and is acceptable to you. <u>Do not</u> change your mind simply to avoid conflict.	
4. When decision-making reaches a stalemate, look for an <u>alternative</u> that is acceptable to all group members.	
5. <u>Do not</u> make decisions by flipping a coin, by taking a vote, or by bargaining ("I'll back your viewpoint if you back mine.")	

ANSWER KEY FOR CALCULATING YOUR INDIVIDUAL SCORE AND YOUR GROUP'S SCORE

LOST ON THE MOON

15 ITEMS	NASA'S RANKS	YOUR INDI-VIDUAL RANKS	INDI-VIDUAL ERROR POINTS	YOUR GROUP RANKS	GROUP ERROR POINTS
Box of matches					
Food concentrate					
Fifty feet of nylon rope					
Parachute silk					
Solar-powered portable heating unit					
Two .45 caliber pistols					
One case of dehydrated milk					
Two 100-pound tanks of oxygen					
Stellar map (of the moon's constellation)					
Self-inflating life raft					
Magnetic compass					
Five gallons of water					
Signal flares					
First-aid kit conatining injection needles					
Solar-powered FM receiver-transmitter					

Add up the total error points you got and your group got:

TOTAL SCORES = _____   _____

INSTRUCTIONS: Calculate "error points" by calculating the absolute difference between your Individual Ranks and NASA's (disregard plus or minus signs); and between your Group Ranks and NASA's.

SCORING FOR INDIVIDUALS: 0-25 = excellent   56-70 = poor
                          26-32 = good   71-112 = very poor
                          33-45 = average

A FAIRY TALE

A woodcutter and his wife lived near a river on the edge of the forest.
The woodcutter was unkind to his wife and shouted at her and beat her. The wife
finally took a lover, a merchant who befriended her, who lived on the other
side of the river in the village. She visited her lover in the day when she
went to the village to shop. There were two ways to reach the village. There
was a boatman who ferried passengers across the river for a price, and a
bridge several miles upstream where the forest was deep and dark. On her visits
to the village in the daytime, the wife always took the bridge. It was safe
in the daytime, but at night a huge Troll which everyone feared came out of
the forest and kept watch over the bridge , killing and eating everyone who
passed over it. One night after the woodcutter beat his wife, she ran out
of the house intent on visiting her lover who would comfort her. Fearing to
cross the bridge, she approached the boatman's house and asked him to ferry
her across the river. He demanded five silver coins for the trip and she
could not pay. She pleaded with the boatman. "I must get across tonight",
she said, "and the only other way is the bridge where the Troll is. Please
help me". But the boatman would not. So the wife decided to take a chance
crossing the bridge at night, and the Troll caught and ate her.

DISCUSSION QUESTION:

Who is the most to blame for what happened?
The Troll, the boatman, the merchant, the
woodcutter, the wife, the villagers?.

EXERCISE #2

OBSERVER REPORT SHEET

NAMES OF GROUP MEMBERS	PLACE A TALLY IN THE SPACE BESIDE A MEMBER'S NAME EACH TIME HE SPEAKS (E.G. JOHN ~~IIII~~ I)	TOTAL
1		
2		
3		
4		
5		
6		
7		

OBSERVATIONS TO BE MADE WHEN THE GROUP HAS FINISHED:

How well did the members of your group work together? (Circle appropriate number).

RATHER POORLY NOT CO-OPERATIVE	1	2	3	4	5	6	7	8	REALLY WELL VERY CO-OPERATIVE

Use the space below to write down any important things you noticed about how the group decided on a solution to its task, and how they worked together in carrying out its solution.

NAME:_____

GROUP:_____

GROUP ROLE SHEET

INSTRUCTIONS:

Write the names of each member of your group in the numbered spaces below. For each name, check two group roles you observed each person exhibiting during the tower building task.

Time: 10 minutes (complete at home if necessary)

GROUP ROLES	WRITE NAMES OF MEMBERS OF YOUR GROUP HERE									TOTAL
	1 Yourself	2	3	4	5	6	7			
TASK LEADER - Initiates discussion, proposes solutions, guides group in solving task										
TASK LEADER'S ASSISTANT performs similar functions as Task Leader but to a lesser extent										
FOLLOWER - Accepts leader's direction, co-operates in working on solution proposed by others										
HARMONIZER - Encourages others, smooths disagreements, helps resolve misunderstandings.										
COURT JESTER - Clowns around, makes jokes.										
POINT PICKER - Argues too much, rejects ideas without really giving them fair evaluation.										
MARTIAN OBSERVER - Doesn't talk or participate very much at all.										

GROUP ROLE ANALYSIS WORKSHEET

INSTRUCTIONS: The group Observer records the advantages and disadvantages of each Group Role in building the tower as the group identifies them.
Time: 15 minutes

GROUP ROLE	ADVANTAGES	DISADVANTAGES
TASK LEADER Initiates discussion, proposes solutions, guides group in solving task.		
TASK LEADER'S ASSISTANT - performs similar functions as Task Leader but to a lesser extent.		
FOLLOWER Accepts leader's direction, co-operates in working on solution proposed by others.		
HARMONIZER Encourages others, smooths disagreements, helps resolve misunderstandings.		
COURT JESTER Clowns around, makes jokes.		
POINT PICKER Argues too much, rejects ideas without really giving them fair evaluation.		
MARTIAN OBSERVER Doesn't talk or participate very much at all.		

SOLVING COMMUNICATION PROBLEMS WITH YOUR OWN STUDENTS

AN ASSIGNMENT FOR PRACTICUM

AIMS: 1. To identify a communication problem you are having with your students during practicum.

2. To solve this communication problem using one or more of the communication techniques presented in this chapter.

RATIONALE FOR DOING THIS ACTIVITY:

TIME REQUIRED FOR DOING THIS ACTIVITY:

Varying amounts of class time during practicum

MATERIALS NEEDED:

Pen; and Worksheet provided in this text

PROCEDURE: (TO ACHIEVE AIMS 1 AND 2)

I.   While you are on practicum, identify a communication problem in your classroom and then solve the problem using one or more of the communication techniques presented in this chapter:

1. icebreakers;
2. the eight interpersonal skills: active listening, warmth, respect, genuineness, concreteness, self-disclosure, immediacy, confrontation;
3. the consensus method of group problem solving;
4. increasing participation rates in a group discussion;
5. enabling your students to develop better group roles.

N.B.   SEE THE RATIONALE FOR EACH OF THE COMMUNICATION ACTIVITIES IN THIS CHAPTER FOR DESCRIPTIONS OF SPECIFIC TECHNIQUES AND THE TYPES OF COMMUNICATION PROBLEMS FOR WHICH EACH TECHNIQUE IS MOST SUITABLE.

II. Use the Worksheet for Solving Communication Problems With Your Own Students to record the specific communication problem you chose to solve, the technique(s) you employed to solve the problem, and the results of your application of the technique(s).

98

1. <u>Identify</u> a specific communication problem in one of your classes. This problem may involve a single student, a group of students, or the entire class, as well as yourself! Briefly, describe the problem below:

2. <u>Describe</u> the communication technique(s) you chose to solve the problem and indicate <u>why</u> you chose to use those techniques:

3. Describe how well the selected communication technique(s) worked:

CHAPTER 3

DEVELOPING SKILLS FOR MOTIVATING YOUR STUDENTS IN NEW WAYS

AIMS: 1. To identify feelings resulting from having one's character or personality praised.

2. To identify feelings resulting from having a specific behavior praised.

3. To identify various types of positive reinforcers.

RATIONALE FOR DOING THIS ACTIVITY:

HELLO, BOB... GLAD I RAN INTO YOU BECAUSE I JUST HAD A MOST UPSETTING EXPERIENCE... I GAVE ONE OF MY BEST STUDENTS A SINCERE COMPLIMENT — BUT HE REJECTED IT AND WALKED AWAY!

TELL ME EXACTLY WHAT HAPPENED, SUE.

ONE OF THE TEACHERS HAD LOST HER WALLET, CONTAINING A LOT OF MONEY, SOMEWHERE IN THE SCHOOL. WELL, JOHN, MY STUDENT, FOUND IT AND GAVE IT TO ME TO RETURN TO THE TEACHER WHO LOST IT... I WAS SO PROUD OF WHAT JOHN HAD DONE THAT I SAID TO HIM, "JOHN, YOU ARE CERTAINLY AN HONEST PERSON"... THAT'S WHEN HE TURNED AND WALKED AWAY !!

HAD JOHN EVER REACTED LIKE THIS BEFORE WHEN YOU GAVE HIM A COMPLIMENT ??

WHY, YES! ONCE WHEN I SAID, "YOU ARE A GOOD STUDENT, JOHN" AFTER HE HAD WRITTEN AN ESPECIALLY INTERESTING BOOK REPORT...

THERE WAS ANOTHER OCCASION, TOO... WHEN I SAID, "JOHN, YOU ARE A VERY NICE PERSON", AFTER HE HAD OPENED A DOOR FOR ME.

SUE, DO YOU SEE ANY SIMILARITY IN ALL THREE STATEMENTS YOU MADE TO JOHN?

WELL, AS A PRETTY GOOD STUDENT OF ENGLISH GRAMMAR, I KNOW ALL THREE STATEMENTS CONTAIN A "PREDICATE ADJECTIVE" ... IS THAT WHAT YOU MEAN?

NOT EXACTLY... I WAS LOOKING AT HOW EACH STATEMENT ASCRIBES A PARTICULAR CHARACTERISTIC TO JOHN'S PERSONALITY OR CHARACTER.

OH, I SEE NOW... I SAID JOHN WAS "HONEST", "GOOD", AND "NICE"... I GUESS BECAUSE THIS IS HOW I VIEW HIM.

THAT'S RIGHT! AND IF JOHN DOES NOT VIEW HIMSELF THIS WAY, HE IS LIKELY TO DO SOMETHING TO REFUTE THESE LABELS.

OH, I SEE NOW—I COULD HAVE SAID, "I LIKE THE WAY YOU HOLD THE DOOR FOR ME— IT HELPS ME WHEN I HAVE AN ARMFUL OF BOOKS"... RATHER THAN: "YOU ARE A CONSIDERATE PERSON."

RIGHT YOU ARE, SUE!... AN EFFECTIVE COMPLIMENT (OR PRAISE) CONTAINS TWO ESSENTIAL ELEMENTS:

(1) A DESCRIPTION OF THE ADMIRABLE BEHAVIOR, AND

(2) A DESCRIPTION OF YOUR FEELINGS ABOUT THAT BEHAVIOR.

THERE IS AN OPTIONAL THIRD ELEMENT IN AN EFFECTIVE COMMUNICATION:

(3) THE SPECIFIC EFFECT THE OTHER PERSON'S BEHAVIOR HAD ON YOU OR ON OTHERS.

TO FIND OUT IF YOU UNDERSTAND THESE THREE ELEMENTS, DO THE FOLLOWING EXERCISE WITH THE THREE "PROPERLY STATED" COMPLIMENTS THAT SHOULD HAVE BEEN GIVEN TO THE STUDENT, JOHN. YOU MADE ONE OF THESE "CORRECT" COMPLIMENTS ABOVE, AND I MADE TWO OTHERS.

(1) UNDERLINE ONCE EACH DESCRIPTION OF JOHN'S ADMIRABLE BEHAVIOR,

(2) UNDERLINE TWICE EACH DESCRIPTION OF THE TEACHER'S FEELINGS,

(3) CIRCLE THE EFFECT JOHN'S BEHAVIOR HAD IN EACH SITUATION.

CHECK HOW YOU DID. IF YOU DON'T
UNDERSTAND WHAT'S BEEN SAID TO
THIS POINT, THEN RE-READ BOB
AND SUE'S DISCUSSION AGAIN

BECAUSE

IT IS NOW TIME FOR YOU TO
EXPERIENCE FOR YOURSELF THE KIND
OF FEELINGS WHICH ARE CREATED IN
YOU WHEN YOU RECEIVE TWO KINDS
OF COMPLIMENTS:
(1) "YOU-ARE" COMPLIMENTS
          AND
(2) "I-AM-FEELING" COMPLIMENTS

BE SURE TO DESCRIBE (1) YOUR FEELINGS
AND (2) THE OTHER PERSON'S SPECIFIC
BEHAVIOR WHEN USING AN "I-AM-FEELING"
COMPLIMENT. YOU MAY ALSO ADD
ELEMENT #3 — THE SPECIFIC EFFECT THE
OTHER PERSON'S BEHAVIOR HAS ON YOU.

1. "I LIKE THE WAY YOU RETURNED THE
   LOST WALLET TO ME BECAUSE MRS.
   JONES NEEDS THE MONEY IN IT."

2. "I APPRECIATE THE HARD WORK YOU PUT
   INTO YOUR BOOK REPORT BECAUSE THIS
   MADE YOUR REPORT DELIGHTFUL TO READ."

3. "I LIKE THE WAY YOU HOLD THE DOOR FOR
   ME -- IT HELPS ME WHEN I HAVE AN
   ARMFUL OF BOOKS."

WHY LEARN TO GIVE POSITIVE COMPLIMENTS
IN AN EFFECTIVE WAY?
... BECAUSE RESEARCH ON BOTH
HUMANS AND ANIMALS HAS SHOWN
THAT POSITIVE REINFORCEMENT —
A REWARD, A COMPLIMENT, FOOD,
A SMILE, ETC. — IS THE MOST
EFFECTIVE MEANS FOR INCREASING
THE FREQUENCY OF A SPECIFIC
BEHAVIOR.

GIVING AND RECEIVING COMPLIMENTS WORKSHEET

INSTRUCTIONS:

1. <u>In pairs</u>, Student A will give Student B two kinds of compliments for each Category of Behavior <u>below</u>. First, use <u>"You-are"</u> <u>compliments</u>--such as "You really listen to me", or "You are the most patient person with children I've seen"--for each Category of Behaviors. Then, use, <u>"I-am-feeling"</u> <u>compliments</u> --such as "I feel important when you look at me when I'm talking to you", or "I admire your patience with children"--for each Category of Behaviors.
   <u>Time: 10 minutes</u>

2. Student B now gives Student A compliments in the same way as explained above.
   <u>Time: 10 minutes</u>

3. Each student now writes down his/her own personal <u>feelings</u> experienced in reaction to both kinds of compliments for each Category of Behaviors. (Use the space provided on the next page.)
   <u>Time: 10 minutes</u>

4. Discuss together the feelings you each wrote down (you may add to your written list). Which kind of compliment made you generally feel best? For which Category of Behavior were you especially sensitive to "You-are" compliments?
   <u>Time: 10 minutes</u>

USE THESE "I-AM-FEELING" STEMS TO SEND COMPLIMENTS FOR EACH TYPE OF BEHAVIORS BELOW	USE THESE "YOU-ARE" STEMS TO SEND COMPLIMENTS FOR EACH TYPE OF BEHAVIORS BELOW
I like	You are ....
I admire	You really ....
I feel good when	You ....
I feel important when	

Continued

CATEGORIES OF BEHAVIOR	FEELINGS RESULTING FROM RECEIVING "YOU-ARE" COMPLIMENTS	FEELINGS RESULTING FROM RECEIVING "I-AM-FEELING" COMPLIMENTS
I. FACIAL MANNERISMS e.g.-eye contact, smiling, listening		
II. SPEAKING MANNERISMS e.g.-eye contact, clarity, accent, idiomatic expressions		
III. PARTICIPATION IN CLASS e.g.-asking questions, adding information, getting other people to participate		
IV. WORKING WITH STUDENTS IN SCHOOL e.g.-use of teaching methods, handling discipline, imagination in preparing materials		
V. GENERAL BODY MOVEMENTS AND CLOTHING e.g.-mannerisms, the way you walk, use of hands when talking or listening		

KINDS OF POSITIVE REINFORCERS WORKSHEET

INSTRUCTIONS:

Each student pair will <u>list</u> specific examples under each Category of Reinforcers below, and beside each example, indicate how they would use that positive reinforcer with their students in school.
Time: 20 minutes

CATEGORIES (KINDS) OF POSITIVE REINFORCERS	SPECIFY HOW POSITIVE REINFORCERS CAN BE USED WITH STUDENTS IN VARIOUS SCHOOL SITUATIONS
I. PHYSICAL KINDS	
II. VERBAL KINDS	
III. CONCRETE OBJECTS	
IV. PRIVILEGES	

QUESTIONS FOR DISCUSSION:

1. Which <u>category</u> of reinforcers do you personally prefer to use?

2. Which <u>specific reinforcer</u> do you personally prefer to use?

3. For what kind of school situation do you especially need to start using more positive reinforcement? What kind will you use?

AIMS: 1. To learn the basic needs that motivate human behavior.

        2. To discover what your own needs are.

        3. To develop skills in recognizing how students' needs affect their classroom behavior.

        4. To identify the kinds of situations that arouse students' needs.

        5. To learn constructive ways of helping students resolve their needs.

<u>RATIONALE FOR DOING THIS ACTIVITY:</u>

IT'S SAD THAT A LOT OF TEACHERS WHO COULD HELP THEIR STUDENTS MEET THEIR BELONGING NEEDS — LIKE I KNOW YOU WANT TO DO WITH LENA — DO NOTHING.

WHAT'S REALLY TRAGIC IS THAT UNTIL THE STUDENT MEETS HIS POWERFUL NEED, HE ISN'T GOING TO LEARN MUCH FROM HIS TEACHERS.

TEACHERS WHO THINK THEY'RE THERE JUST TO TEACH SUBJECT MATTER, TAKE NOTE!! YOU'RE ALSO TEACHING PEOPLE WHO HAVE NEEDS, WHICH "NEED SATISFYING".

WHAT OTHER NEEDS ARE THERE?

AFTER BELONGING NEEDS COMES INDEPENDENCE NEEDS, ACHIEVEMENT NEEDS AND SELF-ESTEEM NEEDS. ALL THREE OF THESE CAN BE GROUPED TOGETHER UNDER ESTEEM NEEDS.

INDEPENDENCE NEEDS INVOLVE MAKING ONE'S OWN DECISIONS, TO "STAND UP ON ONE'S OWN TWO FEET" TO DO THINGS BY ONESELF.

RIGHT! AND BEING INDEPENDENT IS ONE WAY TO HELP YOU FEEL GOOD ABOUT YOURSELF.

YES. WHEN I'M INDEPENDENT IN MAKING IMPORTANT DECISIONS I SAY TO MYSELF "YOU DID IT ALL BY YOURSELF. GOOD FOR YOU!"

INDEPENDENCE NEEDS ARE PARTICULARLY IMPORTANT IN STUDENTS FROM ABOUT AGES 14 - 18

THAT'S THE "BREAKING FREE FROM ONE'S FAMILY" AGE. THE AGE OF TEENAGE REBELLION.

FOR MANY STUDENTS IT DOES BECOME A STRUGGLE BECAUSE THE PARENTS DON'T WANT TO "LET GO" AND SEE THEIR CHILD BECOME INDEPENDENT OF THEM.

116

WHEN YOU THINK YOU'RE NOT O.K. YOU DON'T EXPOSE YOURSELF TO NEW THINGS FOR "FEAR OF FAILURE" AND SO YOU DON'T LEARN ANYTHING NEW.

OR YOU JUST FEEL SO WORTHLESS AND "NOT O.K." THAT YOU DON'T CARE ABOUT WHAT'S BEING TAUGHT.

I CAN SEE THAT IF A STUDENT DOESN'T MEET HIS ESTEEM NEEDS HE CAN'T LEARN MUCH IN SCHOOL.

THE FINAL OR HIGHEST NEED LEVEL IN MASLOW'S HIERARCHY OF HUMAN NEEDS IS CALLED SELF-ACTUALIZATION. THIS IS THE NEED TO FULFILL ONE'S POTENTIAL, TO BE ALL THAT ONE CAN BE IN TERMS OF ONE'S ABILITIES AND SENSITIVITIES, THE NEED TO BE CREATIVE, TO UNDERSTAND THE WORLD ABOUT ONE. WHEN THIS NEED IS UNFULFILLED, BOREDOM IS OFTEN THE RESULT.

I EXPERIENCED THAT IN MY LAST TEACHING JOB. I WAS REQUIRED TO TEACH ONLY THE STRAIGHT SUBJECT MATTER. IT WAS ALL A HEAD TRIP! I KNOW I WAS CAPABLE OF MORE CREATIVE AND EXCITING THINGS BOTH FOR MYSELF AND MY PUPILS. BUT I JUST COULDN'T TEACH THE WAY I WANTED.

YOU JUST COULDN'T BE YOUR NATURAL CREATIVE SELF.

RIGHT! THAT'S THE MAIN REASON I CAME HERE. AT THIS SCHOOL, THEY LET YOU TRY OUT NEW THINGS. NOW THAT I'M USING VALUES CLARIFICATION AND SMALL GROUP TECHNIQUES IN MY CLASSES, THE KIDS JUST LOVE IT AND THEY'RE REALLY LEARNING TWICE AS MUCH AS WHEN I DID THE DRY "CHALK AND TALK."

117

118

IN THIS PYRAMID THE MOST POWERFUL NEEDS ARE AT THE BASE, THE LESS POWERFUL AT THE TOP. MASLOW BELIEVES THAT THE LOWER NEEDS MUST FIRST BE SATISFIED BEFORE THE STUDENT IS LIKELY TO GO ON TO SATISFY THOSE NEEDS HIGHER IN THE SCALE.

I SEE. IF YOU'RE STARVING YOU DON'T REALLY WORRY ABOUT YOUR BELONGING NEEDS

THAT'S RIGHT. THE LOWER NEEDS ARE MORE PRESSING. BUT WHAT NEED LEVEL DO YOU THINK MOST TEACHERS ARE CONCERNED WITH?

FROM WHAT THEY PROFESS TO BE INTERESTED IN: SELF-ACTUALIZATION. AHA! NOW I SEE WHAT YOU'RE GETTING AT. TEACHERS TRY TO SATISFY STUDENTS' SELF-ACTUALIZATION NEEDS (CREATIVITY, UNDERSTANDING) BUT FAIL TO SEE THAT MOST STUDENTS GET BLOCKED AT THE LOWER LEVELS WHERE MORE POWERFUL NEEDS ARE UNSATISFIED.

AND UNTIL STUDENTS CAN SATISFY THEIR NEEDS AT THESE LOWER LEVELS, THEY AREN'T GOING TO LEARN MUCH.

AS THIS DIAGRAM SHOWS, MOST STUDENTS GET BLOCKED AT THE LEVEL OF BELONGING AND ESTEEM NEEDS. THEIR UPWARD COURSE TOWARDS THE HIGHER GOALS OF EDUCATION IS <u>DEFLECTED</u> BY UNMET BELONGING AND ESTEEM NEEDS.

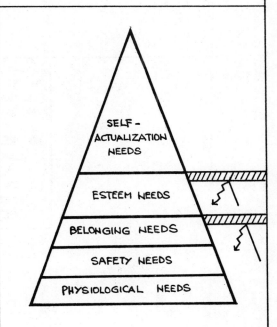

SELF-ACTUALIZATION NEEDS

ESTEEM NEEDS

BELONGING NEEDS

SAFETY NEEDS

PHYSIOLOGICAL NEEDS

IN GLASSER'S TERMS, THE STUDENTS AREN'T MOTIVATED TO LEARN BECAUSE THEY'RE LONELY (THEIR BELONGING NEEDS ARE UNMET) OR BECAUSE THEY HAVE A "FAILURE IDENTITY" (THEIR ESTEEM NEEDS ARE UNMET BECAUSE OF TOO MANY FAILURE EXPERIENCES).

SO IF A TEACHER REALLY WANTS TO DO HIS JOB AND HELP HIS STUDENTS ACHIEVE AND SELF-ACTUALIZE THEMSELVES, HE'S GOT TO KNOW HOW TO HELP THEM SATISFY THEIR OTHER NEEDS! THAT SOUNDS LIKE AN IMPOSSIBLE TASK.

FORTUNATELY, MOST STUDENTS COME TO SCHOOL WITH THEIR PHYSIOLOGICAL AND SAFETY NEEDS SATISFIED. OTHERWISE, TEACHERS WOULD HAVE A TRULY IMPOSSIBLE TASK. BUT FOR THE TWO NEED LEVELS THAT BLOCK MOST STUDENTS' PROGRESS — BELONGING NEEDS AND ESTEEM NEEDS — THERE ARE SOME SIMPLE TECHNIQUES THAT TEACHERS CAN USE TO FREE THEIR STUDENTS TO BECOME EFFECTIVE, SELF-ACTUALIZING LEARNERS.

IN THE FOLLOWING TWO LEARNING ACTIVITIES, YOU WILL LEARN:
(1) TO IDENTIFY YOUR OWN NEEDS

(2) THE WAYS STUDENTS' NEEDS AFFECT THEIR CLASSROOM BEHAVIOR

(3) CONSTRUCTIVE WAYS OF HELPING STUDENTS RESOLVE THEIR NEEDS SO THAT THEY CAN "GET ON" WITH LEARNING.

PERSONAL NEEDS INVENTORY

EXERCISE #1

INSTRUCTIONS:

1. For each of the statements below, place a check (✓) in the appropriate column to the right to indicate the extent to which the statement currently applies to you.

2. Next, re-read each item in the inventory, this time placing an "x" in the appropriate column to the right of each of the statements below to indicate the minimal frequency which you would require in order to be satisfied. (This is not an "ideal" level, but your minimal level of needed satisfaction.)

	Always	Frequently	Occasionally	Seldom	Never
1. I feel secure in the place (apartment, house) in which I live.					
2. I find life stimulating and challenging.					
3. I feel I have no control over what happens to me.					
4. I feel loved.					
5. I have poor health.					
6. I think of original solutions to problems.					
7. I am afraid of being physically harmed.					
8. When someone asks me to do something, my first impulse is to say no.					
9. I lack self-confidence.					
10. Everything I do, I do well.					
11. I am financially self-sufficient.					
12. I am afraid something terrible will happen to me.					
13. I feel tired and run-down.					
14. I feel that my friends really care about me.					
15. I am afraid of being physically assaulted.					
16. I am fulfilling my full potential as a person.					
17. I am bored.					

121

	Always	Frequently	Occastionally	Seldom	Never
18. I feel nervous in large groups.					
19. I am satisfied with my current status level of my career.					
20. I am satisfied with my current level of work achievement.					
21. I feel uneasy being alone.					
22. People who know me respect me.					
23. I feel like an outsider in most groups.					
24. I don't get enough exercise to keep me physically fit.					
25. People value me for my competence.					
26. I make important decisions about my life independent of others.					
27. I am satisfied with my relationships with others.					
28. Physically, I feel strong and lively.					
29. I get enough to eat.					
30. I feel lonely.					
31. I reach the goals I set for myself.					
32. I need someone stronger to rely on.					
33. I don't like the way I am.					
34. I look forward to doing and learning new things.					
35. I have difficulty sleeping at night.					
36. I am successful in my work.					
37. I worry that I might have a serious accident.					
38. Other people give me bad feelings.					
39. My work is very satisfying.					
40. I am an independent person.					
41. I have creative ideas.					
42. I worry about the possibility of personal misfortune or disaster.					

SCORING KEY FOR PERSONAL NEEDS INVENTORY

1. Transfer the "✓" and the "x" you just gave to each statement on the Personal Needs Inventory onto this Scoring Key for each item below. For example: suppose for the first statement on the Personal Needs Inventory, you placed a "✓" in the "Seldom" column, you will now place a "✓" in the "Seldom" column for item #1 on this Scoring Key; similarly, if you placed an "x" in the "Always" column on the Personal Needs Inventory, you will now place an "x" in the "Always" column for item #1 on this Scoring Key.

2. Each item below corresponds to one of seven Types of Human Needs. Add up the six "✓" scores you gave yourself for each Type of Human Need, and then place this total on the Results Sheet (on the next page) under "Current Need Level" for that Type of Human Need. Also, add up the six "x" scores you gave yourself for each Type of Human Need, and then place this total on the Results Sheet under the "Minimal Need Level" for each Type of Human Need.

ITEM	ALWAYS	FREQUENTLY	OCCASIONALLY	SELDOM	NEVER	TYPE OF HUMAN NEED	ITEM	ALWAYS	FREQUENTLY	OCCASIONALLY	SELDOM	NEVER	TYPE OF HUMAN NEED
1.	4	3	2	1	0	Saf	22.	4	3	2	1	0	Est
2.	4	3	2	1	0	S-A	23.	0	1	2	3	4	Bel
3.	0	1	2	3	4	Ind	24.	0	1	2	3	4	Phy
4.	4	3	2	1	0	Bel	25.	4	3	2	1	0	Est
5.	0	1	2	3	4	Phy	26.	4	3	2	1	0	Ind
6.	4	3	2	1	0	S-A	27.	4	3	2	1	0	Bel
7.	0	1	2	3	4	Saf	28.	4	3	2	1	0	Phy
8.	0	1	2	3	4	Ind	29.	4	3	2	1	0	Phy
9.	0	1	2	3	4	Est	30.	0	1	2	3	4	Bel
10.	4	3	2	1	0	Ach	31.	4	3	2	1	0	Ach
11.	4	3	2	1	0	Ind	32.	0	1	2	3	4	Ind
12.	0	1	2	3	4	Saf	33.	0	1	2	3	4	Est
13.	0	1	2	3	4	Phy	34.	4	3	2	1	0	S-A
14.	4	3	2	1	0	Bel	35.	0	1	2	3	4	Phy
15.	0	1	2	3	4	Saf	36.	4	3	2	1	0	Ach
16.	4	3	2	1	0	S-A	37.	0	1	2	3	4	Saf
17.	0	1	2	3	4	S-A	38.	0	1	2	3	4	Est
18.	0	1	2	3	4	Est	39.	4	3	2	1	0	Ach
19.	4	3	2	1	0	Ach	40.	4	3	2	1	0	Ind
20.	4	3	2	1	0	Ach	41.	4	3	2	1	0	S-A
21.	0	1	2	3	4	Bel	42.	0	1	2	3	4	Saf

RESULTS SHEET FOR PERSONAL NEEDS INVENTORY

INSTRUCTIONS: After transferring your score totals to this page, subtract scores for Current Need Level from scores for Minimal Need Level, and place the difference in the last column.

TYPE OF HUMAN NEED	CURRENT NEED LEVEL	MINIMAL NEED LEVEL	NEED SATISFACTION LEVEL (Minimal Need minus Current Need)
PHYSIOLOGICAL (Phy)	24	24	24
SAFETY (Saf)	24	24	24
BELONGING (Bel)	24	24	24
INDEPENDENCE (Ind)	24	24	24
ACHIEVEMENT (Ach)	24	24	24
ESTEEM (Est)	24	24	24
SELF-ACTUALIZATION (S-A)	24	24	24
TOTAL SCORE FOR NEED SATISFACTION LEVEL			168

INTERPRETATION FOR SPECIFIC HUMAN NEEDS

NEED SATISFACTION LEVEL SCORE	INTERPRETATION
0 - 6	Need is very satisfied.
7 - 12	Need is moderately satisfied.
13 - 18	Need is moderately unsatisfied.
19 - 24	Need is very unsatisfied.

LIFE SATISFACTION ASSESSMENT SHEET

INSTRUCTIONS:

1. Indicate how generally satisfied you feel with your life by placing a check (✓) in the appropriate space below. This is your Life Satisfaction score.

Generally Very Satisfied With Life		+7	+6	+5	+4	+3	+2	+1	0	-1	-2	-3	-4	-5	-6	-7		Generally Very Unsatisfied With Life

Needs Are Very Satisfied		0	12	23	34	45	56	67	78	89	100	111	122	133	144	155		Needs Are Very Unsatisfied
		11	22	33	44	55	66	77	88	99	110	121	132	143	154	168		

2. Place a check (✓) in the space immediately above which corresponds to your Total Need Satisfaction Score from the previous page. The range of scores represented by each space is indicated by the number above (lower range) and the number below (upper range) each space.

3. Draw a line <u>from</u> the upper box you checked <u>to</u> the lower box you checked.

QUESTIONS FOR CONSIDERATION:

1. Are your two scores fairly close together?
2. What is the relationship between the extent to which all of a person's needs are satisfied and his or her overall feeling of satisfaction with life?

1. Think of a student you know, or once knew, who seemed to be having difficulty in school. Write a brief description of the student's classroom <u>behavior</u> that indicated he or she was having difficulty.

2. Place a check (✓) beside the need(s) that you think might have motivated this student's behavior.

    Physiological _____   Esteem   _____

    Safety   _____   Achievement   _____

    Belonging   _____   Self-Actualization   _____

    Independence   _____

3. What kind of situation do you think might have aroused this need in the student you observed?

4. What did the student's teachers do that helped or hindered the student in resolving his or her need?

5. If you were this student's regular teacher, what could you do to help the student resolve his or her need?

AIMS: 1. To distinguish between three types of Class
         Meetings.

      2. To identify the aims of Class Meetings.

      3. To identify and develop important organizational
         skills necessary to carry out Class Meetings.

      4. To identify and develop leadership and
         questioning skills necessary for conducting a Class
         Meeting.

      5. To understand realistic expectations for beginning
         Class Meetings.

RATIONALE FOR DOING THIS ACTIVITY:

128

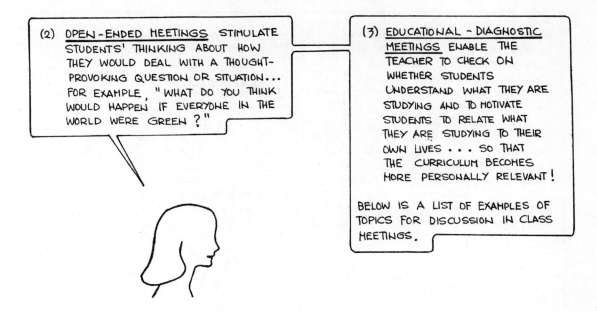

(2) OPEN-ENDED MEETINGS STIMULATE STUDENTS' THINKING ABOUT HOW THEY WOULD DEAL WITH A THOUGHT-PROVOKING QUESTION OR SITUATION... FOR EXAMPLE, "WHAT DO YOU THINK WOULD HAPPEN IF EVERYONE IN THE WORLD WERE GREEN?"

(3) EDUCATIONAL - DIAGNOSTIC MEETINGS ENABLE THE TEACHER TO CHECK ON WHETHER STUDENTS UNDERSTAND WHAT THEY ARE STUDYING AND TO MOTIVATE STUDENTS TO RELATE WHAT THEY ARE STUDYING TO THEIR OWN LIVES . . . SO THAT THE CURRICULUM BECOMES MORE PERSONALLY RELEVANT!

BELOW IS A LIST OF EXAMPLES OF TOPICS FOR DISCUSSION IN CLASS MEETINGS.

EXAMPLES OF TOPICS FOR DISCUSSION IN CLASS MEETINGS

I. TOPICS FOR SOCIAL PROBLEM-SOLVING MEETINGS

1. "What basic rules do we want/need in this classroom?"

2. "How can we prevent bigger students from bullying smaller students on the playground?"

3. "How can we help new students feel welcome in our school (or classroom)?"

II. TOPICS FOR OPEN-ENDED MEETINGS

1. "What would you do if you were in a plane that crashed somewhere in the wilderness? How would you save yourself?"

2. "If you could be any person in the whole world, who would you like to be? Why? What would you do if you were that person?"

3. "How can our society solve the problem of traffic congestion?"
(or pollution, or over-population, or prejudice, etc.)

III. TOPICS FOR EDUCATIONAL-DIAGNOSTIC MEETINGS

1. "What have you studied during the past week that you can apply/use in your life? How can you use it?"

129

GLASSER'S THREE TYPES OF CLASS MEETINGS SEEM TO BE VERY COMPREHENSIVE IN PERMITTING A VARIETY OF DIFFERENT SITUATIONS TO BE DEALT WITH!

YES! AND THEY ALSO PROMOTE A NEW KIND OF "3R'S", WHICH ARE NECESSARY TODAY FOR TEACHING AND LEARNING THE MORE TRADITIONAL 3R'S OF READING, 'RITING, AND 'RITHMETIC.

THE 3R'S I'M REFERRING TO ARE REASONING, BEHAVING RESPONSIBLY AND RELEVANCE IN THE SCHOOL'S CURRICULUM.

WHY IS IT IMPORTANT TO LEARN HOW TO PROMOTE THESE 3R'S?

FOR TWO REASONS!

FIRST, TODAY'S STUDENTS ARE NOT EXPOSED TO VERY MANY SUPERIOR-INFERIOR RELATIONSHIPS BETWEEN PEOPLE ... AND THUS THEY HAVE FEW SUBMISSIVE MODELS TO IMITATE FROM WHOM THEY CAN LEARN TO "DO AS THEY ARE TOLD".

YOU'RE SAYING THAT TRADITIONAL POSITIONS OF POWER AND AUTHORITY ARE NOT BEING OBEYED AS MUCH AS THEY USED TO BE!

RIGHT! JUST THINK OF YOUR OWN EXPERIENCES, OR TRY COMMANDING YOUR STUDENTS TO "DO AS YOU TELL THEM" AND SEE WHAT HAPPENS!

SECOND, LEARNING THESE NEW
3R'S IS IMPORTANT TODAY
BECAUSE STUDENTS ARE NOT AS
WILLING TODAY TO WAIT ON THE
KIND OF SUCCESS THAT RESULTS
FROM ACHIEVING LONG-RANGE,
PERSONALLY IRRELEVANT GOALS
SET FOR THEM BY SOMEONE
ELSE.

LIKE OUR PARENTS DID WHEN
THEY "SACRIFICED THEIR HAPPINESS"
IN ORDER TO PROVIDE THEIR
CHILDREN WITH A "BETTER LIFE"
THAN THEY HAD.

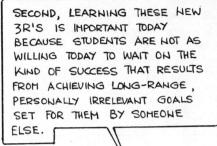

YES! ACCORDING TO THE FAMOUS MEDIA
EXPERT, MARSHALL McLUHAN, TODAY'S
STUDENTS HAVE PUT "ROLES BEFORE GOALS"
... THEY FIRST OF ALL SEEK PERSONAL
HAPPINESS, OR WHAT GLASSER CALLS A
"SUCCESS IDENTITY", AND WILL WORK
TOWARDS GOALS WHICH ARE RELEVANT
TO ACHIEVING THIS.

ACCORDING TO McLUHAN, THIS
IS WHY TODAY'S STUDENTS
ARE SO RESTLESS...
MAKING DEMANDS FOR A
MORE RELEVANT CURRICULUM,
WHICH EMPHASIZES THINKING
INSTEAD OF ROTE MEMORIZATION
OF "TAUGHT FACTS" AND
GIVES STUDENTS MORE
RESPONSIBILITY FOR THEIR
OWN LEARNING...

BELOW IS A LIST OF THE MAJOR AIMS OF GLASSER'S CLASS MEETINGS.

MAJOR AIMS OF WILLIAM GLASSER'S CLASS MEETINGS

1. To increase involvement between the teacher and students and among students themselves. (Involvement is an important way to motivate students to learn.)

2. To develop students' analytical and creative thinking abilities as they tackle open-ended situations in which answers are not dependent on memory and are not categorical (i.e., Yes or No).

3. To develop in students, a "success identity" as they contribute to class meetings and are listened to.

4. To develop students' confidence and skills in expressing their ideas and opinions.

5. To develop students' listening skills as they listen to each other.

6. To develop in students, socially responsible attitudes (e.g. concern for others), and socially responsible behaviors (e.g. respecting the ideas, opinions, and feelings of others).

7. To develop cooperative ways of solving problems which affect individual class members or the class as a whole. (This also helps students feel that they "belong" to the class.)

AT THE SCHOOL I VISITED, I SAW THESE AIMS "COME ALIVE" AS THE TEACHERS GOT THEIR STUDENTS INVOLVED IN CLASS MEETINGS

HOW DO TEACHERS LEAD CLASS MEETINGS?

THERE ARE FOURTEEN ESSENTIAL GUIDELINES TO FOLLOW WHEN LEADING CLASS MEETINGS.

132

A. ORGANIZATIONAL GUIDELINES

1. Form a tight circle with no furniture in the middle. Plan with your
    students a way to effectively and quickly arrange furniture.

2. If necessary, plan a seating arrangement which will promote good
    discussion and the least pupil-to-pupil distraction. (For example, plan
    with "disturbers" to sit apart or next to the teacher).

3. Teacher should sit in a different place in the circle for each meeting.

4. Plan seven to ten minute meetings for young children. Periods should be
    lengthened for older students depending on maturity and interest. As
    growth occurs, meetings will gradually lengthen.

5. Meetings should be held on a regular basis. Every day is best, but at
    least once a week is necessary for students to benefit from them.

6. Experiment with the best time of day to have meetings with your class.
    And schedule your meetings at a specified time so that students expect
    them and can look forward to them as a regular part of their daily (or
    weekly) schedule.

7. Utilize hand-raising in the beginning and whenever necessary or
    comfortable to facilitate discussion.

B. LEADERSHIP GUIDELINES

1. Show warmth and enthusiasm. Children should become aware that you really
    care about listening to them.

2. Be non-judgmental; there are no right or wrong answers in class meetings.
    To encourage deeper thinking on an issue, ask, "What do the rest of you
    think of that idea?"

3. Set simple ground rules; e.g. - one person talks at a time; everyone's
    opinion is to be respected, although not necessarily agreed with, and can
    be challenged. Keep comments constructive.

4. During the first several meetings especially, keep the atmosphere
    comfortable and provide support through as much direction as needed. This
    directiveness will gradually taper off as children grow to trust the
    meeting atmosphere and secure more self-direction. For some groups, this
    may take several months.

5. Develop the art of questioning.
        Refrain from repeating and rephrasing answers.
        Limit "teacher-talk" whenever possible.
        Do not correct poor grammar during the discussions.

6. If discussion is especially involved when it's time to stop, this could be
    a good place to start the next meeting.

7. Work with another teacher to get ideas and obtain feedback on how you're
    doing.

ASKING QUESTIONS IS AN ESPECIALLY IMPORTANT SKILL IN LEADING CLASS MEETINGS. GLASSER RECOMMENDS THREE STAGES IN POSING QUESTIONS:

(1) ASK QUESTIONS WHICH DEFINE THE TOPIC OR PROBLEM BEING DISCUSSED —— "WHAT IS LONELINESS (OR FRIENDSHIP)?"

(2) ASK QUESTIONS USING "YOU" OR "YOUR" TO PERSONALIZE THE TOPIC TO A PARTICULAR STUDENT —— "HAVE YOU EXPERIENCED FEELING ALONE?"

(3) ASK QUESTIONS WHICH CHALLENGE STUDENTS TO THINK. EXAMPLES OF THESE ARE SHOWN BELOW.

CHALLENGING STUDENTS TO THINK

1. Ask questions that pose different answers: "What if.....? Could we.....? Should we.....?"

2. Request clarification: "Are you saying that......?

3. Play "devil's advocate" role: "Why would you do that?"

4. Encourage "way out" answers: "Can anyone think of something really different?"

5. Encourage students to question assumptions and opinions.

6. Encourage students to apply their knowledge: "How can you use what you know about .....?"

7. Encourage students to build onto each other's ideas or opinions: "Can anyone add to what Sally said?"

8. Follow two simple guidelines:

   (a) Listen for interesting ideas which children present in their responses, and follow those ideas with a new Define, Personalize, Challenge sequence.

   (b) Avoid attempting to exhaust a topic or to arrive at an answer ...... either practice tends toward closure, rather than openness.

WHAT SHOULD TEACHERS DO WITH STUDENTS WHO MONOPOLIZE CONVERSATION, OR DON'T PARTICIPATE, OR CREATE MINOR DISTURBANCES?

GLASSER OFFERS GUIDELINES FOR THIS, TOO!

FOR CHILDREN WHO MONOPOLIZE CONVERSATION, CREATE DISTURBANCES, OR DON'T PARTICIPATE, TRY:

1. Strategically sitting in the circle next to them or directly across from them.

2. Placing your hand on their knee or shoulder to encourage them or "tone them down".

3. Talking with them individually at some time other than the meeting to solicit cooperation and emphasize the importance of their contribution to the group.

4. Gently intervening after a reasonable period of time when a child talks endlessly.

5. Encouraging non-participants by supporting them as you call on them; e.g., "You have been listening carefully; I wonder if you want to share your ideas?" or, "I'm sure you have an idea about this, and I'd like to hear it."

DOES GLASSER OFFER GUIDELINES FOR HANDLING MORE SERIOUS DISCIPLINE PROBLEMS DURING CLASS MEETINGS?

YES! HE OFFERS 12 RECOMMENDATIONS.

135

HOST DISCIPLINE PROBLEMS SHOULD BE PRECLUDED AS STUDENTS BECOME PERSONALLY INVOLVED IN DISCUSSING SOMETHING REALLY MEANINGFUL TO THEM DURING THE CLASS MEETING... HOWEVER, IF SERIOUS DISCIPLINE PROBLEMS DO ARISE, CONSIDER THE FOLLOWING . . .

GUIDELINES FOR HANDLING DISCIPLINE PROBLEMS DURING CLASS MEETINGS

1. How is the furniture arrangement? Can everyone see each other?

2. Can the "disruption" be brought up in the meeting for discussion?

3. Control the "clown" by asking if that's what he really meant by that remark. Keep the tone of the meeting businesslike.

4. Physically restrain if necessary until things can get going better.

5. Consider assigned seats if necessary.

6. Talk to continual disruptors privately to get them on your side. Perhaps apply the technique of "Reality Therapy" to help disruptors plan ways of behaving more responsibly and to get a commitment from them that they will follow their plan.

7. Share leadership in the meeting with another teacher or adult. This will give you a different perspective on the "discipline problem".

8. Bring older children into the meeting to help keep interest up. Use resource people.

9. Take your children to observe other class meetings. Discuss.

10. Divide class in half and do a "fishbowl" meeting with one-half watching and taking notes.....   Discuss all together what makes a good meeting.

11. Don't feel guilty about ending a meeting if it's going badly or if nothing much is happening. Be ready to start on time for the next scheduled meeting.

12. Exclude a disruptive child only as a last resort and always with the option open for the child to return when he can make a plan and a commitment to do better.

IT SEEMS LIKE GLASSER HAS THOUGHT OF EVERYTHING—
HOW TO ORGANIZE AND LEAD CLASS MEETINGS, HOW TO
STIMULATE STUDENTS TO THINK, HOW TO MOTIVATE OPTIMAL
PARTICIPATION, AND HOW TO HANDLE DISCIPLINE PROBLEMS
DURING CLASS MEETINGS . . . WHAT ELSE IS THERE?

GLASSER ALSO PROVIDES TEACHERS WITH SOME
VERY REALISTIC EXPECTATIONS ABOUT HOW THE
FIRST 20-30 CLASS MEETINGS MIGHT GO.

REALISTIC EXPECTATIONS FOR THE FIRST 20-30 CLASS MEETINGS

1. "Good students" may be reluctant to talk; often they are uncomfortable with no "right" answers.

2. At the beginning, students may give answers they think teachers want to hear. It takes time to build an atmosphere of trust where students will say what they really think.

3. Students will probably direct most of their responses to the teacher. Again it takes time (and skillful guidance from the teacher) for the children to learn to talk with each other and the group.

4. Students will get excited by some topics and tend to talk together in sub-groups....just as adults do.

5. Some children may initially try to disrupt meetings. Often this is a way out of an unfamiliar situation, and ceases as they grow comfortable with the format, and become involved in the discussion.

6. Class meetings rarely produce miracles. Growth is gradual and comes with experience through consistent efforts. Become aware of small increments of success. Above all, don't give up!

THANK YOU, SUE, FOR TELLING US ABOUT THE GLASSER "CLASS MEETINGS" YOU SAW TEACHERS LEADING IN A SCHOOL IN ORDER TO HELP THEIR STUDENTS LEARN THE 3R'S OF <u>REASONING</u>, BEHAVING <u>RESPONSIBLY</u>, AND SEEING THE <u>RELEVANCE</u> OF THE CURRICULUM AS STUDENTS SEEK TO ATTAIN A "SUCCESS IDENTITY".

BEFORE OUR READERS TRY LEADING (OR PARTICIPATING IN) A "CLASS MEETING" THEMSELVES, LET ME RE-EMPHASIZE TWO IMPORTANT POINTS MADE BY SUE:

1. "CLASS MEETINGS" SHOULD BECOME A REGULARLY SCHEDULED PART OF YOUR CLASSROOM PROGRAM.

2. TEACHERS SHOULD GUIDE STUDENTS TO INTERACT WITH EACH OTHER TO CREATE INVOLVEMENT. "CLASS MEETINGS" WILL NOT LEAD THEMSELVES, NOR WILL THEY WORK IF THE TEACHER DOMINATES OR "LECTURES", OR MAKES VALUE JUDGMENTS THAT STUDENTS' OPINIONS ARE "RIGHT" OR "WRONG".

NOW, IT IS TIME FOR YOU TO EXPERIENCE FOR YOURSELF WHAT A "CLASS MEETING" IS LIKE AS YOU DO ONE OR BOTH OF THE EXERCISES WHICH FOLLOW. I WOULD SUGGEST YOU PARTICIPATE IN A "CLASS MEETING" IN EXERCISE #1 BEFORE YOU LEAD ONE WITH YOUR STUDENTS IN EXERCISE #2.

ANALYSIS OF A CLASS MEETING WORKSHEET

INSTRUCTIONS: Each participant and the leader of the Class Meeting answers the following questions:
Time: 10 minutes

A. WHAT ORGANIZATIONAL GUIDELINES WERE WELL-FOLLOWED?

B. WHAT ORGANIZATIONAL IMPROVEMENTS ARE NECESSARY?

C. WHAT LEADERSHIP GUIDELINES WERE WELL-FOLLOWED?

D. WHAT LEADERSHIP IMPROVEMENTS ARE NECESSARY?

E. WHAT KINDS OF QUESTIONS DID THE LEADER ASK? (Cite examples)

F. HOW MANY CLASS MEMBERS PARTICIPATED IN THE CLASS DISCUSSION?
   (a) 80% - 100%   REASONS:
   (b) 50% - 80%
   (c) 30% - 50%
   (d) 0% - 30%

G. HOW WELL DID THE LEADER PROMOTE THE 3 R's? (Comment below)
   1. REASONING (Thinking)

   2. RESPONSIBLE BEHAVIOR

   3. RELEVANCE (in the topic)

EXERCISE #2: LEADING A CLASS MEETING WITH YOUR OWN STUDENTS

TIME REQUIRED FOR DOING THIS EXERCISE:

> 7 - 15 minutes for each meeting, scheduled daily, if possible, for 3 - 4 weeks (or longer)

MATERIALS NEEDED:

> Guidelines provided in the rationale (above).
> Worksheet provided in this text.

PROCEDURE:

> I. Get authorization and support from your sponsor teacher to lead a series of 7-15 minute Class Meetings over a 3-4 week period (or longer, if possible), so that students can learn the new roles of "active participation" and you can develop competencies for conducting a Class Meeting.
>
> II. Select a topic, or question for class discussion. (Get help from your sponsor teacher, ask your students, or select a topic yourself).
>
> III. Organize the physical setting and lead a Class Meeting. Explain to the class that Class Meetings will become part of the classroom program for the next 3-4 weeks (or longer).
> Time: 7 - 15 minutes
>
> IV. Assess Your Class Meeting (and have your sponsor teacher assess it too), using the Analysis of a Class Meeting Worksheet. (Do this as soon after the Class Meeting as possible, and then, compare your self-assessment with your sponsor teacher's assessment).
> Time: 20 minutes

STUDENT TEACHER'S ANALYSIS OF A CLASS MEETING WORKSHEET | EXERCISE #2

INSTRUCTIONS: The student teacher who leads a Class Meeting answers the following questions:
Time: 10 minutes

A. WHAT ORGANIZATIONAL GUIDELINES WERE WELL-FOLLOWED?

B. WHAT ORGANIZATIONAL IMPROVEMENTS ARE NECESSARY?

C. WHAT LEADERSHIP GUIDELINES WERE WELL-FOLLOWED?

D. WHAT LEADERSHIP IMPROVEMENTS ARE NECESSARY?

E. WHAT KINDS OF QUESTIONS DID THE LEADER ASK? (Cite examples)

F. HOW MANY CLASS MEMBERS PARTICIPATED IN THE CLASS DISCUSSION?
   (a) 80% - 100%   REASONS:
   (b) 50% - 80%
   (c) 30% - 50%
   (d)   0% - 30%

G. HOW WELL DID THE LEADER PROMOTE THE 3 R's? (Comment below)

   1. REASONING (Thinking)

   2. RESPONSIBLE BEHAVIOR

   3. RELEVANCE (in the topic)

141

INSTRUCTIONS: The sponsor teacher (who observes a student teacher leading a Class Meeting) answers the following questions:
Time: 10 minutes

A. WHAT ORGANIZATIONAL GUIDELINES WERE WELL-FOLLOWED?

B. WHAT ORGANIZATIONAL IMPROVEMENTS ARE NECESSARY?

C. WHAT LEADERSHIP GUIDELINES WERE WELL-FOLLOWED?

D. WHAT LEADERSHIP IMPROVEMENTS ARE NECESSARY?

E. WHAT KINDS OF QUESTIONS DID THE LEADER ASK? (Cite examples)

F. HOW MANY CLASS MEMBERS PARTICIPATED IN THE CLASS DISCUSSION?

    (a) 80% - 100%   REASONS:
    (b) 50% - 80%
    (c) 30% - 50%
    (d)   0% - 30%

G. HOW WELL DID THE LEADER PROMOTE THE 3 R's? (Comment below)

    1. REASONING (Thinking)

    2. RESPONSIBLE BEHAVIOR

    3. RELEVANCE (in the topic)

IMPROVING YOUR STUDENT TEACHING BY USING THE "CLINICAL SUPERVISION" METHOD:

AN ASSIGNMENT FOR PRACTICUM

> AIMS: 1. To learn about and to try out a method for self-improvement of your teaching.
>
> 2. To report on teaching improvements as a result of using this method.

RATIONALE FOR DOING THIS ACTIVITY:

144

145

146

147

<u>TIME REQUIRED FOR DOING THIS ACTIVITY</u>:

20 - 40 minutes required altogether (5 - 10 minutes before the lesson starts, and 15 - 35 minutes after its completion) -- not counting the length of time of the lesson itself.

<u>MATERIALS NEEDED</u>:

The "Description of the Five-Step Clinical Supervision Method for Improving One's Teaching"; and various Worksheets provided in this text.

<u>PROCEDURE</u>:

I. Read the "Description of the Five-Step Clinical Supervision Method for Improving One's Teaching", and decide who could best accept this method and use it properly for observing your teaching. Have that person (=the Observer) read it also. Find out if the Observer agrees with this method and is willing to use it as indicated.

II. Arrange for the Observer to observe you teach a lesson or lead a learning activity. You and the Observer should expect to spend time together <u>before</u> and <u>after</u> the lesson (as indicated above under TIME), in order to do all five steps of the method. You and the Observer should use the various Teacher and Observer Worksheets provided.

III. After using this method several times, answer such questions as:

---

1. How has my teaching improved as a result of using this method?

2. Do I feel less evaluated and thus less threatened when this method is used?

3. Do I view the Observer as a Helper or Evaluator when he uses this method?

4. Have I used this method as indicated? Or altered it?

A DESCRIPTION OF THE FIVE-STEP "CLINICAL SUPERVISION"
METHOD FOR IMPROVING ONE'S TEACHING

1. In STEP 1, the Teacher and Observer engage in a PRE-OBSERVATION CONFERENCE so that the Teacher can tell the Observer what he/she wants the Observer to look for during the lesson. To specify these concerns, the Teacher writes down 2 or 3 questions on which he/she wants observational feedback from the Observer.

    For example, the Teacher might want to know: "How successfully do pupils work on their own in small groups?" Or, "How do I help or hinder these pupils?" The Observer then watches what the Teacher and students do in the lesson in order to "answer" these questions for the Teacher.

2. In STEP 2, (OBSERVATION OF THE LESSON), the Observer records objective descriptions of Teacher and student actions taking place during the lesson--actions which are related to the original questions or concerns written down by the Teacher. The Observer does not make subjective value judgments about what he sees the Teacher and students doing. This means that words such as "good" or "bad", or phrases such as "teacher talked too much" or "teacher gave unclear directions" are not used.

    Instead, the Observer might say that the Teacher talked 19 minutes out of a 25 minute period while introducing the learning activity, or that the students asked 6 unanswered questions to request clarification about the Teacher's directions. These statements are objective descriptions of what the Observer saw taking place.

3. STEP 3 involves DATA ORGANIZATION AND ANALYSIS on the part of both the Observer and the Teacher:
    (1) The Teacher writes down brief notes (on the "Self-Assessment Sheet") of what he/she did and what the students did to influence the success of the lesson or learning activity just concluded.
    (2) If appropriate, the Observer summarizes in writing the actions of the Teacher and the actions of students which occurred during the lesson or learning activity just concluded. For example, the Observer might want to indicate the amount of time the Teacher talked in each situation. Or, the Observer's summary might indicate the type of statements the Teacher made and the number of times each type of statement occurred. Thus, the Teacher might have "given orders or commands" five times, "asked recall or main idea questions" once each, "answered student query" twice, and "did not answer student query" six times. The Observer puts tallies beside each type of Teacher action to indicate the frequency of occurrence of each action.
    (3) The Observer also writes down recommendations based on recorded data, which will be discussed with the Teacher in Step 4. For example, the Observer might recommend that the Teacher not dominate the first 20 minutes by talking, or might discuss with the students how they are expected to act in an independent study activity rather than giving them a lot of orders; or that the Teacher might move from one group to another more frequently to help each group stay on task; or that the Teacher might not interrupt a group which is on task; or that the Teacher might require some specified product to result from the independent group activity.

4. In STEP 4 (POST OBSERVATION CONFERENCE), Teacher and Observer sit facing each other:
    (1) The Teacher presents his "Self-Assessment Sheet" to indicate how he thought the lesson or learning activity went.
    (2) The Observer shows the Teacher his "Observer's Observation Sheet" describing the Teacher and student actions he observed and objectively recorded for the total lesson, and also shows his "Summary of Teacher and Pupil Actions", which he has summarized from his written observations. Teacher and Observer then compare their written observations, using these forms.
    (3) Then, the Observer presents his "Data-Based Recommendations" written down previously, and gets agreement from the Teacher on which recommendations he/she will try to implement the next time he/she teaches.

Continued

5. In STEP 5 (THE CRITIQUE), the Teacher indicates how he/she was helped by the Observer --which gives the Observer some indication of exactly how helpful he was, and, the Teacher also indicates ways in which the Observer might be even more helpful in the future.

The Observer writes down how he believed he was helpful in giving the Teacher feedback on the lesson just concluded, and also, how he might be even more helpful to the Teacher in the future.

SUMMARY OF MAIN CHARACTERISTICS FOR THE FIVE STEPS IN THE "CLINICAL SUPERVISION" METHOD FOR IMPROVING ONE'S TEACHING

STEP	MAIN CHARACTERISTICS
1. PRE-OBSERVATION CONFERENCE	(1) ESTABLISHES WHAT OBSERVER IS TO LOOK FOR AND RECORD DURING THE TEACHER'S "LESSON". (2) IS BASED ON THE TEACHER'S CONCERNS, POSED AS WRITTEN QUESTIONS.
2. OBSERVATION OF "LESSON"	(1) IS BASED ON TEACHER'S QUESTIONS. (2) OBSERVER DESCRIBES TEACHER AND PUPIL ACTIONS ON THE "OBSERVER'S OBSERVATION SHEET". (3) IS OBJECTIVE--OBSERVER MAKES NO VALUE JUDGMENTS OF TEACHER'S PERFORMANCE.
3. DATA ORGANIZATION AND ANALYSIS	(1) TEACHER WRITES DOWN OWN OBSERVATIONS OF WHAT HAPPENED IN THE "LESSON" ON "SELF-ASSESSMENT SHEET". (2) OBSERVER SUMMARIZES TEACHER AND PUPIL ACTIONS AS "FREQUENCIES" OF PARTICULAR BEHAVIORS (IF THIS IS APPROPRIATE). (3) OBSERVER WRITES DOWN RECOMMENDATIONS.
4. POST-OBSERVATION CONFERENCE	(1) TEACHER AND OBSERVER COMPARE THEIR WRITTEN OBSERVATIONS OF "LESSON". (2) THEY LOOK AT OBSERVER'S RECOMMENDATIONS AND AGREE ON WHICH ONES THE TEACHER WILL EMPLOY IN THE NEXT "LESSON".
5. CRITIQUE OF OBSERVER BY TEACHER	(1) ANSWER:- "HOW WAS I HELPED BY OBSERVER?" (2) ANSWER:- "HOW CAN OBSERVER HELP FURTHER?"
CRITIQUE BY OBSERVER	(1) ANSWER:- "HOW WAS I HELPFUL TO TEACHER?" (2) ANSWER:- "HOW CAN I BE OF FURTHER HELP?"

OBSERVER'S OBSERVATION SHEET

NAME: _____   LESSON: _____

DATE: _____

STEP 1: TEACHER'S CONCERNS, QUESTIONS, OR PROBLEM AREAS Observer is to look for and record. (Write these here).

STEP 2: OBSERVER'S OBSERVATIONS OF WHAT TOOK PLACE. (A diagram of the physical situation can be drawn to illustrate what the Teacher and pupils are doing.)

TIME	TEACHER & PUPIL ACTIONS (OBJECTIVELY DESCRIBED)

OBSERVER'S SUMMARY SHEET

(Use if Applicable)

STEP 3: SUMMARY OF OBJECTIVELY RECORDED OBSERVATIONS

TYPE(S) OF TEACHER ACTIONS (CATEGORIZE)	FREQUENCY	% TIME SPENT

TYPE(S) OF PUPIL ACTIONS (CATEGORIZE)	FREQUENCY	% TIME SPENT

NAME:_____   LESSON:_____

DATE: _____

STEP 3: OBSERVER'S RECOMMENDATIONS

1. Things to Continue Doing (List)

2. Things to Begin Doing (List)

3. Things to Refrain From Doing (List)

TEACHER'S SELF-ASSESSMENT SHEET

NAME:_____   LESSON:_____

DATE:_____

STEP 3: TEACHER'S OWN RECOMMENDATIONS   (Self-Appraisal)

1. Things to Continue Doing (List)

2. Things to Begin Doing (List)

3. Things to Refrain From Doing (List)

STEP 5: OBSERVER'S CRITIQUE OF HIMSELF

A. Specify ways in which you were helpful to the Teacher in meeting his/her concerns, questions, or problems stated in Step 1.

B. Specify ways in which you think you can be even more helpful to the Teacher in the future.

155

STEP 5:   TEACHER'S CRITIQUE OF OBSERVER

A. Specify ways in which the observer or his/her observations (Step 2) or recommendations (Step 3) were helpful in meeting your concerns, questions, or problems stated in Step 1.

B. Specify ways in which the observer can be even more helpful in the future.

CHAPTER 4

DEVELOPING SKILLS FOR USING HUMANISTIC DISCIPLINE TECHNIQUES

HANDLING AGGRESSIVE STUDENT BEHAVIOR

AIMS: 1. To identify positive and negative consequences that might result from applying a particular solution to the problem of aggressive student behavior.

2. To identify the best solutions to employ.

3. To compare group results.

RATIONALE FOR DOING THIS ACTIVITY:

I USED SOME OF YOUR SUGGESTIONS, SUE, FOR HANDLING INATTENTIVE STUDENTS ...AND THEY WORKED GREAT! NOW LET ME TRY TO HELP YOU WITH YOUR AGGRESSIVE STUDENTS.

I HOPE YOU CAN, BOB BECAUSE I JUST DON'T KNOW WHAT TO DO...

ALL I KNOW FOR SURE IS THAT I CANNOT IGNORE AGGRESSIVE BEHAVIOR WHEN IT THREATENS OR ACTUALLY ENDANGERS OTHER STUDENTS.

WHERE DOES THIS AGGRESSIVE BEHAVIOR OCCUR AND WHAT IS IT LIKE?

THERE ARE A COUPLE OF STUDENTS WHO BULLY STUDENTS ON THE PLAYGROUND DURING RECESS AND LUNCH, AND THEN CONTINUE TO BULLY STUDENTS IN CLASS — ESPECIALLY DURING ACTIVITIES WHERE STUDENTS ARE WORKING ON THEIR OWN WHILE I'M TEACHING SMALLER GROUPS AT THE BACK OF THE ROOM.

PERHAPS I CAN HELP YOU BECAUSE I HAD A SIMILAR SITUATION WHICH I HAD TO RESOLVE.

HERE ARE SIX SUGGESTIONS FOR HANDLING AGGRESSIVE BEHAVIOR...

BUT YOU, TOO, WILL HAVE TO DECIDE WHICH SOLUTIONS MIGHT WORK BEST FOR YOUR PARTICULAR AGGRESSIVE STUDENTS:

(1.) ISOLATE THE AGGRESSIVE STUDENT FROM THOSE WITH WHOM HE OR SHE HAS TROUBLE.

(2.) ARRANGE TO SEND AN AGGRESSIVE STUDENT TO THE PRINCIPAL — AS A PLACE OF RETREAT — WHENEVER THIS MISBEHAVIOR OCCURS.

(3.) WHEN THE AGGRESSIVE STUDENTS ARE NOT PRESENT, HELP THE OTHER STUDENTS UNDERSTAND THIS MISBEHAVIOR AND LET THEM SUGGEST WAYS TO DEAL WITH IT.

(4.) LET AGGRESSIVE STUDENTS EXPRESS AGGRESSIVE FEELINGS IN MORE ACCEPTABLE WAYS.

(5.) EXCLUDE AN AGGRESSIVE STUDENT FROM THE CLASS AND/OR PLAYGROUND WHENEVER THIS MISBEHAVIOR OCCURS.

(6.) ENCOURAGE OTHER STUDENTS TO RETALIATE BY TREATING AGGRESSIVE STUDENTS IN THE SAME WAY SO THEY WILL FIND OUT HOW IT FEELS.

THANKS, BOB... I'LL TRY SOME OF THESE SUGGESTIONS AND LET YOU KNOW HOW THEY WORK

AGGRESSIVE BEHAVIOR WORKSHEET

<u>INSTRUCTIONS</u>:

1. <u>On your own</u>, write down on this worksheet all the possible positive and negative consequences you can think of for each proposed solution.

2. Then, <u>via group consensus</u>, rank order the 6 proposed solutions from best to use (= 1) to worse to use (= 6) based on a group discussion of the possible consequences each group member has listed in step 1.

PROPOSED SOLUTIONS	POSSIBLE POSITIVE CONSEQUENCES	POSSIBLE NEGATIVE CONSEQUENCES
1. Isolate aggressive student		
2. Send to principal's office		
3. Let rest of class make suggestions to handle problem		
4. Express aggression in more acceptable ways		
5. Exclude from class or playground		
6. Urge classmates to retaliate		

What is the rank order given these solutions by the group?

1. _____   3. _____   5. _____

2. _____   4. _____   6. _____

AIMS: 1.   To identify positive and negative consequences
             that might result from applying a particular
             solution to the problem of inattentive student
             behavior.

        2.   To identify the best solution to employ.

        3.   To compare group results.

RATIONALE FOR DOING THIS ACTIVITY:

WHAT'S WRONG, BOB... YOU SURE LOOK GLOOMY TODAY!

IT'S THAT OBVIOUS, EH?

DO YOU WANT TO TELL ME ABOUT IT? PERHAPS I CAN HELP

I HOPE SO, SUE... THERE ARE TWO OR THREE REALLY INATTENTIVE STUDENTS IN MY CLASS... THEY ARE MAKING IT DIFFICULT FOR ME AND FOR THE OTHER STUDENTS!

IN WHAT SPECIFIC WAYS?

WELL... YOU KNOW THAT I'VE BEEN HAVING MY STUDENTS GIVE A BOOK REPORT TO THE CLASS IN A WAY THAT WILL PERSUADE THEIR CLASSMATES TO WANT TO READ THAT BOOK.

THIS SOUNDS LIKE IT WOULD GET EVERYBODY MOTIVATED TO GIVE AN INSPIRING BOOK REPORT.

IT DOES, THE BOOK REPORTS ARE MORE IMAGINATIVE AND REFLECT A BETTER UNDER-STANDING OF THE BOOK READ THAN WHEN I HAD STUDENTS PREPARE BOOK REPORTS FOR ME TO READ.

INATTENTIVE BEHAVIOR WORKSHEET

INSTRUCTIONS:

1. <u>On your own</u>, write down on this worksheet all the possible positive and negative consequences you can think of for each proposed solution.

2. Then, <u>via group consensus</u>, rank-order the 6 proposed solutions from best to use (= 1) to worse to use (= 6) based on a group discussion of the possible consequences each group member has listed in step 1.

PROPOSED SOLUTION	POSSIBLE POSITIVE CONSEQUENCES	POSSIBLE NEGATIVE CONSEQUENCES
1. Seat near front		
2. Student repeats what was said		
3. Ignore		
4. Lessons in listening for class		
5. Reward positive behavior		
6. Explain importance of listening to the student after class		

What is the rank order given these solutions by the groups?

1. _____   4. _____

2. _____   5. _____

3. _____   6. _____

AIMS: 1. To identify the five steps in using Reality Therapy.

2. To identify two principles for using Reality Therapy.

RATIONALE FOR DOING THIS ACTIVITY:

HELLO, SUE! AFTER OUR PREVIOUS DISCUSSION ABOUT USING WILLIAM GLASSER'S "CLASS MEETINGS" TO MOTIVATE STUDENTS, I, MYSELF WAS MOTIVATED TO READ ANOTHER ONE OF HIS BOOKS — REALITY THERAPY!

"REALITY THERAPY" WHAT IS IT?

IT'S A CORRECTIVE TECHNIQUE WHICH GLASSER FIRST USED TO HELP VERY DELINQUENT JUVENILES BECOME RESPONSIBLE FOR IMPROVING THEIR MISBEHAVIOR ... AND IT WORKED SO SUCCESSFULLY THAT HE THEN BEGAN TO TEACH TEACHERS HOW TO USE "REALITY THERAPY" TO HELP THEIR STUDENTS BEHAVE BETTER IN SCHOOL.

WHY DID GLASSER FIRST START USING "REALITY THERAPY"?

HE FOUND THE JUVENILE DELINQUENTS WERE ACTING OUT A "FAILURE IDENTITY" WHICH THEY HAD DEVELOPED AS A RESULT OF "FAILING TO LOVE AND BE LOVED" AND "FAILING TO ACHIEVE SELF-WORTH".

HOW DOES THIS "FAILURE IDENTITY" DEVELOP?

IF A PERSON CANNOT DEVELOP A "SUCCESS IDENTITY" THROUGH THE PATHWAYS OF LOVE AND SELF-WORTH, HE ATTEMPTS TO DO SO THROUGH TWO OTHER PATHWAYS — DELINQUENCY AND WITHDRAWAL!

DELINQUENCY REFERS TO BEHAVING IN AN IRRESPONSIBLE, MORALLY WRONG MANNER ... AND WITHDRAWAL REFERS TO DENYING OR IGNORING THE REALITY AROUND YOU — AND THIS CAUSES YOU TO BEHAVE UNREALISTICALLY.

IS THE GOAL OF "REALITY THERAPY", THEN, TO "CORRECT" PEOPLE'S DELINQUENT AND WITHDRAWAL BEHAVIOR?

YES! THIS IS HOW GLASSER FIRST USED "REALITY THERAPY" AS A CORRECTIVE TECHNIQUE ... BUT THEN HE REALIZED THAT IT COULD ALSO BE USED WITH STUDENTS IN SCHOOL AS A PREVENTIVE TECHNIQUE TO PREVENT THEM FROM DEVELOPING A "FAILURE IDENTITY".

167

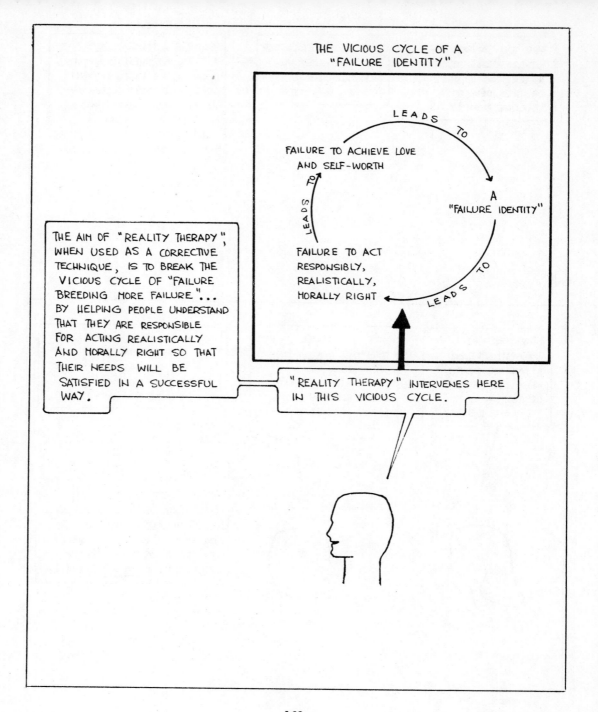

168

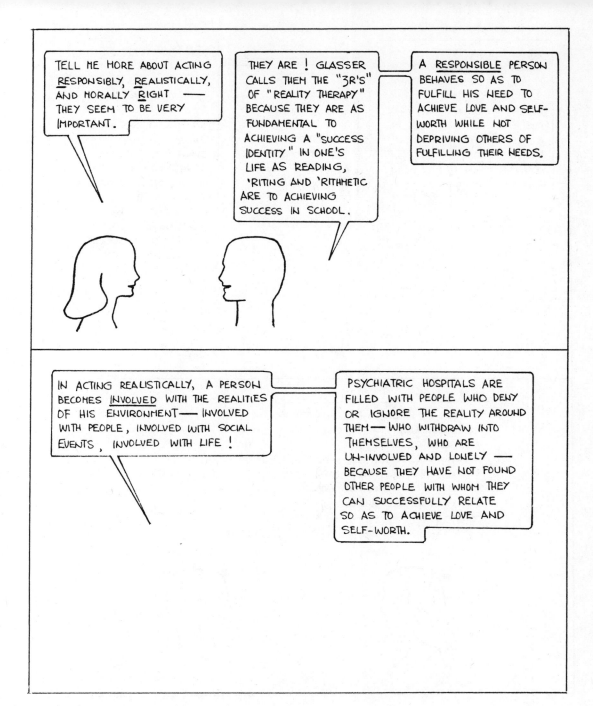

170

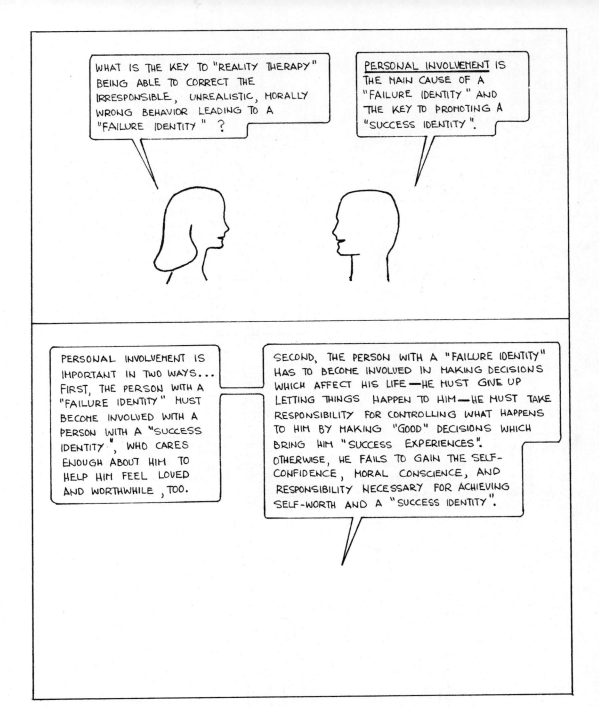

WHAT IS THE KEY TO "REALITY THERAPY" BEING ABLE TO CORRECT THE IRRESPONSIBLE, UNREALISTIC, MORALLY WRONG BEHAVIOR LEADING TO A "FAILURE IDENTITY"?

PERSONAL INVOLVEMENT IS THE MAIN CAUSE OF A "FAILURE IDENTITY" AND THE KEY TO PROMOTING A "SUCCESS IDENTITY".

PERSONAL INVOLVEMENT IS IMPORTANT IN TWO WAYS... FIRST, THE PERSON WITH A "FAILURE IDENTITY" MUST BECOME INVOLVED WITH A PERSON WITH A "SUCCESS IDENTITY", WHO CARES ENOUGH ABOUT HIM TO HELP HIM FEEL LOVED AND WORTHWHILE, TOO.

SECOND, THE PERSON WITH A "FAILURE IDENTITY" HAS TO BECOME INVOLVED IN MAKING DECISIONS WHICH AFFECT HIS LIFE—HE MUST GIVE UP LETTING THINGS HAPPEN TO HIM—HE MUST TAKE RESPONSIBILITY FOR CONTROLLING WHAT HAPPENS TO HIM BY MAKING "GOOD" DECISIONS WHICH BRING HIM "SUCCESS EXPERIENCES". OTHERWISE, HE FAILS TO GAIN THE SELF-CONFIDENCE, MORAL CONSCIENCE, AND RESPONSIBILITY NECESSARY FOR ACHIEVING SELF-WORTH AND A "SUCCESS IDENTITY".

TO SUM UP: "REALITY THERAPY" OPERATES ON THE BELIEF THAT EACH PERSON MUST BECOME RESPONSIBLE FOR MAKING BETTER DECISIONS WHICH ENABLE HIM TO ACHIEVE A "SUCCESS IDENTITY" ... AND THERE IS RESEARCH SUPPORT FOR THIS BELIEF IN JAMES COLEMAN'S REPORT ON THE INFLUENCE OF PUBLIC SCHOOLING, CALLED EQUALITY OF EDUCATIONAL OPPORTUNITY.

"In addition to the school character-istics which were shown to be related to pupil achievement, Coleman found a pupil characteristic which appears to have a stronger relationship to achievement than all the school factors combined. The extent to which a pupil feels he has control over his own destiny is strongly related to achievement. This feeling of potency is less prevalent among Negro students, but where it is present 'their achieve-ment is higher than that of white pupils who lack that conviction'."

Reference: Edmund Gordon, JACD Bulletin, Ferkauf Graduate School, Yeshiva University, Vol. III, No. 5, Nov. 1967.

NOW THAT WE'VE TALKED ABOUT THE "3R'S" OF "REALITY THERAPY", AND ABOUT THE IMPORTANCE OF INVOLVEMENT, TELL ME HOW I, AS A TEACHER, CAN USE "REALITY THERAPY" TO HELP MY STUDENTS ACHIEVE A "SUCCESS IDENTITY".

O.K.!..."REALITY THERAPY" CONSISTS OF FIVE STEPS AND TWO IMPORTANT PRINCIPLES.

The following five steps are intended to help students experience success in school by becoming involved in decision-making, by becoming responsible for their own behavior and its consequences, and by becoming self-confident thinkers who can control their behavior realistically within society.

STEP 1: <u>Get involved</u> with your students by being personal and being friendly, by giving your time to the student experiencing failure (e.g. provide intermittent personal attention or reinforcement throughout the day after each successful activity or behavior the student demonstrates); the aim is to initially replace the student's failure with your involvement, with your time, with your understanding, and your positive expectations that the student can succeed. This personal involvement with the student continues through the other four steps as well.

STEP 2: <u>Emphasize present behavior</u> -- help the student become self-aware of his present behavior and the consequences of it (e.g. ask him what he is doing now? How is it helping you now?). Avoid two dead ends: (1) do not dwell on the student's <u>past history</u> of failure or inappropriate behavior and do not request the student to "reform his past" because this prospect overwhelms him; (2) do not dwell on <u>how the student feels</u> because he cannot do anything about "feeling badly", until he stops behaving badly". Therefore, <u>accept</u> the fact that the student "feels badly" about himself, and then help him "do better".

STEP 3: <u>Help the student make a value judgment</u> that he wants to improve his "bad" behavior by asking questions such as: "Is what you are doing helping you? Your teacher? Your parents? The school? The world?" When the teacher asks questions such as these, the student learns that he has the ability and the responsibility to make value judgments and decisions which can improve what he is doing in life; he can control as contrasted with being externally controlled by external sources. The student must want to change before you can proceed to the next step.

STEP 4: <u>Help the student make a workable plan of action</u> to improve his behavior. This should come from the student; it should not be too big, but rather should be a series of moment-to-moment plans with gradually increased time intervals for the plan to be executed so that each plan is capable of successful execution on the part of the student. Give positive reinforcement following each such success. Plans which are too big, although well intentioned, can result in another failure experience which is antithetical to the approach of Reality Therapy.

STEP 5: <u>Get a commitment from the student</u> -- e.g. his signature, his handshake, or a written contract--saying that he has committed himself to fulfilling the plan he has chosen to execute. If the student uses the ploy, "You don't trust me", and you really don't, say so. You will not break the personal relationship initially established; rather you will show that you care that he cares about himself. Without this commitment, the student's plan will often not be fulfilled.

WHAT WOULD I DO IF I GOT INVOLVED WITH A STUDENT AND FOLLOWED ALL THE STEPS, BUT THE STUDENT DID NOT FOLLOW THE PLAN OF ACTION TO CHANGE HIS BEHAVIOR, WHICH HE HAD COMMITTED HIMSELF TO DOING ?

GLASSER REALIZES THAT "EVEN THE BEST LAID PLAN CAN GO AWRY", SO HE INCLUDES TWO IMPORTANT PRINCIPLES TO HELP THE TEACHER AND STUDENT EVENTUALLY SUCCEED.

TWO PRINCIPLES TO FOLLOW WHEN THE STUDENT DOES NOT FULFILL HIS
PLAN OF ACTION TO IMPROVE HIS BEHAVIOR

PRINCIPLE 1: Do not accept any excuses when the student does not fulfill the plan he has decided to make. Accepting excuses lets the student become irresponsible again, and allows him to believe that you don't care enough to get him to keep trying. Rather than accept any excuses, get the student to make another value judgment or decision to improve what he is doing in life (Step 3), make another plan of action which is more manageable (Step 4), and make another commitment that he will fulfill his plan (Step 5).

PRINCIPLE 2: Do not administer punishment (which Glasser defines as physical pain), because this allows the student to believe that he has paid off his debt for his irresponsible behavior. Instead, use natural consequences appropriate to the student's irresponsible behavior; e.g., if the student has committed himself to completing a particular task during class time and does not, detention after school should be for completing the task and not imposed as retribution (which would be punishment). The rules and regulations, as well as the natural consequences or sanctions, should be decided upon in such a way that students have a voice in the decision being made because this helps the students assume responsibility for their own behavior.

NOW THAT YOU HAVE READ BOB'S DESCRIPTION OF "REALITY THERAPY", YOU WILL HAVE AN OPPORTUNITY TO CHECK YOUR UNDERSTANDING OF ITS FIVE STEPS AND TWO PRINCIPLES BY DOING THE FOLLOWING EXERCISE.

INSTRUCTIONS:

After the role play of a "discipline problem", answer the following questions to indicate how well "Reality Therapy" was used to help the "misbehaving student" to improve his/her behavior. Verbalize your answers to the pair which performed the role play and also write them down in the space provided below.
Time: 15 minutes

I. In what ways did the "teacher" get involved with the "misbehaving student" and show that he cared?

II. How did the "teacher" help the "student" become aware of his present behavior and its consequences?

III. How did the "teacher" help the "student" make a value judgment that his behavior needed improving and a decision to improve it?

IV. How did the "teacher" help the "student" make a workable plan of action to improve his behavior? What was the plan? How did it propose to bring about more responsible, realistic, morally right student behavior?

V. How did the "teacher" get a commitment from the "student" to follow his plan? What was the commitment?

VI. Did the "teacher" accept any excuses from the "student" for his misbehavior or for not following his plan? Describe these excuses.

VII. Did the "teacher" threaten to use or actually use punishment? Describe any instances.

USING RUDOLF DREIKURS' CORRECTIVE PROCEDURES FOR MODIFYING THE FOUR GOALS OF MISBEHAVIOR

AIMS: 1. To identify four goals of misbehavior.

2. To identify appropriate intervention techniques that correct students' mistaken goals.

RATIONALE FOR DOING THIS ACTIVITY:

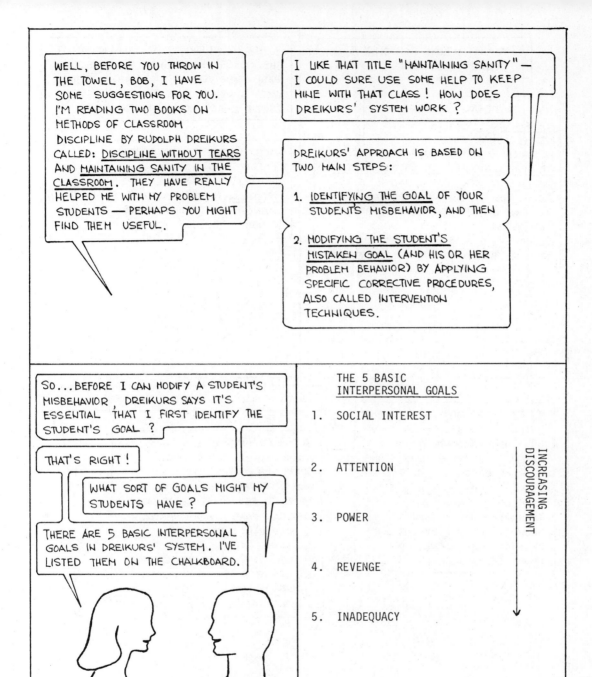

WELL, BEFORE YOU THROW IN THE TOWEL, BOB, I HAVE SOME SUGGESTIONS FOR YOU. I'M READING TWO BOOKS ON METHODS OF CLASSROOM DISCIPLINE BY RUDOLPH DREIKURS CALLED: DISCIPLINE WITHOUT TEARS AND MAINTAINING SANITY IN THE CLASSROOM. THEY HAVE REALLY HELPED ME WITH MY PROBLEM STUDENTS — PERHAPS YOU MIGHT FIND THEM USEFUL.

I LIKE THAT TITLE "MAINTAINING SANITY" — I COULD SURE USE SOME HELP TO KEEP MINE WITH THAT CLASS! HOW DOES DREIKURS' SYSTEM WORK?

DREIKURS' APPROACH IS BASED ON TWO MAIN STEPS:

1. IDENTIFYING THE GOAL OF YOUR STUDENT'S MISBEHAVIOR, AND THEN

2. MODIFYING THE STUDENT'S MISTAKEN GOAL (AND HIS OR HER PROBLEM BEHAVIOR) BY APPLYING SPECIFIC CORRECTIVE PROCEDURES, ALSO CALLED INTERVENTION TECHNIQUES.

SO...BEFORE I CAN MODIFY A STUDENT'S MISBEHAVIOR, DREIKURS SAYS IT'S ESSENTIAL THAT I FIRST IDENTIFY THE STUDENT'S GOAL?

THAT'S RIGHT!

WHAT SORT OF GOALS MIGHT MY STUDENTS HAVE?

THERE ARE 5 BASIC INTERPERSONAL GOALS IN DREIKURS' SYSTEM. I'VE LISTED THEM ON THE CHALKBOARD.

THE 5 BASIC INTERPERSONAL GOALS

1. SOCIAL INTEREST

2. ATTENTION

3. POWER

4. REVENGE

5. INADEQUACY

INCREASING DISCOURAGEMENT

177

YOU MEAN THERE ARE ONLY 5 GOALS OF BEHAVIOR?

NO... THERE ARE ONLY 5 BASIC INTERPERSONAL GOALS. AN INTERPERSONAL GOAL IS A GOAL IN WHICH WHAT YOU WANT IS A SPECIFIC REACTION FROM ANOTHER PERSON. OPENING A DOOR, FOR INSTANCE, IS A GOAL BUT NOT AN INTERPERSONAL ONE. IF, HOWEVER, YOU OPEN A DOOR BECAUSE YOU KNOW THAT IT WILL ANNOY SOMEONE, YOUR GOAL IS REVENGE... TO HURT THEM.

I GET IT, DREIKURS IS TALKING ABOUT THE GOALS PEOPLE HAVE IN CONNECTION WITH OTHER PEOPLE, NOT IN CONNECTION WITH THINGS. WHAT EXACTLY ARE EACH OF THE GOALS YOU'VE MENTIONED?

SOCIAL INTEREST IS THE GOAL OF COOPERATING WITH AND HELPING OTHER PEOPLE. ATTENTION IS THE GOAL OF TRYING TO GET OTHER PEOPLE TO NOTICE YOU...

POWER IS THE GOAL OF TRYING TO CONTROL OTHER PEOPLE OR SHOW THEM THAT YOU ARE THE BOSS. REVENGE IS THE GOAL OF TRYING TO HURT OTHERS... TO "PAY THEM BACK". AND INADEQUACY IS THE GOAL OF DISPLAYING AN INADEQUACY OR IMAGINED DISABILITY IN ORDER TO GET OUT OF SITUATIONS WHERE ONE IS AFRAID OF FAILING.

WHAT DETERMINES ONE'S INTERPERSONAL GOAL?

A CHILD'S INTERPERSONAL GOAL IS STRONGLY RELATED TO HOW ADULTS TREAT HIM. IF A CHILD IS ACCEPTED AND ENCOURAGED BY ADULTS, AND MADE TO FEEL THAT HE BELONGS AND CAN MAKE A WORTHWHILE CONTRIBUTION TO THE FAMILY OR CLASSROOM GROUP, HE WILL TEND TO FEEL "GOOD" ABOUT HIMSELF AND AND OTHERS AND WILL DISPLAY THE COOPERATIVE GOAL OF SOCIAL INTEREST IN HIS RELATIONSHIPS WITH OTHER PEOPLE.

WHAT HAPPENS IF A CHILD IS NOT ACCEPTED OR ENCOURAGED BY ADULTS?
WHAT IF ADULTS JUST IGNORE HIM??

I SEE YOUR POINT... CHILDREN CAN'T STAND BEING IGNORED... TREATED LIKE THEY DON'T EXIST, OR AREN'T IMPORTANT.
HOW DOES A CHILD COME TO DEVELOP THE GOAL OF POWER?

IF A CHILD FEELS IGNORED, HE WILL TRY TO FIND A PLACE IN THE GROUP BY SEEKING THE GOAL OF <u>ATTENTION</u>. THIS TYPE OF CHILD THINKS "I ONLY FEEL ACCEPTED WHEN OTHERS PAY ATTENTION TO ME." HE WANTS TO BE NOTICED BECAUSE THIS MAKES HIM FEEL WORTHWHILE, AS THOUGH HE BELONGS AND "HAS A PLACE" IN THE GROUP.

IF IN ADDITION TO NOT ACCEPTING OR ENCOURAGING A CHILD, ADULTS TRY TO CONTROL HIM AND FORCE HIM IN AN UNFAIR OR AUTHORITARIAN MANNER TO DO THEIR WILL, HE MAY DEVELOP THE GOAL OF <u>POWER</u> — HE WILL TRY TO SHOW OTHERS THAT HE IS THE BOSS BY REFUSING TO COOPERATE. THIS TYPE OF CHILD BELIEVES: "IF YOU DON'T LET ME HAVE MY WAY, YOU DON'T CARE FOR ME."

HE FEELS ACCEPTED — THAT HE "HAS A PLACE" — ONLY IF HE CAN "CONTROL" OTHERS.

EXACTLY. THE POWER-SEEKING CHILD IS A VERY DISCOURAGED CHILD. HE TRIES TO DRAW YOU INTO A "FIGHT" IN ORDER TO DEMONSTRATE HIS POWER.

179

WHAT HAPPENS IF A CHILD IS EVEN MORE DISCOURAGED ?

IF THE SIGNIFICANT ADULTS AROUND A CHILD BEAT OR BRUTALIZE HIM AND ACTUALLY DISPLAY DISLIKE TOWARDS HIM...

...LIKE SOME PARENTS WHO DIDN'T WANT TO HAVE A CHILD, OR PARENTS OR TEACHERS WHO "TAKE THINGS OUT" ON A CHILD, USING HIM AS A SCAPEGOAT...

...THIS MAY CAUSE A CHILD TO DISPLAY THE GOAL OF REVENGE. HE WANTS TO HURT OTHERS AS DEEPLY AS HE FEELS HURT BY THEM. HE BELIEVES: "IF I CAN'T HURT THEM, THEN AT LEAST I HAVE SOME IMPACT ON OTHERS." THE REVENGE-SEEKING CHILD IS DEEPLY DISCOURAGED... HE THINKS OTHERS DISLIKE HIM AND SO HE OFTEN PROVOKES OTHERS TO ACTUALLY DISLIKE HIM.

WHAT CAUSES A CHILD TO DISPLAY THE GOAL OF INADEQUACY ?

IF ADULTS PUNISH A CHILD EVERYTIME HE MAKES A MISTAKE AND CONVEY TO HIM THE IDEA THAT HE HAS NO WORTH, THE CHILD MAY DISPLAY INADEQUACY IN ORDER TO GET OUT OF ATTEMPTING TO DO OR LEARN ANYTHING NEW THAT HE MIGHT FAIL AT. THE CHILD WITH THIS GOAL BELIEVES: "I DON'T WANT ANYONE TO FIND OUT HOW STUPID AND INCAPABLE I AM."

HE FEELS SO HOPELESS AND STUPID THAT HE JUST WANTS TO BE LEFT ALONE. FAILING AT LEARNING TASKS IS SUCH A BLOW TO HIS SELF-ESTEEM THAT HE AVOIDS THE RISK OF FAILURE BY MAKING EXCUSES TO GET OUT OF ATTEMPTING NEW LEARNING TASKS. THIS TYPE OF CHILD IS THE MOST DEEPLY DISCOURAGED OF ALL. HE HAS GIVEN UP !!

I HEAR YOU SAYING THAT AS A CHILD GETS MORE AND MORE DISCOURAGED. BECAUSE ADULTS IGNORE, CONTROL, HURT OR OTHERWISE FAIL TO ENCOURAGE HIM, HE MOVES FROM THE POSITIVE GOAL OF SOCIAL INTEREST TO THE NEGATIVE GOALS OF ATTENTION, POWER, REVENGE, AND INADEQUACY.

THAT'S RIGHT. THESE NEGATIVE INTERPERSONAL GOALS: ATTENTION, POWER, REVENGE AND INADEQUACY ARE ALSO CALLED "MISTAKEN" GOALS.

WHY ARE THEY CALLED THAT?

BECAUSE THE CHILD WHO DISPLAYS ONE OF THESE 4 GOALS BELIEVES THAT PURSUING THAT GOAL IS THE ONLY WAY HE CAN "FIND A PLACE" AND "MAKE AN IMPACT" ON HIS FAMILY OR CLASSROOM GROUP.

I SEE... HIS LOGIC ABOUT HOW TO BELONG AND MAKE A CONTRIBUTION IS FAULTY. THEREFORE, THE GOALS ARE "MISTAKEN" GOALS.

YES... AND THE TEACHER WHO REALLY CARES ABOUT HIS STUDENTS WILL TRY TO SHOW THOSE STUDENTS WHO HAVE MISTAKEN GOALS MORE CONSTRUCTIVE WAYS OF FINDING THEIR "PLACE" IN THE CLASSROOM.

BUT ISN'T THE TEACHER BEING MANIPULATIVE BY DOING THAT?

IN A SENSE... YES. BUT IT IS A POSITIVE MANIPULATION. THE FACILITATIVE TEACHER DOESN'T TRY TO CHANGE HIS STUDENTS JUST TO MAKE LIFE EASIER FOR HIMSELF.

THE FACILITATIVE TEACHER TRIES TO HELP THE STUDENTS WITH MISTAKEN GOALS TO LEARN MORE CONSTRUCTIVE WAYS OF MEETING THEIR NEEDS BECAUSE HE KNOWS HOW DEEPLY DISCOURAGED AND HOW UNHAPPY THESE CHILDREN REALLY ARE.

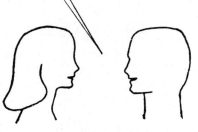

CHART OF INTERPERSONAL GOALS AND RELATED BEHAVIORAL CHARACTERISTICS

INTERPERSONAL GOAL	CONSTRUCTIVE BEHAVIORAL CHARACTERISTICS		DESTRUCTIVE BEHAVIORAL CHARACTERISTICS	
	ACTIVE	PASSIVE	ACTIVE	PASSIVE
1. SOCIAL INTEREST	"Active Social Interest"	"Passive Social Interest"	*	*
2. ATTENTION	"Successful"	"Charming"	"Nuisance"	"Helpless"
3. POWER	*	*	"Rebellious"	"Stubborn"
4. REVENGE	*	*	"Vicious"	"Sullen"
5. INADEQUACY	*	*	*	"Hopeless"

* Absence of a corresponding behavioral characteristic for a particular Interpersonal Goal.

EXAMPLES OF SPECIFIC INTERPERSONAL GOALS

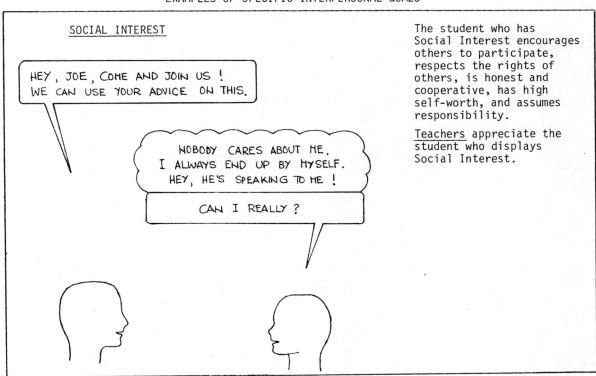

SOCIAL INTEREST

HEY, JOE, COME AND JOIN US!
WE CAN USE YOUR ADVICE ON THIS.

NOBODY CARES ABOUT ME.
I ALWAYS END UP BY MYSELF.
HEY, HE'S SPEAKING TO ME!

CAN I REALLY?

The student who has Social Interest encourages others to participate, respects the rights of others, is honest and cooperative, has high self-worth, and assumes responsibility.

Teachers appreciate the student who displays Social Interest.

183

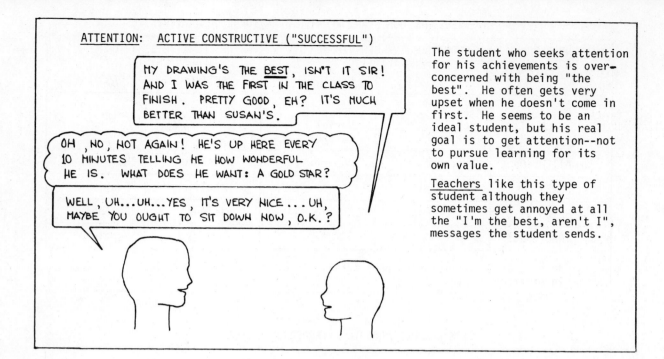

ATTENTION: ACTIVE CONSTRUCTIVE ("SUCCESSFUL")

MY DRAWING'S THE BEST, ISN'T IT SIR! AND I WAS THE FIRST IN THE CLASS TO FINISH. PRETTY GOOD, EH? IT'S MUCH BETTER THAN SUSAN'S.

OH, NO, NOT AGAIN! HE'S UP HERE EVERY 10 MINUTES TELLING ME HOW WONDERFUL HE IS. WHAT DOES HE WANT: A GOLD STAR?

WELL, UH...UH...YES, IT'S VERY NICE ...UH, MAYBE YOU OUGHT TO SIT DOWN NOW, O.K.?

The student who seeks attention for his achievements is over-concerned with being "the best". He often gets very upset when he doesn't come in first. He seems to be an ideal student, but his real goal is to get attention--not to pursue learning for its own value.

Teachers like this type of student although they sometimes get annoyed at all the "I'm the best, aren't I", messages the student sends.

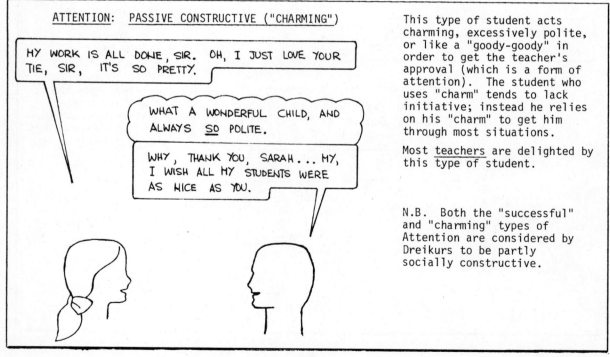

ATTENTION: PASSIVE CONSTRUCTIVE ("CHARMING")

MY WORK IS ALL DONE, SIR. OH, I JUST LOVE YOUR TIE, SIR, IT'S SO PRETTY.

WHAT A WONDERFUL CHILD, AND ALWAYS SO POLITE.

WHY, THANK YOU, SARAH... MY, I WISH ALL MY STUDENTS WERE AS NICE AS YOU.

This type of student acts charming, excessively polite, or like a "goody-goody" in order to get the teacher's approval (which is a form of attention). The student who uses "charm" tends to lack initiative; instead he relies on his "charm" to get him through most situations.

Most teachers are delighted by this type of student.

N.B. Both the "successful" and "charming" types of Attention are considered by Dreikurs to be partly socially constructive.

184

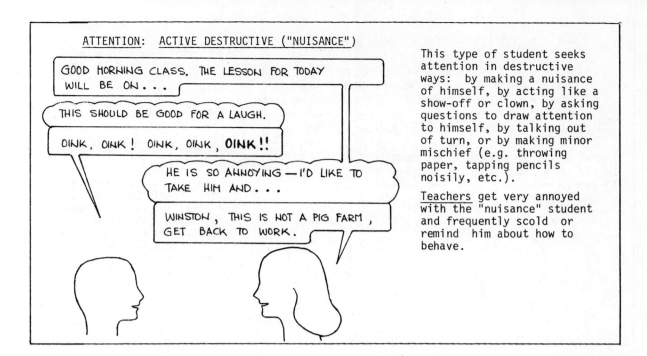

ATTENTION: ACTIVE DESTRUCTIVE ("NUISANCE")

GOOD MORNING CLASS. THE LESSON FOR TODAY WILL BE ON...

THIS SHOULD BE GOOD FOR A LAUGH.

OINK, OINK! OINK, OINK, **OINK!!**

HE IS SO ANNOYING — I'D LIKE TO TAKE HIM AND...

WINSTON, THIS IS NOT A PIG FARM, GET BACK TO WORK.

This type of student seeks attention in destructive ways: by making a nuisance of himself, by acting like a show-off or clown, by asking questions to draw attention to himself, by talking out of turn, or by making minor mischief (e.g. throwing paper, tapping pencils noisily, etc.).

<u>Teachers</u> get very annoyed with the "nuisance" student and frequently scold or remind him about how to behave.

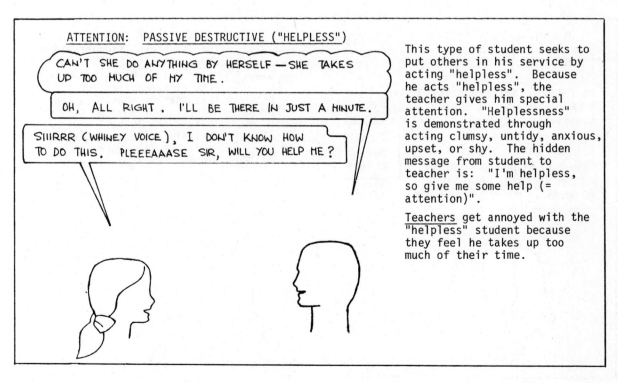

ATTENTION: PASSIVE DESTRUCTIVE ("HELPLESS")

CAN'T SHE DO ANYTHING BY HERSELF — SHE TAKES UP TOO MUCH OF MY TIME.

OH, ALL RIGHT. I'LL BE THERE IN JUST A MINUTE.

SIIIRRR (WHINEY VOICE), I DON'T KNOW HOW TO DO THIS. PLEEEAAASE SIR, WILL YOU HELP ME?

This type of student seeks to put others in his service by acting "helpless". Because he acts "helpless", the teacher gives him special attention. "Helplessness" is demonstrated through acting clumsy, untidy, anxious, upset, or shy. The hidden message from student to teacher is: "I'm helpless, so give me some help (= attention)".

<u>Teachers</u> get annoyed with the "helpless" student because they feel he takes up too much of their time.

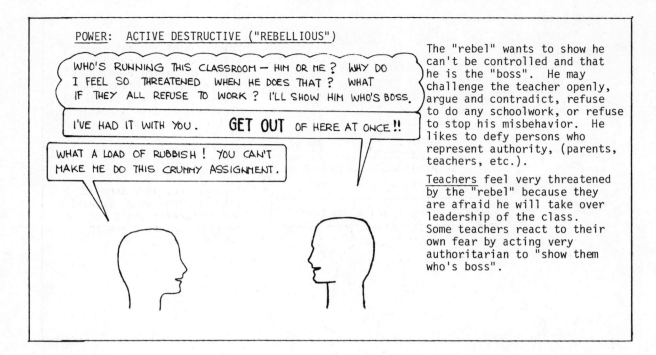

POWER: ACTIVE DESTRUCTIVE ("REBELLIOUS")

The "rebel" wants to show he can't be controlled and that he is the "boss". He may challenge the teacher openly, argue and contradict, refuse to do any schoolwork, or refuse to stop his misbehavior. He likes to defy persons who represent authority, (parents, teachers, etc.).

Teachers feel very threatened by the "rebel" because they are afraid he will take over leadership of the class. Some teachers react to their own fear by acting very authoritarian to "show them who's boss".

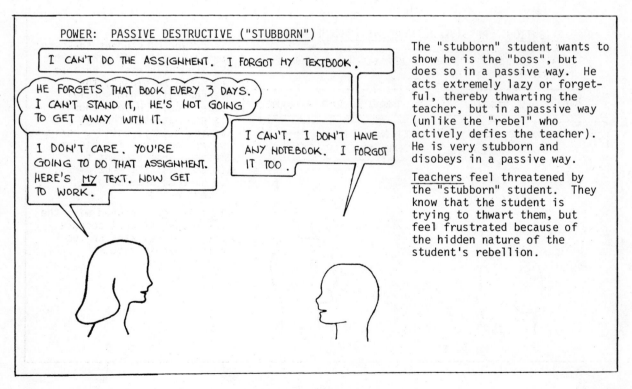

POWER: PASSIVE DESTRUCTIVE ("STUBBORN")

The "stubborn" student wants to show he is the "boss", but does so in a passive way. He acts extremely lazy or forgetful, thereby thwarting the teacher, but in a passive way (unlike the "rebel" who actively defies the teacher). He is very stubborn and disobeys in a passive way.

Teachers feel threatened by the "stubborn" student. They know that the student is trying to thwart them, but feel frustrated because of the hidden nature of the student's rebellion.

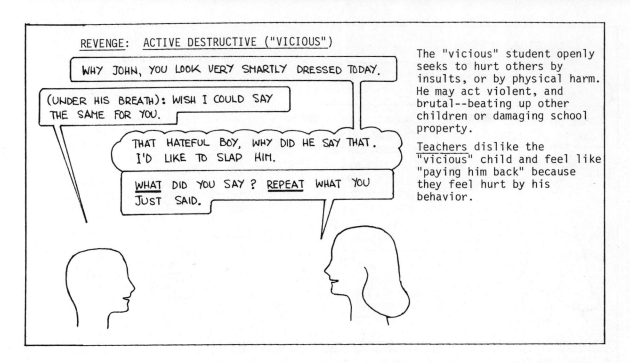

REVENGE: ACTIVE DESTRUCTIVE ("VICIOUS")

WHY JOHN, YOU LOOK VERY SMARTLY DRESSED TODAY.

(UNDER HIS BREATH): WISH I COULD SAY THE SAME FOR YOU.

THAT HATEFUL BOY, WHY DID HE SAY THAT. I'D LIKE TO SLAP HIM.

WHAT DID YOU SAY? REPEAT WHAT YOU JUST SAID.

The "vicious" student openly seeks to hurt others by insults, or by physical harm. He may act violent, and brutal--beating up other children or damaging school property.

Teachers dislike the "vicious" child and feel like "paying him back" because they feel hurt by his behavior.

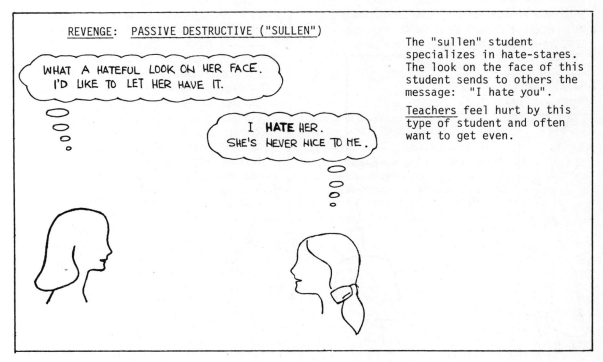

REVENGE: PASSIVE DESTRUCTIVE ("SULLEN")

WHAT A HATEFUL LOOK ON HER FACE. I'D LIKE TO LET HER HAVE IT.

I HATE HER. SHE'S NEVER NICE TO ME.

The "sullen" student specializes in hate-stares. The look on the face of this student sends to others the message: "I hate you".

Teachers feel hurt by this type of student and often want to get even.

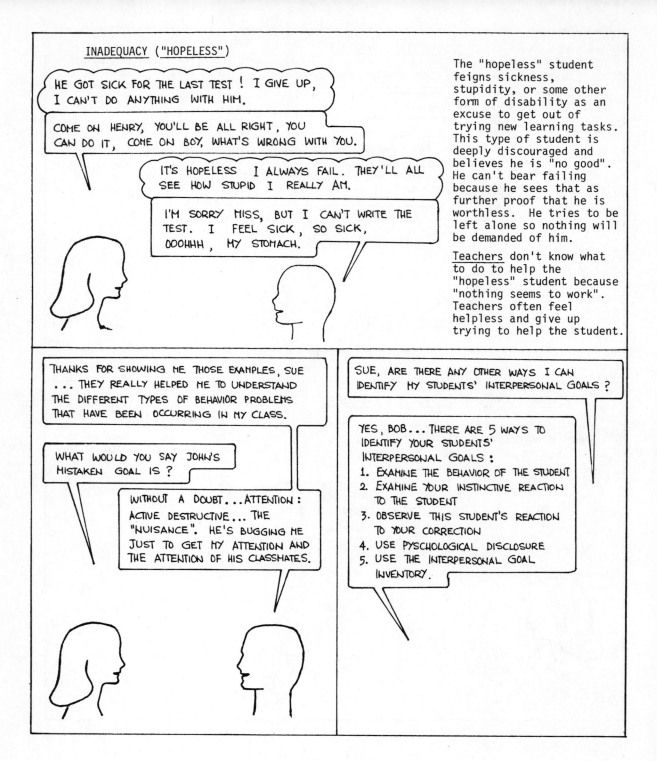

INADEQUACY ("HOPELESS")

The "hopeless" student feigns sickness, stupidity, or some other form of disability as an excuse to get out of trying new learning tasks. This type of student is deeply discouraged and believes he is "no good". He can't bear failing because he sees that as further proof that he is worthless. He tries to be left alone so nothing will be demanded of him.

Teachers don't know what to do to help the "hopeless" student because "nothing seems to work". Teachers often feel helpless and give up trying to help the student.

188

EXAMINING YOUR INSTINCTIVE REACTIONS (FEELINGS) TO A
"PROBLEM STUDENT" AS A WAY OF IDENTIFYING HIS
"MISTAKEN GOALS"

IF YOU FEEL	THE STUDENT'S PROBABLE GOAL IS
1. ANNOYED	ATTENTION-SEEKING
2. THREATENED	POWER-SEEKING
3. HURT	REVENGE-SEEKING
4. LIKE GIVING UP	DISPLAYING INADEQUACY

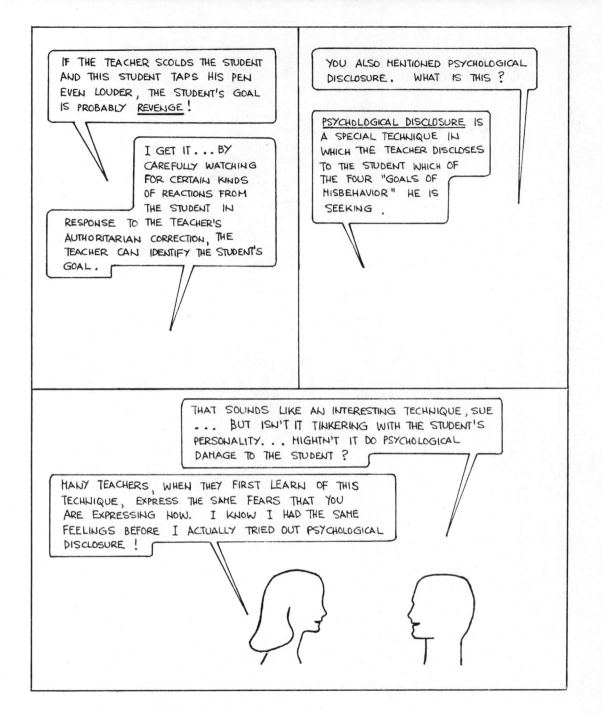

IF THE TEACHER SCOLDS THE STUDENT AND THIS STUDENT TAPS HIS PEN EVEN LOUDER, THE STUDENT'S GOAL IS PROBABLY <u>REVENGE</u>!

I GET IT... BY CAREFULLY WATCHING FOR CERTAIN KINDS OF REACTIONS FROM THE STUDENT IN RESPONSE TO THE TEACHER'S AUTHORITARIAN CORRECTION, THE TEACHER CAN IDENTIFY THE STUDENT'S GOAL.

YOU ALSO MENTIONED PSYCHOLOGICAL DISCLOSURE. WHAT IS THIS?

<u>PSYCHOLOGICAL DISCLOSURE</u> IS A SPECIAL TECHNIQUE IN WHICH THE TEACHER DISCLOSES TO THE STUDENT WHICH OF THE FOUR "GOALS OF MISBEHAVIOR" HE IS SEEKING.

THAT SOUNDS LIKE AN INTERESTING TECHNIQUE, SUE ... BUT ISN'T IT TINKERING WITH THE STUDENT'S PERSONALITY... MIGHTN'T IT DO PSYCHOLOGICAL DAMAGE TO THE STUDENT?

MANY TEACHERS, WHEN THEY FIRST LEARN OF THIS TECHNIQUE, EXPRESS THE SAME FEARS THAT YOU ARE EXPRESSING NOW. I KNOW I HAD THE SAME FEELINGS BEFORE I ACTUALLY TRIED OUT PSYCHOLOGICAL DISCLOSURE!

191

BUT THE ANSWER TO YOUR QUESTION, BOB, IS A RESOUNDING NO! FIRST OF ALL, TEACHERS ASK THE STUDENTS' PERMISSION BEFORE USING PSYCHOLOGICAL DISCLOSURE. SECOND, THERE IS NO EVIDENCE THAT TEACHERS WHO USE PSYCHOLOGICAL DISCLOSURE HARM THEIR STUDENTS IN ANY WAY. THE CHART ON THE NEXT PAGE SHOWS HOW PSYCHOLOGICAL DISCLOSURE ACTUALLY HELPS "PROBLEM STUDENTS" TO STOP MISBEHAVING—TO STOP TRYING TO SATISFY THEIR "MISTAKEN GOALS".

I CAN SEE FROM THE CHART HOW PSYCHOLOGICAL DISCLOSURE HELPS TEACHERS TO IDENTIFY STUDENTS' GOALS, BUT HOW DOES PSYCHOLOGICAL DISCLOSURE HELP THE STUDENT?

BY USING PSYCHOLOGICAL DISCLOSURE, THE TEACHER HELPS THE STUDENT TO UNDERSTAND HIS "MISTAKEN GOAL" AND MAKES HIM AWARE OF THE INFLUENCE OF THIS "HIDDEN GOAL" ON HIS BEHAVIOR. BY HELPING THE STUDENT TO UNDERSTAND HIMSELF BETTER, THE TEACHER ENABLES THE STUDENT TO CHANGE HIS OWN BEHAVIOR.

I SEE... THE TEACHER HELPS THE STUDENT TO GET INSIGHT INTO HIS OWN BEHAVIOR, AND THIS INSIGHT HELPS THE STUDENT TO CHANGE IN A POSITIVE DIRECTION.

EXACTLY! LET ME TELL YOU ABOUT A PERSONAL EXPERIENCE: I HAD A PROBLEM GRADE 8 STUDENT, LAURA, WHO ALWAYS SEEMED AFRAID TO TAKE PART IN CLASSROOM ACTIVITIES. SO I TRIED PSYCHOLOGICAL DISCLOSURE WITH HER. HERE'S WHAT HAPPENED . . .

192

1. Never attempt Psychological Disclosure during a conflict situation with the student. Find a time when you and the student can sit down alone <u>uninterrupted</u>. (You can arrange a meeting at recess or after class).

2. Say to the student: "I've noticed in class that you (describe the student's problem behavior in a non-evaluative way)...."

3. Next, say: "Do you know why you act that way?"
   Most students will say, "No", because they honestly don't understand the goals of their behavior (which is why Psychological Disclosure is helpful to them).

4. Get the student's <u>permission</u> to guess his goal (i.e., to do Psychological Disclosure): "May I tell you why I think you act the way you do?" If the student says no, respect his wishes. You can always try again at a later date. Most students, however, will say yes...they're curious to find out what you know about them.

5. If the student has given you his permission, ask him the following four questions, one at a time, pausing briefly to note any reaction on the part of the student:

   (a) Could it be you act this way to get attention? (Attention goal)

   (b) Could it be you act this way to show me that you are the boss and that I can't make you do anything you don't want to do? (Power goal)

   (c) Could it be you act this way because you feel hurt and you want to hurt others back? (Revenge goal)

   (d) Could it be you feel stupid and don't want people to know? (Inadequacy goal)

6. According to Dreikurs, the student <u>may</u> say no to each question. But, when you ask the question that accurately describes the student's "hidden" goal, you will get a "recognition reflex" from the student: his eyes will suddenly become wider ("Wow, how did the teacher know that!"), or he will blush, or he will show some other facial or bodily gesture that indicates he is reacting strongly to what you said. The student's "recognition reflex" in response to a specific Psychological Disclosure question by the teacher discloses the student's interpersonal goal.

   N.B. It is important to ask all four goal questions in the order indicated since more than one goal may be present in the student.

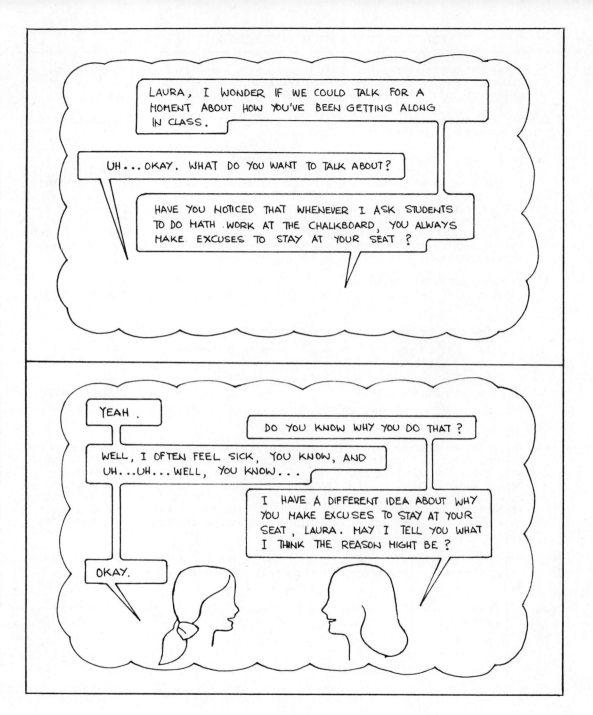

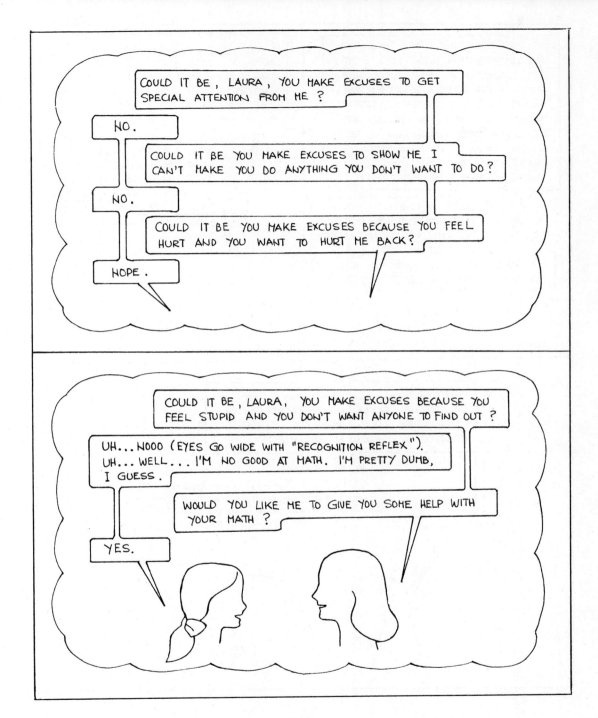

BUT THE REALLY INTERESTING THING, BOB, WAS THAT ABOUT A WEEK AFTER I DID THAT PSYCHOLOGICAL DISCLOSURE WITH LAURA — AND BEFORE I HAD ANY TIME TO GIVE HER SPECIAL TUTORING WITH MATH — SHE STARTED TO DO WORK AT THE CHALKBOARD ALONG WITH THE REST OF THE CLASS. SHE STILL MADE EXCUSES NOW AND THEN, BUT STILL ...THE CHANGE WAS REMARKABLE.

THAT'S FANTASTIC! IT SOUNDS LIKE PSYCHOLOGICAL DISCLOSURE NOT ONLY HELPED YOU IDENTIFY HER "MISTAKEN GOAL", BUT IT WAS ALSO A SUCCESSFUL INTERVENTION TECHNIQUE.

IT WAS VERY SUCCESSFUL IN HELPING LAURA TO UNDERSTAND THE "HIDDEN" MOTIVES BEHIND HER BEHAVIOR. ONCE SHE GOT INSIGHT INTO HER "MISTAKEN GOAL", SHE TOOK ACTION TO CHANGE IT.

THAT'S A POWERFUL INTERVENTION TECHNIQUE. I'M GOING TO TRY IT WITH JOHN! BUT TELL ME, WHAT IS THE INTERPERSONAL GOAL INVENTORY YOU MENTIONED EARLIER?

THE INTERPERSONAL GOAL INVENTORY IS A SPECIAL RATING SCALE WHICH TEACHERS CAN USE TO IDENTIFY THE INTERPERSONAL GOALS OF STUDENTS WITH PROBLEM BEHAVIORS.

BY FILLING OUT THIS RATING SCALE ON A STUDENT, A TEACHER CAN IDENTIFY THE STUDENT'S "MISTAKEN GOAL"?

THAT'S RIGHT.

196

CORRECTIVE PROCEDURES FOR ATTENTION-SEEKING

1. Use Psychological Disclosure to help the student understand the goal of his misbehavior.

2. Ignore the student when he is misbehaving. Remember that scolding, reminding, and punishing are forms of "negative attention". You must be consistent in using ignoring for it to work successfully.

3. Give the student attention when he is working or cooperating with others.

4. Use logical consequences - i.e., if a student fools around and doesn't get his assignment finished during class time, the logical consequence is that he must stay in during recess and complete the work. Logical consequences are arranged by the teacher, but the student is always given a choice, e.g. "You can do your work now, or you'll have to do it later". If the student makes an irresponsible choice (e.g. doesn't do work now), then the teacher enforces the logical consequence (e.g. student has to stay in and do the work later).

CORRECTIVE PROCEDURES FOR POWER-SEEKING

1. Use Psychological Disclosure to help the student understand the goal of his misbehavior.

2. Withdraw from the power conflict. Remember: it takes two to fight. Take your "sail" out of the student's "wind". This is a form of ignoring his negative behavior. Fighting with a power-seeking student reinforces his rebellious behavior. Keep your "cool".

3. Acknowledge to the student that he has power.

4. Give the student some meaningful responsibility in the classroom. Channel his power-seeking into constructive channels. Enlist his cooperation.

5. Make friends with him. Show interest in his interests.

CORRECTIVE PROCEDURES FOR REVENGE-SEEKING

1. Use Psychological Disclosure to help the student understand the goal of his misbehavior.

2. Ignore the student's revenge-seeking behavior. Don't act hurt or seek to retaliate against him yourself.

3. Make friends with the student. Show a personal interest in him. Try to "win" him over. Show him that you like him; he believes people dislike him--show that he's wrong.

4. Find him a friend in the class whom he can sit beside.

5. Obtain the help of the class in encouraging the revenge-seeking student.

CORRECTIVE PROCEDURES FOR DISPLAY OF INADEQUACY

1. Use Psychological Disclosure to help the student understand the goal of his misbehavior.

2. Don't give up on the student. Avoid getting discouraged hourself. Keep trying.

3. Give the student lots of encouragement. When the student has difficulty with a task, convey to him that you have faith in his ability to succeed. Let him know you think he can do it.

4. Avoid giving "smothering" help, that robs the student of his independence.

5. Make friends with the student. Show him you like him for himself--not for what he can do.

6. Point out the smallest of improvements and tell the student how much you like what he has done.

THESE CORRECTIVE PROCEDURES ARE VERY INTERESTING, SUE... BUT I WONDER IF THEY'RE NECESSARY. I MEAN, WHY NOT USE PUNISHMENT LIKE MY TEACHERS USED TO USE ON THEIR STUDENTS. PUNISHMENT WORKS, DOESN'T IT?

PUNISHMENT WORKS—BUT ONLY FOR A SHORT PERIOD OF TIME (MAYBE A FEW DAYS OR A FEW MINUTES) AND THEN THE MISBEHAVIOR RETURNS. PUNISHMENT ONLY SUPPRESSES A MISBEHAVIOR TEMPORARILY. THE COMPETENT TEACHER WANTS PERMANENT RESULTS SUCH AS ARE OBTAINED BY USING THE DREIKURS TECHNIQUE.

DOES PUNISHMENT HAVE ANY OTHER DRAWBACKS?

YES. IF YOU PUNISH A CHILD REGULARLY, HE WILL COME TO ASSOCIATE YOU WITH THE PUNISHMENT AND WILL TRY TO AVOID YOU AND YOUR CLASS; HE MAY DEVELOP FEAR OR ANXIETY REACTIONS IN YOUR PRESENCE, AND THESE MAY INTERFERE WITH HIS LEARNING AND CLASSROOM PARTICIPATION, OR HE MAY COME TO HATE YOU AND THE ACADEMIC SUBJECT HE IDENTIFIES WITH YOU.

WOW, PUNISHMENT CAN HAVE A REALLY DESTRUCTIVE EFFECT ON A STUDENT AND ON HIS LEARNING! ARE THERE ANY SITUATIONS WHERE A TEACHER'S USE OF PUNISHMENT IS APPROPRIATE?

YES, BOB... THERE ARE TWO SITUATIONS WHERE IT'S SUITABLE TO USE PUNISHMENT:
1. WHEN A STUDENT IS IN DANGER OF BEING PHYSICALLY HARMED (e.g. STUDENT RUNS INTO A BUSY STREET).
2. WHEN A STUDENT IS DOING SOMETHING THAT WILL PHYSICALLY HARM SOMEONE ELSE (e.g. PUNCHING ANOTHER STUDENT)

SO PUNISHMENT IS DESIRABLE IN SITUATIONS WHERE QUICK RESULTS MUST BE OBTAINED ON THE SPOT TO PREVENT STUDENTS FROM BEING PHYSICALLY HARMED.

THAT'S RIGHT.

199

IF PUNISHMENT IS SO INEFFECTIVE — AND I CAN SEE THAT IT IS — WHY DO SO MANY TEACHERS USE IT ?

BECAUSE THEY DON'T KNOW ANY OTHER DISCIPLINE TECHNIQUES. MOST TEACHERS DON'T REALIZE THAT THERE ARE MORE EFFECTIVE WAYS OF CORRECTING STUDENTS' MISBEHAVIOR . . . WAYS THAT GET PERMANENT RESULTS AND DON'T HAVE ANY OF THE DISADVANTAGES OF PUNISHMENT.

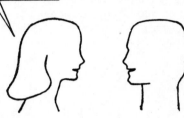

THE DREIKURS TECHNIQUE IS ONE OF THE MOST EFFECTIVE OF THESE "NEW" APPROACHES TO CLASSROOM DISCIPLINE. THOUSANDS OF TEACHERS HAVE USED DREIKURS' CORRECTIVE PROCEDURES TO PERMANENTLY ELIMINATE PROBLEM BEHAVIORS IN THEIR CLASSROOMS. THE DREIKURS' APPROACH IS EASY TO USE AND IT REALLY HELPS YOUR STUDENTS.

IT SOUNDS LIKE AN EXCITING APPROACH, SUE. I'M GOING TO TRY IT WITH MY STUDENT JOHN. MAYBE IT WILL HELP ME "MAINTAIN SANITY" IN MY CLASSROOM !

GOOD LUCK !

IN THE FOLLOWING FIVE EXERCISES YOU WILL LEARN HOW TO IDENTIFY AND CORRECT STUDENTS' "MISTAKEN GOALS" AND MISBEHAVIORS IN THE CLASSROOM. IN THE FIRST THREE EXERCISES, YOU WILL LEARN TO BECOME AN EXPERT AT IDENTIFYING THE GOALS OF STUDENTS' MISBEHAVIOR. IN THE REMAINING TWO EXERCISES, YOU WILL PRACTISE SKILLS IN APPLYING CORRECTIVE PROCEDURES THAT WILL PERMANENTLY ELIMINATE PROBLEM BEHAVIORS FROM YOUR CLASSROOM.

INTERPERSONAL GOAL IDENTIFICATION WORKSHEET   EXERCISE #1

INSTRUCTIONS:

Together with your partner, read each of the following nine Student Responses to the Teacher's Statement. Then <u>match</u> each Student Response with the appropriate Interpersonal Goal shown in the list of Interpersonal Goals. Do this by taking the number beside the Interpersonal Goal selected and writing it in the space provided beside the appropriate Student Response.

Time: 15 minutes

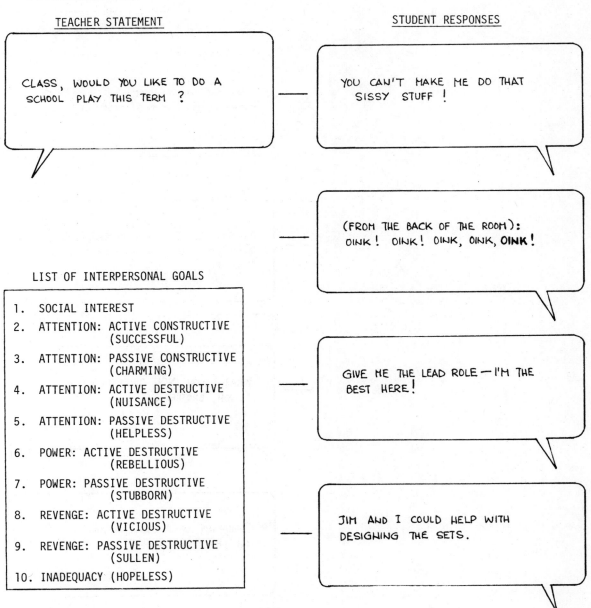

TEACHER STATEMENT

CLASS, WOULD YOU LIKE TO DO A SCHOOL PLAY THIS TERM ?

STUDENT RESPONSES

YOU CAN'T MAKE ME DO THAT SISSY STUFF !

(FROM THE BACK OF THE ROOM): OINK! OINK! OINK, OINK, OINK!

GIVE ME THE LEAD ROLE — I'M THE BEST HERE!

JIM AND I COULD HELP WITH DESIGNING THE SETS.

LIST OF INTERPERSONAL GOALS

1. SOCIAL INTEREST
2. ATTENTION: ACTIVE CONSTRUCTIVE (SUCCESSFUL)
3. ATTENTION: PASSIVE CONSTRUCTIVE (CHARMING)
4. ATTENTION: ACTIVE DESTRUCTIVE (NUISANCE)
5. ATTENTION: PASSIVE DESTRUCTIVE (HELPLESS)
6. POWER: ACTIVE DESTRUCTIVE (REBELLIOUS)
7. POWER: PASSIVE DESTRUCTIVE (STUBBORN)
8. REVENGE: ACTIVE DESTRUCTIVE (VICIOUS)
9. REVENGE: PASSIVE DESTRUCTIVE (SULLEN)
10. INADEQUACY (HOPELESS)

DON'T GIVE ME A PART, I'M TOO CLUMSY TO PLAY A PART.

YOU MADE A MISTAKE. IT'S "CLASS" PLAY, NOT "SCHOOL" PLAY.

OH SIR, YOU'RE SO WONDERFUL TO THINK OF SUCH A WONDERFUL IDEA FOR US.

WHAT, WITH YOU DIRECTING? OH, BROTHER . . .

(TRIPPING OVER CHAIR, AGAIN): OH, MY FOOT, I HURT MY FOOT !

INTERPERSONAL GOAL INVENTORY (Form A: Teacher Rating Scale)

BACKGROUND INFORMATION:

NAME OF STUDENT:_____ DATE:_____

AGE: _____ SEX:_____

GRADE: _____ SCHOOL:_____

RATED BY: _____

INSTRUCTIONS:

Show the extent to which you feel the student you are rating displays each of the following characteristics by placing a check (✔) in the appropriate column to the right.

CHARACTERISTICS	A GREAT DEAL	MODER-ATELY	MILDLY	NOT AT ALL
1. Seeks praise for good work.				
2. Is excessively nice.				
3. Acts the clown.				
4. Is untidy.				
5. Argues with others.				
6. Is stubborn.				
7. Is interested in others.				
8. Tries to be left alone.				
9. Seems to feel hopeless.				
10. Physically hurts others.				
11. Is extremely lazy about doing assignments.				
12. Always disagrees.				
13. Acts nervous.				
14. Is noisy.				
15. Thinks of "we" rather than just "I".				
16. Makes cute remarks.				
17. Refuses to do assigned work.				
18. Is shy, bashful.				
19. Acts the show-off.				

CHARACTERISTICS	A GREAT DEAL	MODER- ATELY	MILDLY	NOT AT ALL
20. Is excessively polite.				
21. Tries to get attention through performing well.				
22. Likes to help others.				
23. Says hurtful things.				
24. Gives up easily.				
25. Will not do what he (she) is told.				
26. Forgets things he (she) is supposed to do.				
27. Acts in a violent or brutal manner.				
28. Thinks he (she) is stupid.				
29. Is easily frightened.				
30. Is a warm, friendly person.				
31. Is a quiet "nice guy" or "nice girl".				
32. Gets upset if he (she) doesn't come in first.				
33. Acts helpless.				
34. Makes a nuisance of himself (herself).				
35. Tries to be "teacher's pet".				
36. Enjoys learning about new things.				
37. Makes excuses to avoid situations he (she) is afraid he (she) will do poorly in.				
38. Steals.				
39. Pretends not to hear.				
40. Wants to be the boss.				
41. Calls others names.				
42. Ignores the teacher.				
43. Keeps teacher busy by asking silly questions.				
44. Does stunts to get attention.				
45. Is a good student, but likes to keep in the background.				

SCORING KEY FOR INTERPERSONAL GOAL INVENTORY

EXERCISE #2

INSTRUCTIONS:

1. <u>Circle</u> the number in the space below which corresponds to the check mark you gave to each "characteristic of a Problem Student" on the Interpersonal Goal Inventory. (E.g. if you checked "A GREAT DEAL" for the first "Characteristic" on the Inventory, then circle the number "3" for the first "Characteristic" below.

2. <u>Total</u> the scores for each of the nine Interpersonal Goals below (their name is abbreviated below). Then, transfer these "totaled scores" onto the Results Sheet (on the next page).
Time: 20 minutes

"CHAR-ACTER-ISTIC"	A GREAT DEAL	MODER-ATELY	MILDLY	NOT AT ALL	GOAL ABBRE-VIATION	"CHAR-ACTER-ISTIC"	A GREAT DEAL	MODER-ATELY	MILDLY	NOT AT ALL	GOAL ABBRE-VIATION
1	3	2	1	0	A-AC	23	3	2	1	0	RS
2	3	2	1	0	A-PC	24	3	2	1	0	IN
3	3	2	1	0	A-AD	25	3	2	1	0	P-AD
4	3	2	1	0	A-PD	26	3	2	1	0	P-PD
5	3	2	1	0	P-AD	27	3	2	1	0	RS
6	3	2	1	0	P-PD	28	3	2	1	0	IN
7	3	2	1	0	SI	29	3	2	1	0	A-PD
8	3	2	1	0	IN	30	3	2	1	0	SI
9	3	2	1	0	IN	31	3	2	1	0	A-PC
10	3	2	1	0	RS	32	3	2	1	0	A-AC
11	3	2	1	0	P-PD	33	3	2	1	0	A-PD
12	3	2	1	0	P-AD	34	3	2	1	0	A-AD
13	3	2	1	0	A-PD	35	3	2	1	0	A-PC
14	3	2	1	0	A-AD	36	3	2	1	0	SI
15	3	2	1	0	SI	37	3	2	1	0	IN
16	3	2	1	0	A-AC	38	3	2	1	0	RS
17	3	2	1	0	P-AD	39	3	2	1	0	P-PD
18	3	2	1	0	A-PD	40	3	2	1	0	P-AD
19	3	2	1	0	A-AD	41	3	2	1	0	RS
20	3	2	1	0	A-PC	42	3	2	1	0	P-PD
21	3	2	1	0	A-AC	43	3	2	1	0	A-AD
22	3	2	1	0	SI	44	3	2	1	0	A-AC
						45	3	2	1	0	A-PC

RESULTS SHEET FOR INTERPERSONAL GOAL INVENTORY

INTERPERSONAL GOAL ABBREVIATION		INTERPERSONAL GOALS	SCORE
1. SI	=	Social Interest	15
2. A-AC	=	Attention: Active Constructive (Successful)	15
3. A-PC	=	Attention: Passive Constructive (Charming)	15
4. A-AD	=	Attention: Active Destructive (Nuisance)	15
5. A-PD	=	Attention: Passive Destructive (Helpless)	15
6. P-AD	=	Power: Active Destructive (Rebellious)	15
7. P-PD	=	Power: Passive Destructive (Stubborn)	15
8. RS	=	Revenge (Vicious)	15
9. IN	=	Inadequacy (Hopeless)	15

* *

Total "Constructive Characteristics" Score (Add 1 + 2 + 3)	45
Total "Destructive Characteristics" Score (Add 4 + 5 + 6 + 7 + 8 + 9)	90
Total "Active Characteristics" Score (Add 2 + 4 + 6)	45
Total "Passive" Characteristics" Score (Add 3 + 5 + 7 + 9)	60

206

DREIKURS' EXERCISE #3:   USING THE INTERPERSONAL GOAL SOCIOGRAM TO
                         UNDERSTAND YOUR CLASSROOM GROUP DYNAMICS
                         (A PROJECT FOR PRACTICUM)

TIME REQUIRED FOR DOING THIS EXERCISE:

About 2 hours

MATERIALS NEEDED:

As many copies of the Description Sheet for the Interpersonal Goal Sociogram
(one copy provided in this text) as there are students in your class.

PROCEDURE: (TO ACHIEVE AIM 1)

   I.   Reproduce a copy of the Interpersonal Goal Sociogram Description Sheet
        for each member of the class. Administer the Description Sheet to the
        class. Begin by reading the instructions on the Description Sheet to the
        class--make sure that everyone understands how to complete the form. If
        the students do not know each other's names very well, it may be helpful
        to distribute a class list of names along with the Description Sheet.
        Stress that the results will be confidential and that they will be used to
        help you (the teacher) to assign students to work groups for special class
        projects.
        After about 20 minutes, collect the sheets.

  II.   Go through the sheets and add up on the Results Sheet the number of
        persons rating each student on each of the 5 Interpersonal Goal categories.
        The 45 items on the Description Sheet are divided into nine 5 item
        categories representing Dreikurs' basic interpersonal goals. The
        categories and corresponding item numbers are shown below.

Category Number		Name (And Abbreviation) of Interpersonal Goal Category	Measured by Items
1	SI	= Social Interest	1 - 5
2	AS-AC	= Attention-Seeking Active Constructive	6 - 10
3	AS-PC	= Attention-Seeking Passive Constructive	11 - 15
4	AS-AD	= Attention-Seeking Active Destructive	16 - 20
5	AS-PD	= Attention-Seeking Passive Destructive	21 - 25
6	PS-AD	= Power-Seeking Active Destructive	26 - 30
7	PS-PD	= Power-Seeking Passive Destructive	31 - 35
8	RS	= Revenge-Seeking Active and Passive Destructive	36 - 40
9	IN	= Inadequacy	41 - 45

Total + = Total Constructive (add 1 + 2 + 3)

Total - = Total Destructive (add 4 + 5 + 6 + 7 + 8 + 9)

In tallying scores to be placed onto the <u>Results Sheet</u>, ignore the number of times a ratee is referred to in one 5 item category on one rater's sheet. <u>Example</u>: for Category 1 - Social Interest, count the number of persons rating the first subject once or more than once in that category. If 15 people rate Mary as being in the Social Interest category, the score for Mary on SI is 15. If each of those 15 persons writes Mary's name down beside each of the 5 items for Social Interest, the SI score for Mary is still 15. Count only <u>the number of persons</u> viewing Mary within the SI category (irregardless of the number of times she is referred to by each person within a single category). When you are finished with the table, circle the highest score received by each person. You may wish to translate the raw scores into percentage scores $\left(\dfrac{\text{Raw Score}}{\text{No. of Students Completing Description Sheet}} \times 100\right)$ to facilitate comparison between different classes.

III. Using the information from the questions on who the "very best" and "second best" friend of each student was, prepare a sociogram showing the friendship choices for the class. Identify students using the numbers beside their names on the Results Sheet. For each student, write down on the sociogram the abbreviation for the Interpersonal Goal for which that person received the highest score.

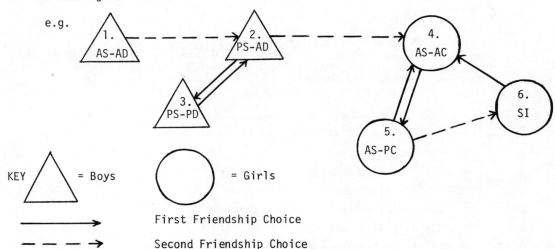

The completed diagram is called an Interpersonal Goal Sociogram because it shows not only friendship clusters but also identifies sub-groups based on different interpersonal goals such as Social Interest, Attention, Power, Revenge or Inadequacy. Using this information, the teacher can explore the personality and group dynamics of his class in a way not permitted by sociograms based on friendship choice alone.

QUESTIONS TO THINK ABOUT:

1. What sort of group relationships do the problem students in your class have?

2. Look at the students who received the most friendship choices. What interpersonal goals do these "stars" have? Are any of these popular students also problem students? What influence do you think these popular students have on their friends?

3. Look at the students whom no one chose as a friend. What interpersonal goals do those "isolates" have? Can you think of somewhere to sit the "isolates" so they can find some friends and become a part of the classroom group?

4. What are the dominant interpersonal goals in your classroom? What is the relationship between the dominant type of interpersonal goal in your classroom and the "atmosphere" or "mood" in your classroom?

5. Do students with particular interpersonal goals have a favorite place to sit in the classroom? Where do Inadequate students sit? Where do Power-seeking students sit? Where do the Active and Passive Constructive Attention Seeking Students ("success" and "charm") like to sit?

6. Complete an Interpersonal Goal Inventory on your number 1 problem student in this class. Is the way you perceive this student (the score you obtain in the inventory) similar to how the class perceives him (scores on the Interpersonal Goal Sociogram Results Sheet)?

DESCRIPTION SHEET

How well do you know your classmates?
Below are some word pictures of members of your class.
Read each statement and write down the names of the persons whom you think the descriptions fit. For each person, write down both his first name and his last name.
Remember that one description may fit several persons. You may write as many names as you think belong beside each description.
The same person may be named for more than one description.
If you cannot think of anyone to match a particular description, go on to the next one.
Take as much time as you need to finish. Do not hurry.

WHO IN YOUR CLASS:	NAMES
1. Is interested in others	
2. Thinks of "we" rather than just "I"	
3. Likes to help others	
4. Enjoys learning about new things	
5. Is a warm, friendly person	
6. Makes cute remarks	
7. Seeks praise for good work	
8. Does stunts to get attention	
9. Gets upset when he (she) doesn't come in first	
10. Tries to get attention through performing well	
11. Is excessively nice	
12. Is a quiet "nice guy" or "nice girl"	
13. Is a good student, but likes to keep in the background	
14. Tries to be "teacher's pet"	
15. Is excessively polite	
16. Acts the clown	
17. Is noisy	
18. Acts the show off	
19. Makes a nuisance of himself/herself	
20. Keeps the teacher busy by asking silly questions	

WHO IN YOUR CLASS:	NAMES
21. Is untidy	
22. Acts nervous	
23. Is shy, bashful	
24. Is easily frightened	
25. Acts helpless	
26. Argues with others	
27. Refuses to do assigned work	
28. Will not do what he is told	
29. Always disagrees	
30. Wants to be the boss	
31. Is stubborn	
32. Is extremely lazy about doing assignments	
33. Forgets things he (she) is supposed to do	
34. Pretends not to hear	
35. Ignores the teacher	
36. Physically hurts others	
37. Says hurtful things	
38. Acts in a violent or brutal manner	
39. Steals	
40. Calls others names	
41. Tries to be left alone	
42. Seems to feel hopeless	
43. Gives up easily	
44. Thinks he (she) is stupid	
45. Makes excuses to avoid situations he (she) is afraid he (she) will do poorly in	
MY TWO BEST FRIENDS IN THIS CLASS ARE:	
1. My very best friend:	
2. My second best friend:	

211

CLASSROOM MISBEHAVIOR ROLE PLAY WORKSHEET

ROLE PLAY SITUATION #1: ALICE

Alice was repeatedly absent from class. She had many forms of excuses for her absence. She had excuses to go to her counsellor, or her doctor. On other occasions, she had to help in the staff dining room or she was just absent because she did not feel well. These absences gave her excuses to avoid her assignments in both Family Life and Interior Decorating.

She frequently "cornered me" to tell me about her counselling. (This was not in school guidance. It is private vocational counselling). She said the tests were bothering her eyes, and she could not read and concentrate in class. She was shaking, stammering and nervous during this one particular conversation.

Several days passed on and she still was not producing any work in class. Private conferences or simply instructions did not seem to encourage her.

My reaction was one of understanding but with a little impatience, since she was taking quite a bit of my time. Her class teacher's reaction was one of annoyance. Another class teacher was annoyed but understanding.

The results of inquiries about Alice yielded the fact that she is an epileptic. She is moderately well controlled, but has personality problems that make control difficult. She uses the threat of a seizure as a tool for attention and sympathy. She has a twin sister who does not have any of the difficulties Alice displays.

All this information helped me greatly with the intervention strategies. I could describe some incidents, but the final day will make a good summary for the intervention strategies.

Interior decorating evaluation required a well organized note book for all projects. On the final day of the class, Alice requested a private conference. Her appeal of sympathy and crying made it very tempting for me to give in to her request to not have to do an assignment, but neither Alice or I would have benefited from that solution. She sat in a little back room with me (while I marked books), for one hour and 20 minutes. During this time, with encouragement and prodding, she completed "something" for each assignment. Some of her ideas were very good! Of course, she had gained the "hoped for" attention, and had my company for this space of time. When she started to talk about anything not related to the assignment, I ignored her. When she had a good idea, I praised her. With encouragement, a display of faith in her, helping her to get organized, we had success. This project was quite successful. I think I could have improved my procedures if I had started earlier to have Alice do an assignment while I was with her. She then may have had success on her own, with some parts of her work. Time is the big factor. A teacher finds it difficult to neglect other members of the class while devoting so much time to one student.

Also, I could have gained benefit from the results of the Interpersonal Goal Inventory if I had completed it before the last week of practicum. It is a very useful and successful tool in diagnosis.

ROLE PLAY SITUATION #2: BEN

Ben was one student who made sure that the teacher realized he was in the room. The first things that caught my attention were the way Ben would talk out of turn, make cute remarks, and generally be noisy. Ben's antics would cause the two or three students around him to act up.

My first reaction was to give Ben more attention. By this, I mean that I prompted him to do his assignments, and I tended to spend more time in the part of the room where he was seated, so that he would not talk to his neighbors. But Ben would continue to cause a disturbance as soon as I moved to a different part of the room.

The situation got to the point where I would tell Ben to shut up, and he would practically continue talking without even a pause. I began to become aware that I was entering into a power struggle with Ben.

During the third week of the practicum, I changed my tactics. After an outbreak of unnecessary talking, I gave Ben the choice of either sitting quietly and behaving, or of moving to an isolated part of the room where he would have nobody to talk to. After a long pause, he said he wanted to remain with his friends, and that he would behave himself. After about 15 minutes, he began to talk noisely with his friends. I said to him: "Since you cannot work quietly with your friends, you must sit on your own", and I sat him by himself. Once Ben was isolated, I tended to ignore him. I let him experience the consequence of his decision.

After class, I asked Ben if he wanted to say anything about his new seat. Ben said he did not like it. I asked him if he knew why he acted up in class. Ben acted uncomfortable, and said he did not know why. I asked him if he wanted my opinion. Ben gave no answer, so I asked him if he acted up to get my attention. Ben flatly denied that this was the case, but before he could deny it, his mouth fell open and his eyes widened.

After this incident, Ben sat in the isolated part of the room for the remaining classes during the third week. Before a class started in the fourth week, Ben approached me and asked if he could move back to his old seat. I hesitated. Then, Ben promised he would behave himself. So I agreed.

Ben was quite well behaved for the rest of the week. There were a couple of times when Ben would start talking out of turn again. Whenever this occurred, I would quietly remind him of his promise. This was sufficient to get him to calm down. However, towards the end of the week, I felt as if I was having to remind Ben of his promise too often.

I feel that I had some short-term success in dealing with Ben. I say short-term because I think the effect of his promise was beginning to weaken. I am not sure if reminding him of his promise was a good tactic.

RESULTS SHEET

CATEGORY

NAME	1 SI 1-5	2 AS-AC 6-10	3 AS-PC 11-15	4 AS-AD 16-20	5 AS-PD 21-25	6 PS-AD 26-30	7 PS-PD 31-35	8 RS 36-40	9 IN 41-45	10 TOTAL +	11 TOTAL −
1.											
2.											
3.											
4.											
5.											
6.											
7.											
8.											
9.											
10.											
11.											
12.											
13.											
14.											
15.											
16.											
17.											
18.											
19.											
20.											
21.											
22.											
23.											
24.											
25.											
26.											
27.											
28.											
29.											
30.											
31.											
32.											
TOTAL NO. OF NAMES IN EACH CATEGORY											

This lifestyle project is based on a Grade 12 male, who was a student in my Family Life Course. Ron made himself well heard from the first day of practicum. He usually arrived late to class, entering by loudly announcing himself or making a "witty" comment. He would continually "crack jokes", or fool around during class; get up in the middle of the lesson and talk to everyone he passed as he walked to the back of the portable hut to get a drink of water. He would never ask permission or excuse himself. Ron was non-cooperative in group work. He would insist on working by himself always, even though he sat with four friends. He would repeatedly ask for review of instructions after they were given or would come to me and ask for further explanations of the requirements of the assignment. Whenever instructions were repeated directly to him, he would frown, shake his head and still say he didn't understand what to do. Often, he would ask me to explain the assignment or instructions to him; but interrupt me by talking about skiing or golfing.

Ron also teased or made insulting comments to other students when they were contributing an idea to the class. In turn, these students were embarrassed, and often showed anger towards Ron by telling him to "shut-up". Often, if I asked Ron to "wait his turn" to make a comment, the other students would agree with me, and again tell him to be quiet. Whenever students spoke, Ron would tell them they were wrong, would always argue with them, but would rarely give the student the correct answer if he requested it.

My reactions to Ron changed from frustrating annoyance to strong interest. On a one-to-one basis, he was a very polite, vitalic person. I felt he was potentially a very capable person and had a lot to offer to the class once his behavior was modified to allow positive functioning and interaction within the class.

The first action I took with Ron was to ignore his interruptions and try to overtalk his talking. But it ended up being a contest of who could overtalk who; so I immediately stopped this action. After telling him to be quiet several times, (Ron talked out and fooled around even more then), I approached him by saying; "I know you would like me to tell you to be quiet, but I have too much to cover in class today". This action quieted him down only for about five minutes.

The last steps of action I took with Ron was to ask him why he liked to show off all the time. His actions subsided somewhat after I confronted him, but not enough to continue the class adequately. After that, I spoke with him and agreed to let him have the first couple of minutes of the class to tell his jokes; but only on the condition he didn't disturb the class anymore during the rest of the period.   At this time, I would try to give Ron as much positive reinforcement as possible whenever he was working quietly on an assignment or not interrupting. Most of the reinforcement was verbal or non-verbal gestures. Occasionally, when he came to class early, I would try to give him a bit of attention before class started, by asking him about his skiing or golfing. Also, after he told his jokes or whatever, I often would tell him he was more clever than I as I couldn't tell jokes like that, or be as witty as him, etc. These steps proved to work quite well, as we could get through a period with only a few distractions from Ron.

The students offered their ideas to the class more so towards the end of the practicum, and the students were much more friendlier towards Ron. They would ask him to join them in group work rather than reject him.

I entered my Grade 6 English Class and began making friends with the class by asking them their names. This was pleasant. Unfortunately, however, Laura was there. She mockingly said, "Have you got something "special" for names?" She said this in such a way that it made me feel stupid and abnormal. The class, of course, laughed at me with Laura.

My reaction was, "Is she running this class or am I running it?" I did not, however, want to confront this situation, so I put it away by beginning with the lesson. During the lesson, Laura said, "There is something wrong with your definition of Animals: Animals do not have a thinking mind like us. My dog has a mind". At this point, the class became very interested in Laura's criticism, and three people pointed out that their pets all can think.

Laura was getting the class on her side. I do not disagree with disagreement, but with disagreement for disagreement's sake—Laura's brand of disagreement. The next day, Laura would begin fooling around and whispering, etc. This would bother me. But I would not tell her directly. I would address the whole class hoping that she would stop. But of all the students, Laura would still be talking.

I had had enough; I felt furious. I didn't know what to do. That evening I remembered that I had a project to do for my Ed Psych class. I didn't want to do it because I felt too busy with all my other problems. But I decided to do it.

The following day, I asked Laura to see me after class. I said to her, "Could it be that you want to disagree with everything I say?" At this, Laura stopped. Her eyes gazed at the floor. She looked shocked, so I said, "Could it be that you want to show me that everything I do is all wrong?"

After this incident, Laura stopped criticizing; she began to cooperate with me. Indeed, Laura and another girl were the only students to bring food for the party at the end of the practicum.

The transformation was unbelievable. With a few sentences which exposed her game, I was able to change a rebellious, power-hungry student, to a kind, cooperative student.

Jane, a Grade 8 student in my girls' Physical Education class, came to my attention on the very first day that I observed her in class. She looked the "hopeless" student, would not participate in the gymnastic activities as the other students did, and seemed completely disinterested in what was going on. She didn't want anything to do with the other girls, and I noticed that even when other classmates tried to encourage her to take her turn on the vaulting box, she just wanted to be left alone. I had the feeling that she didn't want to participate because she felt that she was incapable of doing what the other girls did, and if she as much as made an attempt, they would then know how incapable she was. She gave the outward appearance of being hopeless and not caring.

The other students generally left her alone, but in speaking to her whilst trying to get her to participate, I detected a tone of annoyance.

I approached her with: "It appears to me that you feel you are unable to do these gymnastic activities, and would rather not try". She replied, "You're right, I can't do them, and any way, they are stupid to do. And I don't want to try". Jane also readily complained about some physical ailment as a reason for not wanting to participate.

Because I had such a short time with Jane -- out of 5 periods, I only saw her three times (she was absent for 2 periods). After that first period, I spoke to her regular P.E. teacher about her, and learned that she came from a home with many problems and that she really doesn't try very much in P.E. as she feels incapable. Although she appeared to be a strong, healthy, girl.

At the beginning of the next class, I subtly chose her to return my attendance book to the P.E. office and to take a note to the main office. I was very polite about asking her, and very friendly. Then, during the P.E. lesson, which was generally informal, educational gymnastics with each girl working on her own or in partners, I gave her as much encouragement, quietly, to her alone, as I could without it appearing that I was spending so much time with her. I noticed that she was happier to start trying, and the other girls were more aware of her trying, so didn't reject her as readily. I told her that I was sure she could do some of the things I suggested in the lesson (because it was not formal gymnastics this class was particularly appropriate for her to work at her level without feeling that she had to perfect certain feats).

Jane reacted very well to my encouragement and friendliness.

The third period, we did circuit training -- Jane complained but with a smile, as the other girls did. She hit herself with a small barbell which was a good excuse to stop. I suggested she get a wet paper towel, and put it on her forehead, and when she felt relieved to come back and join in. After about 10 minutes, she returned and continued with the exercises.

I feel my project was as successful as it could be in the short time--at least it was a beginning of a success!

For the 4th period, Jane came at the end of the class because she had been in the nurse's office attending to a sprained finger. But she took her shoes off right away, and quite happily joined in the last 5 - 10 minutes of the class building pyramids. She was smiling, and the other students seemed to accept her well.

ROLE PLAY SITUATION #6:   LOUISE

The Grade 10 Art Class made use of five large tables. The boys grouped themselves around the two front tables; the girls at the two back ones, with the exception of Louise, who sat at the remaining table by herself. She was quick to grasp abstract concepts of form and composition, but she tried to hide her work from me when I walked by, or she would fold it in half, or rip it up. She reacted with bitter sarcasm to any comments directed towards her by either her classmates, or myself. If any of the boys in the class were bothering the others, they would say, "Cut it out, or we'll make you sit with Louise", and the whole class would laugh. Louise would attack savagely and then withdraw even more. She was very good at giving "hate stares".

Her paint colors were heavy, dark and muddy. Almost all of her work contained a woman with her back turned and a small hand reaching from one of the corners.

When I enquired about her, the Sponsor Teacher informed me that her father was an alcoholic who, when tired of beating his wife, would begin on Louise.

She was sullen and defiant - violent and brutal when challenged. I thought she might have an inferiority complex when she displayed reluctance to show me her work. But when she ripped up her drawings directly after I would compliment her, it seemed more as though she was trying to hurt me. I didn't act hurt. I completely ignored her sarcastic comments. When she did not get the appropriate feedback, she realized the approach she was using was a waste of time. I made sure I was not "sugar sweet".

I did the unexpected. I used some of the pieces of her ripped-up drawings in a demonstration about composition. She seemed a little warmer when she realized my compliments were not just flattery.

I showed her she was liked. I made sure that whenever I saw her, I said hello, and said something about her drawings.

She seemed to begin to want to please me, and followed through on her theme better than most of the class. I made her feel she had talent - and because she knew I meant my criticism, she really began to develop her work well.

She began to open up and ask my opinion.

WORKSHEET FOR IDENTIFYING EFFECTIVE AND INEFFECTIVE CORRECTIVE PROCEDURES

INSTRUCTIONS:

Read through the Case Study about Mark on the next several pages, and then, with your partner, obtain consensus on (and write down) answers to the following questions:

1. What _negative_ things do you feel the teacher did in working with Mark?

2. What _positive_ things do you feel the teacher did in working with Mark?

3. What corrective procedures would you recommend if this were your student?

Mark was a very restless student and did not seem to fathom at all, the idea that there were "rules" one should follow. He liked to bug the other students and no one liked him, although they didn't show it; they simply ignored him. He seemed to have one friend, Don, with whom he sat at the table. Mark seemed to try to work, but he was very slow.

The second day I was there, Mark and Don were fooling around excessively, so I told them to remain after class. I then asked them to explain their behavior to me. Don tried, but Mark thought it was a joke. Don could see I was serious and tried to get Mark to settle down. Mark refused. As I let them go, Don said to Mark, "You'd better smarten up". I said, "That's it, Don, see if you can make Mark behave". I realized the next day that this was the wrong thing to say because Mark now made more noise than ever and was all over the room bothering people.

Then Don was transferred out to Remedial Reading and Mark was worse than ever. I moved him off in a corner and tried to ignore him, or simply gave him constructive comments. We had begun to work on projects, so I was helping more than teaching. The kids were helping each other and there was quite a bit of noise in the classroom for this week. Mark couldn't decide what to do as he felt the Rennaissance was "boring". So I sat with him and tried to help him decide on a topic. We finally decided on Egypt, but Mark's hands and arms were shaking the whole time. For awhile Mark worked on Egypt, but then he was all over the room again: throwing paper airplanes out of the window and bothering the students.

I felt I had to clamp down on him again, and began to reprimand his actions. He did give his presentation; made a big production out of it though, and shook again. He had to sit quietly while the others were giving theirs and he didn't like this. As a matter of fact, in between two presentations, he got up and told me I should change the calendar. I decided to let him do it, so we stopped while he changed it. Well, he ripped February off, and the whole calendar fell--the class roared, and Mark, for a split second, was at a loss. Then, he decided to make a big production again in stapling it back up.

I was never infuriated or insensed or at my wits end by anything Mark did. Sometimes I was bothered and wondered why he was like this. I knew nothing about him and decided after about two weeks to ask about him in the staff room. Well, everyone was aghast when they heard I had him on my practicum. Apparently, he is a real "problem" and has been kicked out of three classes, after the teachers had really tried. His background was horrendous: Mother re-married, three sisters all pregnant at sixteen, no parental control or guidance of him at all.

I felt then that the whole situation was completely out of my league. Mark had also skipped several classes, but I chose not to make an issue of this. He arrived the last day late to write a test after missing nearly four days of classes, and all the material. I simply said as he entered, "Mark, here's the test, sit over there and write it". He didn't object at all. Then I gave him an extra assignment, as he finished the test early, to enable him to upgrade his marks. He did the assignment, handed it in, and wanted to leave, but I wouldn't let him. Next thing I knew, Mark pulled a knife on another kid. The whole room became silent when I asked him to sit down and put the knife away. After a few seconds and a look of utter rebellion, he did just that. Then I asked him if indeed it was a knife. At first he disagreed, but with prompting from the class, he finally agreed that it was indeed a knife. So I sent him to the principal, saying I would be down immediately after class. He refused to go a couple of times, but I stood my ground. Then he left. The bell rang a minute later and I went to the principal's office. Mark hadn't reported.

Continued

We phoned the parents. At first, the Mother said her son wouldn't do anything like that and commented on the school having no control these days. She phoned back when Mark got home, and apologized and expressed her concern about Mark. Mark said the whole thing was a joke.

I concluded that Mark was a Rebel. He was openly defiant and didn't think "rules" applied to him. It was almost as though he thought he was the only one in the class and could do exactly as he pleased. He was truant several times and defied authority.

I tried several different discipline techniques on Mark. First of all, I was firm with him. I stuck to whatever I had said. This did not seem to work. I also tried to ignore him when he misbehaved. This had no effect whatsoever except to upset the other students. They resented the things that Mark got away with and also how he interrupted their studying. I tried to keep telling myself during this time that punishing, reminding, coaxing, and scolding are all forms of "negative attention". I tried treating Mark on an adult level but this was disasterous. I also appealed for Mark's help and enlisted his cooperation, but I could never bring myself to admit that he had all the power as I did not feel this was the case. I felt Mark had a psychological problem deeper than I could ever penetrate.

Mark's revenge attitude did not bother me. I was not hurt by what he said, I simply didn't care. I guess I gave up, although sometimes I did try to encourage him. The outcome was that whatever I did worked, but only for the moment.

I could have improved the situation by not letting Mark frustrate me as I did. I do not like being frustrated and this is why I gave up. It wasn't that I felt threatened, I just had no answer for his behavior. I had never seen anyone that mixed up before. Mark's regular teacher felt he simply needed attention. I do not believe this is the case. It is this and more. I think he is so spiteful of his lot in life that he is trying to make others pay for it. By continually giving him attention, this teacher is not really helping Mark, and he is also alienating the rest of the class.

AIMS: 1. To identify the attitudes a teacher must
have to employ this method.

2. To identify the six steps in this method.

3. To distinguish between this "no lose"
method and two "win/lose" methods.

4. To apply this method to resolve a real
"conflict-of-needs" problem.

RATIONALE FOR DOING THIS ACTIVITY:

WHEN TEACHERS EMPLOY THIS "NO-LOSE" METHOD FOR SOLVING PROBLEMS, THEY ARE PROVIDING DEMOCRATIC LEADERSHIP RATHER THAN AUTHORITARIAN IMPOSITION OR LAISSEZ-FAIRE "NON-INTERVENTION".

YEAH, IT IS DEMOCRATIC IN THE FOLLOWING WAYS :

1. EVERYONE PARTICIPATES

2. NO POWER OR COERCION IS INVOLVED

3. COOPERATION (NOT COMPETITION) IS ENCOURAGED

4. TEACHERS GUIDE STUDENTS TO BECOME MORE RESPONSIBLE AND MATURE.

RIGHT, BOB ! AND IMPORTANT ADVANTAGES RESULT FROM USING THIS DEMOCRATIC PROBLEM-SOLVING PROCESS :

1. EVERYONE IS COMMITTED TO CARRYING OUT THE SOLUTION THEY DECIDED UPON.

2. PARTICIPANTS DO NOT HAVE TO BE "SOLD" ON THE SOLUTION.

3. A BETTER SOLUTION RESULTS BECAUSE MORE "HEADS" ARE INVOLVED.

4. THE SOLUTION IS BASED ON AN UNDERSTANDING OF REAL PROBLEMS (i.e., CONFLICTING NEEDS).

5. TEACHERS AND STUDENTS LIKE IT BETTER SINCE ALL ARE "WINNERS."

STEP 1:   DEFINING THE PROBLEM (GETTING CONFLICTING NEEDS INTO THE OPEN)

1. Explain how this procedure differs from the two power struggles where either the teacher or student wins, while the other loses.

2. Involve only those students in this problem-solving procedure who are a part of the conflict.

3. These students must volunteer to participate.

4. Use "I messages" to state your needs as the teacher (e.g. "I do not like to leave the group I'm working with to repeat my instructions".)

5. Use "active listening" to help students express their unmet needs (this is the problem from their point of view). Do not encourage them to state solutions they want--only their unmet needs.

STEP 2:   GENERATING POSSIBLE SOLUTIONS (BY BRAINSTORMING)

1. Get as many participants as possible to pose as many solutions as they can think of.

2. Record these proposed solutions on paper or on a tape recorder.

3. No evaluations are allowed as to whether an idea is "good" or "bad".

4. No justifications (reasons) are required for any idea proposed.

STEP 3:   EVALUATING THE SOLUTIONS (ELIMINATING UNACCEPTABLE SOLUTIONS)

1. Now it's time to determine which solutions are best and which ones you like most.

2. Cross off the list any solution that produces a negative evaluation from anyone for any reason.

3. Use "I messages" to let students know your assessment about each solution-- especially ones that are unacceptable to you.

4. Use "active listening" to clarify for everyone what students say about each solution.

Continued

STEP 4:   MAKING THE DECISION (AGREEING ON ONE SOLUTION ACCEPTABLE TO ALL)

1. By means of group consensus, find one solution which everyone agrees to try
    to see if it will work. Do not take a majority vote because this will
    make those who have not agreed to the solutions "losers". A non-binding
    "straw vote" may be taken to determine "where everyone is".

2. Write down the agreed upon solution—perhaps as a contract, which everyone
    signs to indicate their willingness to try out the solution. If someone
    refuses to sign the contract, a consensus may not have been reached yet.
    (Repeat Step 4 if necessary—because grudging submission to a contract
    probably indicates it will not be fulfilled).

STEP 5:   DETERMINING HOW TO IMPLEMENT THE DECISION (SPECIFYING RESPONSIBILITIES)

1. Ask the group "Who is to be responsible for doing what? And by when?"

2. Write down and post a list containing this information, as well as who
    is responsible for enforcement.

STEP 6:   ASSESSING THE SUCCESS OF THE SOLUTION

1. If the solution has worked, there will be positive feelings towards each
    other, the original conflict-of-needs will have disappeared.

2. However, solutions can fail to work for everyone—which means going
    through Steps 1-5 again to find another solution acceptable to all.

NOW IT IS TIME FOR OUR READERS TO PRACTISE USING THOMAS GORDON'S "NO-LOSE METHOD" FOR SOLVING PROBLEMS. THIS CAN BE DONE IN YOUR ED. PSYCH. CLASS TO SOLVE A PROBLEM (i.e., CONFLICT-OF-NEEDS) SITUATION WHICH INVOLVES MEMBERS OF THE ED. PSYCH. CLASS. OR, IT CAN BE USED DURING A PRACTICUM TO SOLVE A PROBLEM BETWEEN YOU AND YOUR STUDENTS. IN EITHER SITUATION, FOLLOW THE PROCEDURE BELOW.

* *

TIME REQUIRED FOR DOING THIS ACTIVITY:

   One or two 50 minute periods (perhaps longer!)

MATERIALS NEEDED:

   Chalkboard for displaying ideas; Worksheet provided in this text.

PROCEDURE:

   I.   Discuss the rationale (above) -- and perhaps read Thomas Gordon's
         Teacher Effectiveness Training -- in order to fully understand the
         difference between this "No-Lose" Problem-Solving Method and the two less
         effective "win/lose" methods of (a) authoritarian imposition of the
         solution by the teacher, or (b) laissez-faire abandonment of leadership
         by the teacher to accept a solution posed by the student.

   II.   Use this "No-Lose" Method when there is a real conflict-of-needs
         (i.e. problem) between you and your students. If only the student has
         a problem of needs not being met (while your needs are being met), use
         "active listening" to help your student understand his needs and propose
         ways of satisfying them. If only you have a problem of your needs not
         being met (while your students needs are being met), then state your
         needs through "I messages" so that your students can understand your
         needs and can help you satisfy them.

   III. Use this "No-Lose" Method only after you have gained competence in
         using "I messages" and   "active listening" (see Chapter I).

IV. Do not rush through the "No-Lose" Method—the extra time required to involve everyone in agreeing on a solution that is acceptable to all will be "made up" because the solution does not later have to be "sold" as a good one. Moreover, if an acceptable solution has been reached, the problem will be resolved so that class time will not subsequently have to be taken up each day debating it.

V. All six steps need not be completed at one time. You should, however, complete a step which is started so that a new step can be focused on the next time.

VI. Go through all six steps. Each one is important for the success of the next. If the problem still persists, do not view the students in a negative way, but rather view the solution as a "bad" one because it was obviously unacceptable to everyone.

VII. View solutions as changeable—not fixed and permanent for all times—because as the situation changes, another solution might be required. This "No-Lose" Method is a process for involving people in determining workable solutions—not a "cookbook" for establishing "answers".

VIII. View conflicts as relation-strengthening—not relation-damaging—because the solution that results will enhance personal feelings towards one another since no one loses and everyone wins in having his/her needs met.

APPLYING HUMANISTIC DISCIPLINE TECHNIQUES WITH YOUR "PROBLEM STUDENTS"

AN ASSIGNMENT FOR PRACTICUM

<u>AIMS</u>:
1. To identify a "problem student" in a class you will be teaching during practicum.

2. To identify one (or more) Humanistic Discipline Technique(s) that you can use to modify your "problem student's" behavior.

3. To modify your problem student's behavior on practicum by applying the Humanistic Discipline Techniques you have selected.

4. To evaluate the success of your Classroom Discipline Project.

RATIONALE FOR DOING THIS ACTIVITY:

IN THIS CHAPTER YOU HAVE LEARNED THREE MAJOR HUMANISTIC DISCIPLINE TECHNIQUES:
1. WILLIAM GLASSER'S "REALITY THERAPY".
2. THOMAS GORDON'S "NO-LOSE" METHOD OF SOLVING CONFLICTS.
3. RUDOLF DREIKURS' "CORRECTIVE PROCEDURES FOR HANDLING THE 4 GOALS OF MISBEHAVIOR".

IN A CLASSROOM DISCIPLINE PROJECT, YOU WILL ACTUALLY APPLY ONE (OR MORE) OF THESE HUMANISTIC DISCIPLINE TECHNIQUES TO MODIFY THE MISBEHAVIOR OF ONE OF YOUR OWN "PROBLEM STUDENTS".

CLASSROOM DISCIPLINE PROJECT WORKSHEET

Give as detailed a description of your project as you can, using the structured guidelines shown below: Complete questions 1 and 2 in class; complete question 3 during your practicum; complete question 4 after your practicum.

1. Describe in _detail_, the behavior of one "problem student" that came to your attention during your pre-practicum visit to the classes you will be teaching during your practicum. What were your reactions and the reactions of other students and teachers to this "problem student"?

2. What Humanistic Discipline Techniques would you use to improve the situation when you next see this "problem student"? Be specific, describing how you would apply each Humanistic Discipline Technique and give your _reason_ for using each.

3. What was the behavior of the "problem student" <u>during</u> your practicum? What
   Humanistic Discipline Techniques did you actually apply? What were the reactions
   of the student to the Humanistic Discipline Techniques you applied?

4. Indicate your evaluation of how successful your project was by answering the following questions:

    A. What did you do that improved the situation? What was the most effective technique you used?

    B. What did you do that was ineffective or made the student's behavior worse?

    C. If you were doing this project again, with a different "problem student", what would you do differently?

    D. Overall, how would you evaluate the success of your Classroom Discipline Project?

233

CHAPTER 5

DEVELOPING SKILLS FOR PROMOTING AND ASSESSING YOUR STUDENTS' LEARNING AND COGNITIVE DEVELOPMENT

A DIAGNOSING AND ADAPTING TO DIFFERENT LEARNING STYLES

AIMS:
1. To identify common student behavior which reflect four different styles of learning.

2. To propose teaching/learning techniques appropriate for four styles of learning.

RATIONALE FOR DOING THIS ACTIVITY:

BOB, AM I GLAD TO RUN INTO YOU!... I'VE GOT A GROUP OF STUDENTS ON MY PRACTICUM, WHO DON'T SEEM TO BE LEARNING WHAT I'M TEACHING EVEN THOUGH I'M USING A VARIETY OF METHODS AND MATERIALS LIKE WE WERE TAUGHT TO DO IN OUR "METHODS COURSES".

IT SOUNDS LIKE YOU ARE WELL-PREPARED FROM A "TEACHING" STANDPOINT... BUT, TELL ME — ARE YOU PLANNING YOUR LESSONS TO TAKE INTO ACCOUNT DIFFERENT "LEARNING STYLES"?

GOSH!... I'M NOT SURE... COULD YOU TELL ME WHAT YOU MEAN?

HAVE YOU NOTICED THAT DIFFERENT STUDENTS USE A DIFFERENT STYLE, OR APPROACH, TO LEARNING? DON'T SOME STUDENTS NEED MORE HELP OR LESS HELP FROM YOU? OR CAN HANDLE ONLY LIMITED ALTERNATIVES? OR REBEL WHEN ASKED TO DO THE ASSIGNMENTS YOU PRESCRIBE?

235

YES, I HAVE NOTICED DIFFERENT STUDENTS DOING EACH OF THESE THINGS... AND, I GUESS I WAS NOT REALLY PLANNING MY LESSONS WITH THESE DIFFERENCES IN "LEARNING STYLE" IN MIND... I WAS MAINLY TRYING TO INDIVIDUALIZE MY INSTRUCTION BY PACING IT TO STUDENT'S DIFFERENT LEARNING RATES, AND, ALSO, TO PERSONALIZE MY INSTRUCTION TO MEET STUDENTS' PERSONAL INTERESTS.

IT'S CERTAINLY COMMENDABLE THAT YOUR PLANNING IS GEARED TO INDIVIDUALIZING AND PERSONALIZING YOUR TEACHING ... BUT, THIS IS NOT ENOUGH, AS YOU'VE FOUND OUT. TO BE AN EFFECTIVE TEACHER, YOU MUST ALSO PLAN YOUR LESSONS TO TAKE STUDENTS' "LEARNING STYLES" INTO ACCOUNT.

I THINK YOU'RE RIGHT, BOB... I DO WANT MY STUDENTS TO LEARN... ESPECIALLY AFTER I PUT SO MUCH TIME AND EFFORT INTO PLANNING MY LESSONS... WHAT DO YOU SUGGEST I DO?

I'M NO EXPERT IN THIS EITHER, SUE... BUT IT SEEMS LOGICAL, FIRST OF ALL, TO DIAGNOSE A PARTICULAR "LEARNING STYLE" AND, THEN, TO PROVIDE TEACHING/ LEARNING TECHNIQUES WHICH ARE APPROPRIATELY SUITED TO EACH "LEARNING STYLE"...

236

ALLOW ME TO HELP ! BOB IS RIGHT ... THE FIRST STEP IS TO <u>DIAGNOSE</u> WHETHER A STUDENT HAS ONE OF THE FOUR COMMON "LEARNING STYLES" — "RIGID", "UNDISCIPLINED", "ANXIOUS", OR "CREATIVE" — BY IDENTIFYING STUDENT BEHAVIORS RELATED TO EACH "LEARNING STYLE."

THE NEXT STEP IS CALLED THE "PROBLEM OF THE <u>MATCH</u>" BECAUSE THE EFFECTIVE TEACHER PROVIDES TEACHING/LEARNING TECHNIQUES (EXPERIENCES, ACTIVITIES, METHODS, MATERIALS, PERSONAL RELATIONSHIPS) WHICH ARE APPROPRIATELY SUITED TO A STUDENT'S "LEARNING STYLE" SO THAT LEARNING TAKES PLACE.

BEFORE I CONTINUE, LET ME DEFINE WHAT I MEAN BY "LEARNING STYLE" ... EVERYONE HAS A CHARACTERISTIC LEARNING STYLE, OR APPROACH TO LEARNING, WHICH, IN TURN, DETERMINES <u>HOW</u> THAT PERSON WILL UTILIZE HIS VARIOUS LEARNING ABILITIES TO LEARN AND TO SOLVE PROBLEMS.

THE CHARACTERISTIC LEARNING STYLE A PERSON DEVELOPS DEPENDS UPON BOTH HIS INFORMATION-PROCESSING ABILITY AND HIS PERSONALITY:
(1) HIS <u>ATTITUDINAL OPENNESS</u> TO PROCESSING INFORMATION IS AN IMPORTANT PERSONALITY CHARACTERISTIC, AND
(2) HIS <u>CONCEPTUAL LEVEL</u> OF COGNITIVE DEVELOPMENT IS AN IMPORTANT INFORMATION-PROCESSING CHARACTERISTIC.

(1) "ATTITUDINAL OPENNESS TO INFORMATION - PROCESSING"
REFERS TO HOW MUCH A PERSON LETS HIMSELF BE
INFLUENCED BY <u>INTERNAL</u> SOURCES OF INFORMATION
(SUCH AS HIS THOUGHTS, BELIEFS, VALUES, FEELINGS,
DESIRES) AND BY <u>EXTERNAL</u> SOURCES OF INFORMATION
(SUCH AS EVENTS, OBJECTS, OTHER PEOPLE, SOCIAL
EXPECTATIONS, PEOPLE'S APPROVAL/DISAPPROVAL OF HIM).
A MORE OPEN PERSON IS MORE INFLUENCED BY BOTH
SOURCES OF INFORMATION.

(2) "CONCEPTUAL LEVEL OF COGNITIVE
DEVELOPMENT" REFERS TO WHETHER
A PERSON IS STIMULUS-BOUND
TO <u>CONCRETE</u> SOURCES OF
INFORMATION (e.g. PEOPLE, OBJECTS,
THINGS) OR CAN UTILIZE <u>ABSTRACT</u>
<u>CONCEPTS</u> (e.g. IDEAS, SYMBOLS
LIKE $E = MC^2$) AS SYMBOLS
WHICH STAND FOR CONCRETE
REFERENTS.

THE CHART ON THE NEXT PAGE
INDICATES HOW A PERSON'S
INFORMATION - PROCESSING ABILITY
AND PERSONALITY COMBINE TO
PRODUCE FOUR DISTINCTIVE
"LEARNING STYLES".

THE DISTINGUISHING CHARACTERISTICS OF FOUR COMMON LEARNING STYLES

CHARACTERISTICS OF A PERSON WITH A "RIGID" LEARNING STYLE

This person has such a <u>tightly closed</u> system for processing information that he does not let either internal or external sources of information influence his behavior. This person cannot symbolically manage information in a problem-solving situation, but must have lots of concrete examples in order to understand or learn.

CHARACTERISTICS OF A PERSON WITH AN "UNDISCIPLINED" LEARNING STYLE

This person is strongly influenced by <u>internal</u> sources of information but has not learned to effectively utilize external sources of information. This person has developed a moderately symbolic level of conceptual ability, which he mainly uses to seek immediate gratification of his internal needs/desires rather than responding to external influences.

CHARACTERISTICS OF A PERSON WITH AN "ANXIOUS" LEARNING STYLE

This person is strongly influenced by <u>external</u> sources of information, but tends to "close out" internal sources of information. This person has developed a moderately symbolic level of conceptual ability, which he mainly uses to impress other people so as to get their admiration and approval rather than to act on his own convictions.

CHARACTERISTICS OF A PERSON WITH A "CREATIVE" LEARNING STYLE

This person is maximally open to the influences of both internal and external sources of information. Because he has a high level of conceptual development, he can symbolically process both internal and external sources of information in deciding which source to let influence his behavior.

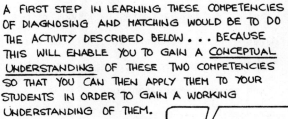

A FIRST STEP IN LEARNING THESE COMPETENCIES OF DIAGNOSING AND MATCHING WOULD BE TO DO THE ACTIVITY DESCRIBED BELOW... BECAUSE THIS WILL ENABLE YOU TO GAIN A <u>CONCEPTUAL UNDERSTANDING</u> OF THESE TWO COMPETENCIES SO THAT YOU CAN THEN APPLY THEM TO YOUR STUDENTS IN ORDER TO GAIN A WORKING UNDERSTANDING OF THEM.

WHAT YOU'VE SAID SOUNDS VERY USEFUL FOR BECOMING AN EFFECTIVE TEACHER... BUT, HOW CAN WE LEARN TO DIAGNOSE COMMON "LEARNING STYLES" AND THEN "MATCH" OUR TEACHING TO THEM SO THAT MORE LEARNING TAKES PLACE?

INSTRUCTIONS:

In groups of 4 - 6, match the number (1, 2, 3, 4, etc) of each Common Learner Behavior listed on the left with its corresponding Learning Style listed on the bottom of the next page.
Time: 25 minutes

COMMON LEARNER BEHAVIORS

1. Lacks tolerance for a task he does not enjoy.

2. Interdependent in his relationship with the teacher.

3. Asserts independence of others in negative ways.

4. Strives to be "well liked" by others.

5. Responds stereotypically when solving problems.

6. Sees errors and criticisms as rejections of himself.

7. Has trouble choosing between alternative tasks.

8. Takes responsibility for his own learning.

9. Excessively dependent on others to structure learning tasks for him.

10. Misinterprets simple statements.

11. Prone to blame external circumstances when things "go wrong".

12. Most comfortable when the teacher gives the "right" answer.

13. Keeps making the same error over and over.

14. Becomes confused and disoriented easily.

15. Tries to outdo classmates by producing more quantity.

16. Makes sound decisions when presented with alternatives.

17. Overly sensitive to criticism or correction.

18. Tends toward temper tantrums.

19. Refuses to perform tasks.

20. Cannot follow complex instructions.

Continued

COMMON LEARNER BEHAVIORS - CONTINUED

21. Fails to apply himself to finishing a task.

22. Self-critical: can admit mistakes.

23. Disrespectful towards people and things.

24. Reflective; introspective.

25. Won't try a task for fear of failing.

26. Self-motivated.

27. Can be extremely competitive.

28. Negative: "I won't..."

29. Tries too hard.

30. Not a good listener.

31. Upset by changes in routine.

32. Worries about pleasing others.

33. Purposeful, goal-directed.

34. Doesn't trust people in authority.

35. Outwardly nervous during tests.

36. Learns quick from mistakes.

COMMON LEARNING STYLES

(Write the number of the Learner Behavior under the Learning Style with which it corresponds.)

1. "RIGID" LEARNING STYLE

3. "ANXIOUS" LEARNING STYLE

2. "UNDISCIPLINED" LEARNING STYLE

4. "CREATIVE" LEARNING STYLE

ADAPTING TEACHING/LEARNING TECHNIQUES TO LEARNING STYLES WORKSHEET

<u>INSTRUCTIONS</u>:

In groups of 4 - 6, propose specific Teaching/Learning Techniques (including specific activities and experiences, methods, materials, personal relationships, etc.), which are <u>appropriately suited</u> to teaching learners with four different Learning Styles.

<u>Time</u>: 25 minutes

I. <u>APPROPRIATE TEACHING/LEARNING ACTIVITIES FOR A "RIGID" LEARNING STYLE</u>

II. <u>APPROPRIATE TEACHING/LEARNING ACTIVITIES FOR AN "UNDISCIPLINED" LEARNING STYLE</u>

III. <u>APPROPRIATE TEACHING/LEARNING ACTIVITIES FOR AN "ANXIOUS" LEARNING STYLE</u>

IV. <u>APPROPRIATE TEACHING/LEARNING ACTIVITIES FOR A "CREATIVE" LEARNING STYLE</u>

AIMS: 1. To identify common student behavior which reflects six basic learning disabilities.

2. To propose teaching/learning techniques for remediating these basic learning disabilities.

I'M GLAD YOU FEEL THAT WAY, BOB, BECAUSE I'VE SEEN TOO MANY TEACHERS WHO DO NOT REALIZE THAT ONE OF THEIR MOST BASIC RESPONSIBILITIES IS TO HELP STUDENTS DEVELOP BASIC LEARNING ABILITIES SO THAT THEY THEN "HAVE THE ABILITY" TO LEARN THE CURRICULUM BEING TAUGHT OR DO THE TEACHING/LEARNING ACTIVITIES PROVIDED BY THE TEACHER.

YES! ...TOO MANY TEACHERS ERRONEOUSLY ASSUME THAT STUDENTS COME TO SCHOOL AREADY HAVING DEVELOPED BASIC LEARNING ABILITIES, AND THUS PROCEED TO TEACH IN A WAY WHICH CAUSES THESE "LEARNING DISABLED" STUDENTS TO FALL FURTHER AND FURTHER BEHIND OTHER STUDENTS...

...OR —WHAT'S EVEN WORSE —SOME TEACHERS WILL SIMPLY LABEL THESE STUDENTS AS "LD'S" AND THEN EXCUSE THEIR OWN INABILITY TO TEACH THEM "BECAUSE THEY ARE LEARNING DISABLED".. WHAT AN INCREDIBLE EXAMPLE OF CIRCULAR THINKING TO AVOID ONE'S PROFESSIONAL RESPONSIBILITIES!

BUT... TO GET BACK TO MY ORIGINAL QUERY— WHAT SUGGESTIONS CAN YOU OFFER TO HELP ME DO A PROFESSIONAL JOB OF HANDLING THIS CLASS ON MY PRACTICUM?

EXCUSE ME! PERHAPS I CAN HELP....FIRST OF ALL BY EXPLAINING WHAT A "LEARNING DISABILITY" MEANS TO ME...

TO ME, A "LEARNING DISABILITY" REFERS TO THE DEFICIT THAT RESULTS FROM A FAILURE TO FULLY DEVELOP AT A PARTICULAR AGE LEVEL A SPECIFIC ABILITY OR SKILL REQUIRED FOR ADEQUATE LEARNING... IN OTHER WORDS, THE DEFICIENCY IN AN ABILITY IS OF SUCH A DEGREE AS TO SIGNIFICANTLY INTERFERE WITH LEARNING IN TASKS REQUIRING THAT ABILITY.

THE DEFINITIONS OF SIX BASIC LEARNING DISABILITIES — GIVEN ON THE NEXT PAGE—WILL CLARIFY WHAT "LEARNING DISABILITY" MEANS.

244

DEFINITIONS OF SIX BASIC LEARNING DISABILITIES

1. ATTENTION DISABILITY

The learner lacks ability to focus his attention on a task; instead he responds to irrelevant stimulation. It's not that he is disinterested or unwilling to attend to relevant stimulation in a task--he simply lacks this ability.

2. MOTOR DISABILITY

The learner lacks ability to use his gross body muscles in a coordinated manner because of deficient development of a "body schema" to act as a frame of reference for directional judgment in time and space, and because of insufficient development of correct posture and balance. Fine motor disabilities can also occur--e.g. in the ocular pursuit muscle of the eye, in the small muscles of the fingers and wrists, resulting in uncoordinated motor vehavior in these areas.

3. VISUAL-RECEPTIVE DISABILITY

The learner can see alright, but lacks ability to receive, interpret, and comprehend visual information. That is, (1) he is unable to discriminate between visual configurations, between objects differing in external form, relative size, position in space, texture, and internal detail; (2) he is unable to understand the meaning of visual symbols, and, (3) he is unable to recognize and comprehend visual information involving higher levels of cognition. (Also called a visual-perceptual disability).

4. AUDITORY-RECEPTIVE DISABILITY

The learner can hear alright, but lacks ability to detect, perceive, and comprehend auditory information. That is, he is unable to understand the meaning of auditory symbols.

5. CONCEPTUAL DISABILITY

The learner lacks ability to deal with concrete objects and events in terms of their symbolic verbal labels, but must depend on observable objects and events themselves in order to solve problems or "see things as they might be". Mostly, however, thought is limited to concrete things "as they are" because the learner has not symbollically internalized the concept which stands for the concrete, observable referents.

Continued...

The learner lacks the ability to automatically integrate visual and auditory information and the ability to correctly reproduce a sequence of symbols (such as written or spoken grammar) in its syntactical and grammatical sense.

* *

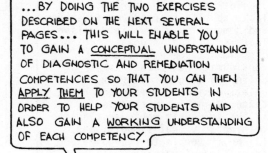

WHAT YOU'VE SAID SOUNDS VERY USEFUL...BUT, HOW CAN WE LEARN TO DIAGNOSE THESE SIX COMMON, SPECIFIC "LEARNING DISABILITIES" AND THEN PROVIDE SUITABLE REMEDIATION TO HELP OUR STUDENTS DEVELOP THESE DEFICIENT ABILITIES?

...BY DOING THE TWO EXERCISES DESCRIBED ON THE NEXT SEVERAL PAGES... THIS WILL ENABLE YOU TO GAIN A CONCEPTUAL UNDERSTANDING OF DIAGNOSTIC AND REMEDIATION COMPETENCIES SO THAT YOU CAN THEN APPLY THEM TO YOUR STUDENTS IN ORDER TO HELP YOUR STUDENTS AND ALSO GAIN A WORKING UNDERSTANDING OF EACH COMPETENCY.

INSTRUCTIONS:

1. In groups of 4 - 6, match the number (1, 2, 3, 4, etc.) of each Common Learner Behavior listed at the left with its corresponding Specific Learning Disability listed on the right.
   Time: 25 minutes

COMMON LEARNER BEHAVIORS

1. Holds head close to what he is reading.

2. Sloppy writing and printing.

3. Confuses "them" for "then".

4. Does not use "precise" words to explain something.

5. Asks for oral instructions to be repeated.

6. Easily distracted by noise and movement.

7. Jumbles word order in sentence.

8. Copying off the board causes fatigue.

9. Has difficulty classifying objects verbally.

10. Rote memory is below normal.

11. Hyperactive: "can't sit still".

12. Speech is "herky-jerky".

13. Skips words and lines when reading.

14. Work "runs off the page".

15. Large handwriting.

16. Makes reversals in reading.

17. Needs reduction of stimulation in order to perform adequately.

18. Has trouble expressing feelings in words.

SPECIFIC LEARNING DISABILITIES

(Write the number of the Learner Behavior under the Learning Disability with which it corresponds.)

1. ATTENTION DISABILITIES:

2. MOTOR DISABILITY:

3. VISUAL-RECEPTIVE DISABILITY:

4. AUDITORY-RECEPTIVE DISABILITY:

Continued...

COMMON LEARNER BEHAVIORS (continued)   SPECIFIC LEARNING DISABILITIES

19. Has difficulty expressing "time" in words.

20. Cannot repeat accurately what he heard
    said.

21. Cannot easily determine similarities and
    differences in objects.

22. Has difficulty using scissors.

23. Does not recognize differences in similar
    phonic sounds.

24. Unless teacher speaks slowly, cannot
    follow instructions.

25. Letters of alphabet not smoothly formed.

26. Easily upset by physical discomfort.

27. Does poorly on written tests but knows
    work in class discussions.

28. Confused when following directions with
    more than one step.

29. Clumsy on the playground.

30. Cannot follow a series of verbal directions.

31. Unable to "listen fast enough" - hears
    only the first several words.

32. Poor sitting posture while reading.

5. CONCEPTUAL DISABILITY

6. AUTOMATIC-SEQUENCING
    DISABILITY

248

REMEDIATING SPECIFIC LEARNING DISABILITIES WORKSHEET

INSTRUCTIONS:

1. In groups of 4 - 6, propose specific Teaching/Learning Techniques, (specific experiences, activities, methods, materials, personal relationships, etc.), which are appropriate for remediating each of the six common Learning Disabilities listed below.
   Time: 30 minutes

LEARNING DISABILITY	PROPOSED REMEDIAL TECHNIQUES
1. ATTENTION SKILLS DISABILITY	
2. MOTOR SKILLS DISABILITY	
3. VISUAL-RECEPTIVE SKILLS DISABILITY	
4. AUDITORY-RECEPTIVE SKILLS DISABILITY	
5. CONCEPTUAL SKILLS DISABILITY	
6. AUTOMATIC-SEQUENCING SKILLS DISABILITY	

AIMS: 1. To identify different ways in which you have learned.

2. To propose learning activities that are appropriate to the different ways in which students learn.

RATIONALE FOR DOING THIS ACTIVITY:

COMMON WAYS IN WHICH LEARNING OCCURS

1. CLASSICAL CONDITIONING

This involves learning either positive or negative emotional reactions in response to a previously neutral stimulus. For example, a student will learn to dislike a subject if he or she is severely frightened by harsh reprimands after making errors. Conversely, he or she will learn to like a subject if a positive emotional experience (such as being praised by a teacher) occurs in conjunction with his or her school work. Understanding this is important because positive or negative student attitudes towards school work and teachers are learned in this way.

2. CONTIGUITY LEARNING

This involves linking or connecting a stimulus and a response because they come closely together in time. Contiguity learning is involved when the teacher presents a stimulus (e.g. "4 + 4" on a flash card), and obtains a quick, accurate response (e.g. = "8") to it, as the student learns the connection that "4 + 4 = 8" . The student learns how to recognize a new word he sees written on the board as the teacher says the word because he links the visual image of the word to its pronounced sound .

3. REINFORCEMENT LEARNING
(LEARNING VIA REINFORCEMENT)

A behavior becomes learned if it is immediately followed by a positive consequence (reward, or reinforcement). For example, a student learns to write more neatly after the teacher has pointed out and praised a few neatly written words, or he learns to enunciate more clearly after the teacher congratulates him for those words he did say clearly. On the other hand, criticising mistakes does not tell the student what he is doing correctly so that he can keep doing it; criticism tells the student "what not to do", not "what to do". It has been estimated that 60%-70% of all human behavior is learned as a consequence of receiving positive reinforcement or reward.

4. IMITATION LEARNING
(LEARNING BY IMITATION)

The student learns new behaviors or attitudes by observing them in a model --i.e., "monkey see, monkey do". For example, a student learns how to print by watching a teacher demonstrate how to hold the pencil and move the hand, and then by practising himself or herself what he/she saw the teacher do. Or the student learns social courtesies, such as saying, "Please" or "thank you" by watching the teacher say these things to other people and then imitating exactly what the teacher did.

5. CONCEPT LEARNING
   (LEARNING CONCEPTS)

This involves understanding the common characteristics making up a class.
For example, the learner groups "cat" and "dog" into the class known as
mammals, and groups "mammals", "birds", and "reptiles" into the larger
class called animals. Such classification, or grouping, improves recall
ability--e.g. when asked to distinguish between the characteristics of a
dog and a snake, the student can call on his recollection of their "class"
characteristics as mammals and reptiles, respectively, even though he may
not be able to remember the specific characteristics of a dog or snake.
Such "concept learning" is employed when the teacher structures specific
experiences together which underly the concept and gets the student to
verbalize the characteristics making up the concept. For example,
teachers could have students learn the identifying characteristics of a
square by having students verbalize the characteristics of a variety of
shapes and state whether they are or are not the identifying
characteristics of a square.

6. PRINCIPLE LEARNING
   (LEARNING PRINCIPLES)

This involves seeing/understanding the relationship among concepts. Many
"inquiry" or "discovery" learning activities are structured so that the
student (by examining the component concepts in a situation), can see
the relationship between these concepts. For example, a student can
"discover" where major cities are located on a map by knowing what people
in major cities require to live (e.g. proximity to waterways and
transportation routes, land suitable for constructing big buildings, etc.)

7. INSIGHT LEARNING
   LEARNING VIA "INSIGHT"

This involves creative thinking in which two or more previously learned
concepts or principles are mentally combined in a novel way so that a
novel product can be produced or a problem can be solved with a novel
solution. For example, having learned to write poetry in iambic
pentameter and having identified and named some emotional reaction to
prejudice, a student could combine these to write a poem in iambic
pentameter in which he/she gives personal emotional reactions to having
experienced prejudice personally.

"WAYS IN WHICH I HAVE LEARNED" WORKSHEET

INSTRUCTIONS: 1. Discuss with your partner, the ways in which each of you has learned (in school, outside of school) in terms of the seven types of Learning specified below. 2. As you finish discussing each type of Learning, briefly write down your personal examples for that type of Learning.

SEVEN TYPES OF LEARNING	PERSONAL EXAMPLES
1. CLASSICAL CONDITIONING	
2. CONTIGUITY LEARNING	
3. LEARNING VIA REINFORCEMENT	
4. LEARNING BY IMITATION	
5. LEARNING CONCEPTS	
6. LEARNING PRINCIPLES	
7. LEARNING VIA INSIGHT	

SPECIFIC WAYS IN WHICH I WOULD PROMOTE MY STUDENT'S LEARNING

INSTRUCTIONS: 1. Discuss with a partner, <u>specific ways</u> in which you could utilize each of the seven types of Learning listed below as your students learn in school. (Specific ways include specific experiences, activities, methods, materials, interpersonal relationships you would provide).
Time: 25 minutes

2. Then write this down under the appropriate Type of Learning below.
Time: 25 minutes

SEVEN TYPES OF LEARNING	CLASSROOM ACTIVITIES TO PROMOTE STUDENT'S LEARNING
1. CLASSICAL CONDITIONING	
2. CONTIGUITY LEARNING	
3. LEARNING VIA REINFORCEMENT	
4. LEARNING BY IMITATION	
5. LEARNING CONCEPTS	
6. LEARNING PRINCIPLES	
7. LEARNING VIA INSIGHT	

PROMOTING THE DEVELOPMENT OF STUDENT'S THINKING SKILLS

AIMS: 1. To learn how children's thinking can be improved by developing their thinking skills.

2. To prepare "Thinking Skill Activity Cards" for developing student's thinking skills.

3. To identify ways of utilizing these "Thinking Skill Activity Cards" in your classroom program.

RATIONALE FOR DOING THIS ACTIVITY:

IN FACT, THESE STUDENTS CAN USUALLY WORK VERY WELL ON THEIR OWN, NEEDING LITTLE EXTRA HELP FROM ME.

BUT THERE ARE A LOT OF STUDENTS WHO NEEDS LOTS OF EXTRA PRACTICE USING THESE THINKING SKILLS IF THEY ARE TO DEVELOP THEM SUFFICIENTLY FOR DOING COURSEWORK AND ASSIGNMENTS REQUIRING THE USE OF THESE VERY SAME THINKING SKILLS.

SOUNDS LIKE THE OLD CHICKEN AND EGG DILEMMA — WHICH CAME FIRST? YOU'RE SAYING THAT STUDENTS DEVELOP THINKING SKILLS BY USING THEM, BUT THAT THEY CAN'T USE THEM VERY WELL IN DOING COURSEWORK ACTIVITIES IF THEY HAVE NOT ALREADY STARTED TO DEVELOP THEM.

THAT'S EXACTLY WHAT I'M SAYING, SUE...

AND I'M SAYING IT BECAUSE I'VE FOUND TOO MANY STUDENTS, WHO REALLY ENJOY THE LEARNING ACTIVITIES THEY DO IN EACH SUBJECT AREA, JUST DO NOT SEEM TO BE DEVELOPING THE THINKING SKILLS THESE ACTIVITIES ARE INTENDED TO PROMOTE...

WHAT'S WORSE — THESE STUDENTS DON'T USUALLY STAY ON TASK — THEY WANDER AROUND DISTURBING OTHERS!

AND, YOU BELIEVE IT'S BECAUSE THESE STUDENTS LACK THE VERY THINKING SKILLS REQUIRED TO STAY ON TASK TO DO THE LEARNING ACTIVITIES IN SCIENCE, SOCIAL STUDIES, LANGUAGE, ARTS, ETC.

THAT'S RIGHT...

AND THAT'S WHY YOU MADE "THINKING SKILL ACTIVITY CARDS"?

YES!... SO MY STUDENTS CAN USE THEM TO GET THE EXTRA PRACTICE THEY NEED IN USING THOSE SPECIFIC THINKING SKILLS IN WHICH THEY ARE WEAK.

WHERE DID YOU GET THE IDEA TO MAKE "THINKING SKILL ACTIVITY CARDS"?

PRIMARILY FROM LOUIS RATH'S BOOK, TEACHING FOR THINKING, AND FROM BENJAMIN BLOOM'S TAXONOMY OF EDUCATIONAL OBJECTIVES FOR THE COGNITIVE DOMAIN.

TELL ME MORE!

AFTER USING THESE TWO BOOKS TO IDENTIFY MAJOR THINKING SKILLS, I THEN MADE 3 OR 4 ACTIVITY CARDS WHICH ALLOWED MY STUDENTS TO USE AND THUS TO DEVELOP EACH SKILL.

WHEN I FOUND A STUDENT WHO WAS WEAK IN ONE OF THESE THINKING SKILLS, I HAD HIM OR HER DO THE ACTIVITIES ON THE SET OF CARDS WHICH PROMOTED THE DEVELOPMENT OF THAT SPECIFIC THINKING SKILL.

DID IT WORK?

IT CERTAINLY DID — AND THE STUDENTS LIKE DOING THE THINKING ACTIVITIES ON THE ACTIVITY CARDS.

NOW... IN THE ACTIVITY THAT FOLLOWS, YOU WILL HAVE AN OPPORTUNITY TO MAKE SOME "THINKING SKILL ACTIVITY CARDS" FOR YOUR STUDENTS TO USE IN ORDER TO GET THE EXTRA PRACTICE THEY NEED TO OVERCOME WEAKNESSES IN THEIR THINKING SKILLS.

DEFINITIONS OF 16 THINKING SKILLS

1. __OBSERVING__ - Noticing details; using any of our five senses to gain information about what is taking place.

2. __COMPARING__ - Determining similarities and differences on the basis of some criteria.

3. __COMPREHENDING__ - Understanding the main idea or theme being communicated in what one sees, reads, or hears.

4. __INTERPRETING__ - Getting personal meaning out of an experience; making sense out of what you experience.

5. __SUMMARIZING__ - Stating in brief the substance of what has already been presented; identifying the main points in a lengthy discourse.

6. __CATEGORIZING__ - Placing things (ideas, objects, events, places, etc.) into an already established classification system, where each group of things has common characteristics.

7. __CLASSIFYING__ - Sorting things (ideas, people, places, events, etc.) into groups according to some principle you devise so that all the things in each group has the same common characteristic(s).

8. __ANALYZING__ - (a) Breaking down a concept, problem, or event into its component parts, (b) so that the relationship between these component parts can be clearly seen and, (c) the organizing principle that holds the parts together can be recognized.
(Analysis may involve 1, 2 or 3 of these thinking operations).

9. __SYNTHESIZING__ - Putting together the parts to create a whole.

10. __CREATIVE THINKING__ - Developing or reorganizing ideas, objects, or words to make a new product.

11. __CRITICAL THINKING__ - Making evaluations or judgments based on analyzing how well something meets a set of standards. (It is not just a matter of finding fault or pointing out shortcomings, but looking for good qualities as well -- in terms of a set of standards.)

12. __LOOKING FOR ASSUMPTIONS__ - Determining if something is true or false by looking at supporting facts or evidence rather than just taking for granted that something is probably true or false.

13. __IMAGINING__ - Pretending that something is real; inventing something "make believe" out of your imagination.

14. __COLLECTING AND ORGANIZING DATA__ - Gathering information and then putting it into groups (classifying it) so that it makes more sense than does the information in its unorganized form.

15. __HYPOTHESIZING__ - Making a guess about something and then gathering information to find out if your guess was right or wrong. (Guesses might be made about the best way to solve a problem or to explain why something is like it is.)

16. __DECISION MAKING__ - Choosing what you would do or choosing what you like best, when presented with options.

FOUR EXAMPLES OF "THINKING SKILL ACTIVITY CARDS"   (Reduced from original size of 5 x 8 inches)

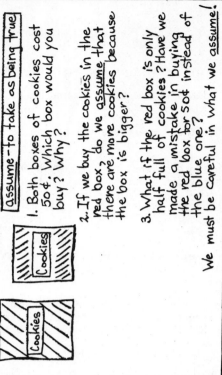

assume—to take as being true

1. Both boxes of cookies cost 50¢. Which box would you buy? Why?

2. If we buy the cookies in the red box, do we assume that there are more cookies because the box is bigger?

3. What if the red box is only half full of cookies? Have we made a mistake in buying the red box for 50¢ instead of the blue one?

We must be careful in what we assume!

1. Could the people in the picture be looking at a fish? Why or why not?

2. Could they be looking at a rocket?

3. Do the people look like your mom and dad? Do they look like anyone you know?

4. Compare the woman with your teacher. How are they the same and how are they different?

5. Write a story about this picture. Tell what the people are looking at. Does anything fall on their heads?

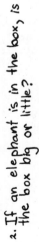

1. Imagine that there is something in the box. What are 3 things that could be in the box?

2. If an elephant is in the box, is the box big or little?

3. Could it be a jack-in-the-box?

4. Could the box be empty?

5. Is the box a circle or a square?

6. Draw a jack-in-the-box. If you don't know what one looks like, ask a friend.

1. Imagine that you have a milk carton like the one in the picture. If the carton is full and has not been opened, can we assume that there is milk inside?

2. If the carton is full, can we assume that it has no holes?

3. If you have a carton of milk with a hole in it, what does the milk do?

4. If the carton has the word "milk" on it, can we assume that at one time it had milk in it?

assume—to take as being true

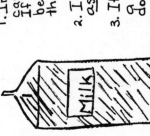

260

QUESTIONS: Which cards promote which Thinking Skills? Which cards promote more than one type of Thinking Skill? For what grade levels (age levels) do you think these four cards are suitable? What would you have done differently if you had made these four cards?

DEVELOPING CREATIVITY IN PROBLEM-SOLVING

AIMS: 1. To develop skills in creative thinking and in problem-solving.

2. To develop cooperation skills in working together with others.

RATIONALE FOR DOING THIS ACTIVITY:

AIMS: 1. To identify the Goals of Education you most prefer to promote.

2. To compare the Goals of Education you prefer to promote with the goals your classmates prefer to promote.

3. To identify the Value Orientation you have towards the Purpose of Schools.

4. To compare your Value Orientation towards the Purpose of Schools with the Goals of Education you prefer to promote.

5. To identify classroom activities for promoting the Goals of Education.

RATIONALE FOR DOING THIS ACTIVITY:

265

266

267

268

GOALS OF EDUCATION WORKSHEET

INSTRUCTIONS: 1. <u>On your own</u>, rank-order these 20 Goals of Education from 1 (=most important for you to promote) to 20 (=least important for you to promote).
2. By means of <u>group consensus</u>, group rank these 20 goals from the one which is most important to be promoted (=1) to the one which is least important to promote (=20).

YOUR PERSONAL RANKING	GROUP RANKING	20 GOALS OF EDUCATION
_____	_____	1. TO DEVELOP CULTURAL APPRECIATION AND CULTURALLY RELATED TALENTS (in art, music, writing, foreign languages, etc.)
_____	_____	2. TO DEVELOP AN ATTITUDE FOR USING LEISURE TIME PRODUCTIVELY AND LEISURE-TIME ABILITIES (in physical, intellectual, and creative areas)
_____	_____	3. TO DEVELOP WORK-RELATED SKILLS AND AN ATTITUDE OF "GOOD WORKMANSHIP".
_____	_____	4. TO DEVELOP GOOD HEALTH AND SAFETY ATTITUDES AND HABITS (both for one's own well-being and for society's as well).
_____	_____	5. TO DEVELOP ATTITUDES AND SKILLS FOR MANAGING ONE'S FINANCES, PROPERTY AND RESOURCES.
_____	_____	6. TO GAIN INFORMATION NEEDED FOR MAKING SUITABLE JOB SELECTIONS.
_____	_____	7. TO DEVELOP ATTITUDES AND SKILLS FOR LIVING IN A FAMILY SITUATION.
_____	_____	8. TO DEVELOP NON-PREJUDICIAL ATTITUDES AND BEHAVIORS TOWARDS PERSONS OF DIFFERENT CULTURES, RACES, RELIGIONS, SEXES,
_____	_____	9. TO DEVELOP DEMOCRATIC ATTITUDES AND PRACTICES (to insure the rights of others through our democratic form of government).
_____	_____	10. TO DEVELOP ATTITUDES AND SKILLS FOR ADAPTING TO CHANGES (in one's life, in one's society, in the world).
_____	_____	11. TO DEVELOP ATTITUDES AND ABILITIES FOR BEING A GOOD CITIZEN (e.g. civic responsibility, protection of personal rights, respect for property and resources).
_____	_____	12. TO BECOME "WELL-EDUCATED" (i.e., having a "store of factual knowledge" in all subject disciplines of the curriculum).
_____	_____	13. TO DEVELOP INTELLECTUAL ABILITIES (for thinking logically, critically, and creatively, and for using the scientific method to solve problems).
_____	_____	14. TO DEVELOP RESPECT AND HABITS FOR "GETTING ALONG" WITH PEOPLE WITH WHOM WE WORK AND LIVE.
_____	_____	15. TO DEVELOP A DESIRE FOR AND ABILITIES FOR "LIFETIME LEARNING" (e.g. self-discipline to learn, analytic ability to examine social issues.)
_____	_____	16. TO DEVELOP "GOOD CHARACTER" (for acting responsibly, for disciplining oneself to work, study, and play constructively).
_____	_____	17. TO DEVELOP A SENSE OF "SELF-WORTH" AND "SELF-CONFIDENCE".
_____	_____	18. TO DEVELOP BASIC COMMUNICATION SKILLS (in reading, writing, speaking, listening).
_____	_____	19. TO DEVELOP AN ATTITUDE OF ACHIEVEMENT AND ABILITIES FOR SUCCEEDING.
_____	_____	20. TO DEVELOP PRACTICAL KNOWLEDGE AND ABILITIES (like those used by each subject specialist in order to understand the world and its inhabitants).

"VALUE ORIENTATIONS TOWARD THE PURPOSE OF SCHOOL" WORKSHEET

INSTRUCTIONS: 1. <u>On your own</u>, rank order the 5 Value Orientations below from 1 (=most important to you) to 5 (=least important to you).

2. <u>In your group</u>, use the group consensus method to <u>match</u> the 20 Goals of Education with the particular "Value Orientation" with which each is related.

DIFFERENT VALUE ORIENTATIONS TOWARDS THE PURPOSE OF SCHOOLS	IMPORTANCE TO YOU (RANK ORDER)	RELATED GOALS OF EDUCATION
I. Emphasize children's personal interests	( )	
II. Emphasize children's personal psychological needs	( )	
III. Emphasize children's mastery of "covered" subject matter	( )	
IV. Emphasize the solving of "real life" problems	( )	
V. Emphasize general education which is useful/practical	( )	

QUESTIONS FOR GROUP DISCUSSION

Look at your own Personal Ranking and your group's Group Ranking of the Goals of Education done on the previous Worksheet.

1. Were the goals you ranked highest assigned to the "Value Orientations" you ranked highest on this Worksheet? Were the goals you ranked lowest assigned to the "Value Orientation" you ranked lowest? Why?

2. Were the goals your group ranked highest on the previous Worksheet assigned to the "Value Orientation" you ranked highest on this Worksheet? Were the goals your group ranked lowest assigned to the "Value Orientation" you ranked lowest? Why?

TEACHING/LEARNING ACTIVITIES WORKSHEET (#1)

INSTRUCTIONS: In your group, list under each Goal of Education those Teaching/ Learning activities which members of your group would like to provide as teachers in order to promote each Goal of Education.

1. TO DEVELOP CULTURAL APPRECIATION AND CULTURALLY RELATED TALENTS

2. TO DEVELOP AN ATTITUDE FOR USING LEISURE TIME PRODUCTIVELY AND LEISURE-TIME ABILITIES

3. TO DEVELOP WORK-RELATED SKILLS AND AN ATTITUDE OF "GOOD WORKMANSHIP"

4. TO DEVELOP GOOD HEALTH AND SAFETY ATTITUDES AND HABITS

5. TO DEVELOP ATTITUDES AND SKILLS FOR MANAGING ONE'S FINANCES, PROPERTY AND RESOURCES

6. TO GAIN INFORMATION NEEDED FOR MAKING SUITABLE JOB SELECTIONS

7. TO DEVELOP ATTITUDES AND SKILLS FOR LIVING IN A FAMILY SITUATION

8. TO DEVELOP NON-PREJUDICIAL ATTITUDES AND BEHAVIORS TOWARDS PERSONS OF DIFFERENT CULTURES, RACES, RELIGIONS, SEXES

9. TO DEVELOP DEMOCRATIC ATTITUDES AND PRACTICES

10. TO DEVELOP ATTITUDES AND SKILLS FOR ADAPTING TO CHANGES

11. TO DEVELOP ATTITUDES AND ABILITIES FOR BEING A GOOD CITIZEN

12. TO BECOME "WELL-EDUCATED"

13. TO DEVELOP INTELLECTUAL ABILITIES

14. TO DEVELOP RESPECT AND HABITS FOR "GETTING ALONG" WITH PEOPLE WITH WHOM WE WORK AND LIVE

15. TO DEVELOP A DESIRE FOR AND ABILITIES FOR "LIFETIME LEARNING"

16. TO DEVELOP "GOOD CHARACTER"

17. TO DEVELOP A SENSE OF "SELF-WORTH" AND "SELF-CONFIDENCE"

18. TO DEVELOP BASIC COMMUNICATION SKILLS

19. TO DEVELOP AN ATTITUDE OF ACHIEVEMENT AND ABILITIES FOR SUCCEEDING

20. TO DEVELOP PRACTICAL KNOWLEDGE AND ABILITIES

UNDERSTANDING ALTERNATIVE GRADING SYSTEMS FOR
ASSESSING STUDENT LEARNING

AIMS: 1. To understand nine different alternatives to the traditional grading system.

2. To identify the strengths and weaknesses of different grading systems.

3. To develop skills in designing a grading system.

RATIONALE FOR DOING THIS ACTIVITY:

DEFINITIONS OF VARIOUS GRADING SYSTEMS

1. TRADITIONAL GRADING BY LETTER GRADES

This is the traditional system of assigning grades by using letters of the alphabet.

Grade	Quality of Work
A	Excellent
B	Superior
C	Average
D	Marginal
F	Failure

2. TRADITIONAL GRADING BY PERCENTAGES

This is the traditional system of assigning grades by using percentages.

Percentages	Quality of Work
80% - 100%	Excellent
67% - 79%	Superior
50% - 66%	Average
Below 50%	Failure

3. SELF GRADING

This is the system where the student determines his own mark for part or all of his course work. The student is given written (or other) feedback on the quality of his assignments and uses this instructor feedback, together with his own assessment of his performance, to arrive at a grade.

4. UNREPORTED GRADES

In this system, the instructor gives grades but doesn't tell the students the specific grades they obtained or the criteria used for giving the grades. Students are instead given feedback on their progress through interviews with the instructor or through written reports in which grades are not mentioned.

5. GROUP CONTRACT

In the contract system, as applied to a whole class, students automatically receive a given grade if they do a specified type, quantity, and quality of work.
For example:
Students who don't come to class or do the required work receive an F.
Students who only come to class regularly or only complete the required work receive a D.
Students who attend class regularly and complete the required work receive a C.
Students who attend class regularly and complete the required work at a specified level of quality receive a B.
Students who meet all requirements for a B grade and turn in a high quality extra project receive an A.

6. CREDIT/NO CREDIT

In this system any student who meets the instructor's criteria of acceptable work is given "credit". If the student fails to meet the instructor's performance criteria, he receives "no credit". In using this system it is important to note that "no credit" does not mean failing work.

7. NORMAL CURVE GRADING

> This is the system of grading students by determining in advance
> what percentage of the class will get A's, what percentage B's,
> and so on, according to a pre-established normal curve
> distribution of marks: A's (7%), B's (24%), C's (38%), D's (24%),
> F's (7%).

8. SELF-EVALUATION

> In this system, the student submits a report to the instructor
> giving the student's self-evaluation of his own progress in
> a course. The student does not grade himself, however. The
> instructor determines the student's grade using the self-
> evaluation as one additional source of information on the
> student's progress.

9. ANECDOTAL WRITTEN EVALUATIONS

> In this approach, students do not receive grades. Instead they
> get written anecdotal comments from the instructor regarding
> their strengths and weaknesses on specific assignments, or on
> the course overall. The use of checklists, in which the teacher
> can check off specific strengths or areas needing improvement,
> is also a form of anecdotal written evaluation.

10. INDIVIDUAL CONTRACT

> In this form of the contract grading system, individual students
> make a separate contract with the teacher as to what he, the
> student, will do to demonstrate learning in a subject area. For
> example, in an English class, one student might elect to read a
> specified number of poems and then to write an exam on the poems.
> A second student might contract to write an essay comparing different
> works of literature. A third student could contract to produce a
> class play together with several other students. In Individual
> Contracting, each student sets his own educational goals, specifies
> the ways he will reach these goals, and identifies how he will be
> assessed on his level of achievement. The contract must be agreed
> to by the teacher and in some instances, both student and teacher
> will negotiate as to what type, quality, and quantity of work the
> student will do to achieve what grade.

11. PASS/FAIL

In this grading system, there are only two grades: Pass and Fail. Students who meet the instructor's criteria for a passing grade receive a Pass. Students who do not meet the required course criteria receive a Fail.

12. MASTERY APPROACH

In this approach, the teacher sets up pre-established competencies and acceptable levels of attainment, which students are required to meet in a particular unit of a subject before they can be considered to have mastered the material in that unit. A particular course will be made up of a number of units which may be divided further into subunits. Students complete the units in a prearranged sequence and must demonstrate mastery of each unit before proceeding to a higher unit. Students who wish to try for an overall A or B grade stay with a particular unit until they demonstrate an A or B level of mastery as determined by criteria set by the instructor. Each student works at his own pace using a variety of resource materials to master the unit at the level he chooses. When a student is ready to be examined on a unit, he will take an examination. If he fails the exam, he stays with the unit until he reaches the pre-established level of mastery. A different examination (or assessment device) is used for subsequent testing. Course credits are determined not by the length of time a student spends on a subject, but by the performance level (i.e., mastery) attained by the student in the subject.

THANKS FOR TELLING ME ABOUT THESE DIFFERENT GRADING SYSTEMS, SUE. THERE ARE SEVERAL INTERESTING ONES I INTEND TO TRY OUT!

GRADING SYSTEM ANALYSIS WORKSHEET A

INSTRUCTIONS: Make brief comments on what you feel are the strengths and
weaknesses of each of the grading systems shown below:

GRADING SYSTEM	STRENGTHS	WEAKNESSES
1. TRADITIONAL GRADING: LETTER GRADE		
2. TRADITIONAL GRADING: PERCENTAGES		
3. SELF-GRADING		
4. UNREPORTED GRADES		
5. CLASS CONTRACT		
6. CREDIT/NO CREDIT		

GRADING SYSTEM ANALYSIS WORKSHEET B

INSTRUCTIONS: Make brief comments on what you feel are the strengths and weaknesses of each of the grading systems shown below:

GRADING SYSTEM	STRENGTHS	WEAKNESSES
7. TRADITIONAL GRADING: NORMAL CURVE GRADING		
8. SELF-EVALUATION		
9. WRITTEN ANECDOTAL EVALUATIONS		
10. INDIVIDUAL CONTRACT		
11. PASS/FAIL		
12. MASTERY APPROACH		

GROUP CONSENSUS WORKSHEET A

INSTRUCTIONS: One person should act as group secretary and write down the group's consensus as to the main strength and weakness for each grading system listed below:

GRADING SYSTEM	MAIN STRENGTH	MAIN WEAKNESS
1. TRADITIONAL GRADING: LETTER GRADES		
2. TRADITIONAL GRADING: PERCENTAGES		
3. SELF-GRADING		
4. UNREPORTED GRADES		
5. CLASS CONTRACT		
6. CREDIT/NO CREDIT		

INSTRUCTIONS: One person should act as group secretary and write down the group's consensus as to the main strength and weakness for each grading system listed below:

GRADING SYSTEM	MAIN STRENGTH	MAIN WEAKNESS
7. TRADITIONAL GRADING: NORMAL CURVE GRADING		
8. SELF-EVALUATION		
9. WRITTEN ANECDOTAL EVALUATIONS		
10. INDIVIDUAL CONTRACT		
11. PASS/FAIL		
12. MASTERY APPROACH		

GRADING SYSTEM DESIGN WORKSHEET

1. <u>GRADE LEVEL BEING ASSESSED</u>:

2. <u>SUBJECT AREA</u>:

3. <u>METHOD OF ASSESSMENT</u> (<u>assignments, tests, exams, skills, etc.</u>):

4. <u>GRADING SYSTEM USED</u> (<u>one of the 12 grading systems, or a combination of them</u>):

GRADING SYSTEM DESIGN FEEDBACK SHEETS

INSTRUCTIONS: Place a check (✓) in the space provided only if you strongly agree that the statement applies to the grading system design being reported.

---

1. Stimulates creativity   _____

2. Motivates brighter students _____

3. Motivates poorer students   _____

4. Is objective (reliable)   _____
   GROUP 1

I would enjoy being assessed this way. _____

Other comments:

---

1. Stimulates creativity   _____

2. Motivates brighter students _____

3. Motivates poorer students   _____

4. Is objective (reliable)   _____
   GROUP 2

I would enjoy being assessed this way. _____

Other comments:

---

1. Stimulates creativity   _____

2. Motivates brighter students _____

3. Motivates poorer students   _____

4. Is objective (reliable)   _____
   GROUP 3

I would enjoy being assessed this way. _____

Other comments:

---

1. Stimulates creativity   _____

2. Motivates brighter students _____

3. Motivates poorer students   _____

4. Is objective (reliable)   _____
   GROUP 4

I would enjoy being assessed this way. _____

Other comments:

---

1. Stimulates creativity   _____

2. Motivates brighter students _____

3. Motivates poorer students   _____

4. Is objective (reliable)   _____
   GROUP 5

I would enjoy being assessed this way. _____

Other comments:

GRADING SYSTEM DESIGN FEEDBACK SHEETS

INSTRUCTIONS: Place a check (✓) in the space provided only if you strongly agree that the statement applies to the grading system design being reported.

---

1. Stimulates creativity _____
2. Motivates brighter students _____
3. Motivates poorer students _____
4. Is objective (reliable) _____
   GROUP 6

I would enjoy being assessed this way. _____

Other comments:

---

1. Stimulates creativity _____
2. Motivates brighter students _____
3. Motivates poorer students _____
4. Is objective (reliable) _____
   GROUP 7

I would enjoy being assessed this way. _____

Other comments:

---

1. Stimulates creativity _____
2. Motivates brighter students _____
3. Motivates poorer students _____
4. Is objective (reliable) _____
   GROUP 8

I would enjoy being assessed this way. _____

Other comments:

---

1. Stimulates creativity _____
2. Motivates brighter students _____
3. Motivates poorer students _____
4. Is objective (reliable) _____
   GROUP 9

I would enjoy being assessed this way. _____

Other comments:

---

1. Stimulates creativity _____
2. Motivates brighter students _____
3. Motivates poorer students _____
4. Is objective (reliable) _____
   GROUP 10

I would enjoy being assessed this way. _____

Other comments:

H

DESIGNING A LEARNING CENTER:

AN ASSIGNMENT FOR PRACTICUM

AIMS: 1. To identify the basic procedures for getting students and teachers to use a learning center properly.

2. To identify the main characteristics of a learning center.

3. To design a learning center which you can use on Practicum.

RATIONALE FOR DOING THIS ACTIVITY:

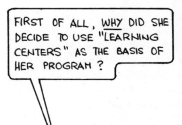

FIRST OF ALL, WHY DID SHE DECIDE TO USE "LEARNING CENTERS" AS THE BASIS OF HER PROGRAM?

SHE TOLD ME FIVE MAJOR REASONS FOR USING A "LEARNING CENTERS" APPROACH:

FIRST, SHE BELIEVES STUDENTS LEARN AND REMEMBER BEST WHEN THEY "LEARN BY DOING SOMETHING" WITH CONCRETE MATERIALS OR WITH OTHER STUDENTS. "LEARNING CENTERS" CONTAIN CONCRETE ACTIVITIES FOR STUDENT TO DO AND CONCRETE MATERIALS FOR THEM TO USE SO THAT THEY CAN ENGAGE IN "ACTIVE LEARNING" AS DISTINGUISHED FROM THE "PASSIVE LEARNING" OF SYMBOLIC MATERIAL CONNECTED WITH READING OR BEING LECTURED TO. THIS PREFERENCE FOR "ACTIVE LEARNING" WITH CONCRETE MATERIALS IS ALSO HELD BY SEVERAL PEOPLE WHO HAVE HAD A PROFOUND INFLUENCE ON EDUCATION — NAMELY, JOHN DEWEY, MARIA MONTESSORI, JEAN PAGET, JEROME BRUNER.

THAT MAKES SENSE... I REMEMBER BEST THOSE THINGS I LEARNED BY MEANS OF "ACTIVE LEARNING" — LIKE LEARNING TO ADD AND SUBTRACT USING COLORED RODS.

SECOND, "LEARNING CENTERS" PROVIDE A VARIETY OF MULTI-MEDIA MATERIALS, WHICH ENABLE STUDENTS TO LEARN BY USING THEIR PREFERRED SENSORY MODALITY (i.e., SIGHT, HEARING, TOUCH).

"LEARNING CENTERS" ARE NOT INTENDED, HOWEVER, TO REPLACE A DEVELOPMENTAL, SEQUENTIAL LEARNING PROGRAM — BUT RATHER REINFORCE AND EXTEND IT.

AGAIN, THAT MAKES SENSE TO ME ... BECAUSE I'M BASICALLY A "VISUAL" LEARNER.

ABOUT 70% OF US ARE "VISUAL" LEARNERS... "LEARNING CENTERS" PROVIDE FOR ALL OUR SENSORY MODALITIES OF LEARNING.

THIRD, "LEARNING CENTERS" PROVIDE A MEANS FOR INTEGRATING THE SUBJECT AREAS IN THE CURRICULUM BY PROVIDING LEARNING ACTIVITIES WHICH INCLUDE SEVERAL SUBJECT AREAS. THIS ALLOWS STUDENTS TO BECOME ENGROSSED IN "DOING THE ACTIVITY" OVER A LONGER PERIOD OF TIME THAN IN A CONVENTIONAL PROGRAM IN WHICH THEY HAVE TO "CHANGE PERIODS" EVERY 40 MINUTES FOR ANOTHER SUBJECT AREA.

A FOURTH ADVANTAGE OF USING "LEARNING CENTERS" IS THAT THEY PROVIDE A MEANS OF KEEPING SOME STUDENTS ACTIVELY INVOLVED IN LEARNING WHILE THE TEACHER WORKS PERSONALLY WITH A SMALL GROUP OF STUDENTS ELSEWHERE ... PERHAPS RETEACHING A CONCEPT THEY DO NOT UNDERSTAND, PERHAPS PROVIDING EXTRA ASSISTANCE ON A SPECIAL PROJECT THEY ARE DOING ...

FIFTH, "LEARNING CENTERS" ALLOW THE "BUDDY SYSTEM" TO BE USED WHERE ONE STUDENT "TEACHES" OR HELPS ANOTHER DO A LEARNING ACTIVITY AT THE CENTER ... FOR EXAMPLE, IN A CREATIVE WRITING CENTER, A SLOWER LEARNER MIGHT DICTATE HIS STORY TO A FASTER LEARNER, WHO WRITES IT DOWN. THEN BOTH COLLABORATE IN "ACTING IT OUT" FOR THE CLASS.

THOSE SOUND LIKE FIVE GOOD REASONS OR ADVANTAGES FOR USING "LEARNING CENTERS" AS A BASIC PART OF A TEACHER'S OVERALL PROGRAM ... BUT SURELY THERE MUST BE DISADVANTAGES TOO ??

MRS. STANBURY PREFERS TO CALL THESE "SENSIBLE CAUTIONS"... SHE POINTED OUT SEVERAL OF THEM —
FIRST, TEACHERS MUST REALIZE THAT PREPARING "LEARNING CENTERS" REQUIRES MORE TIME. MANAGING THEIR USE REQUIRES BETTER ORGANIZATION THAN PREPARING LESSON PRESENTATIONS FOR THE WHOLE CLASS IN EACH SUBJECT AREA.

ALSO, THERE ARE NO "TRIED AND TRUE" FORMULAS FOR HAVING STUDENTS USE "LEARNING CENTERS" PROPERLY. SOME TEACHERS REQUIRE STUDENTS TO FINISH THEIR SEATWORK BEFORE GOING TO WORK AT A "LEARNING CENTER". OTHER TEACHERS, WHO FAVOR "ACTIVE LEARNING", HAVE THEIR STUDENTS WORK AT THE "LEARNING CENTERS" INSTEAD OF ANSWERING QUESTIONS AT THEIR SEATS FROM THE CHALKBOARD OR FROM STENCILS.

THERE ARE TWO "SENSIBLE CAUTIONS", HOWEVER, ON WHICH ALL TEACHERS AGREE :
FIRST, TEACHERS MUST "GO SLOWLY" IN INTRODUCING ONE OR TWO "LEARNING CENTERS" AT A TIME SO THAT STUDENTS CAN LEARN HOW THIS NEW ROUTINE FITS INTO THEIR OVERALL PROGRAM.
SECOND, STUDENTS MUST BE TAUGHT HOW TO USE EACH NEW "LEARNING CENTER" PROPERLY SO THAT THEY WILL KNOW WHAT TO DO AND HOW TO BEHAVE WHILE DOING IT.

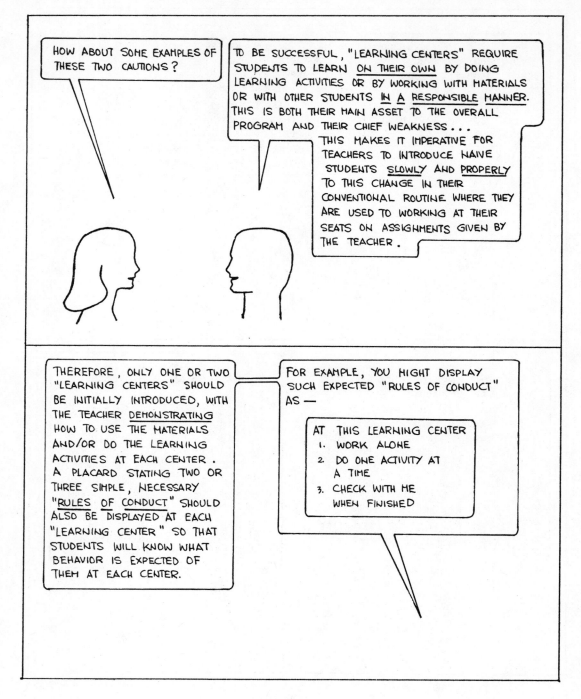

HOW ABOUT SOME EXAMPLES OF THESE TWO CAUTIONS?

TO BE SUCCESSFUL, "LEARNING CENTERS" REQUIRE STUDENTS TO LEARN ON THEIR OWN BY DOING LEARNING ACTIVITIES OR BY WORKING WITH MATERIALS OR WITH OTHER STUDENTS IN A RESPONSIBLE MANNER. THIS IS BOTH THEIR MAIN ASSET TO THE OVERALL PROGRAM AND THEIR CHIEF WEAKNESS...

THIS MAKES IT IMPERATIVE FOR TEACHERS TO INTRODUCE NAIVE STUDENTS SLOWLY AND PROPERLY TO THIS CHANGE IN THEIR CONVENTIONAL ROUTINE WHERE THEY ARE USED TO WORKING AT THEIR SEATS ON ASSIGNMENTS GIVEN BY THE TEACHER.

THEREFORE, ONLY ONE OR TWO "LEARNING CENTERS" SHOULD BE INITIALLY INTRODUCED, WITH THE TEACHER DEMONSTRATING HOW TO USE THE MATERIALS AND/OR DO THE LEARNING ACTIVITIES AT EACH CENTER. A PLACARD STATING TWO OR THREE SIMPLE, NECESSARY "RULES OF CONDUCT" SHOULD ALSO BE DISPLAYED AT EACH "LEARNING CENTER" SO THAT STUDENTS WILL KNOW WHAT BEHAVIOR IS EXPECTED OF THEM AT EACH CENTER.

FOR EXAMPLE, YOU MIGHT DISPLAY SUCH EXPECTED "RULES OF CONDUCT" AS —

AT THIS LEARNING CENTER
1. WORK ALONE
2. DO ONE ACTIVITY AT A TIME
3. CHECK WITH ME WHEN FINISHED

290

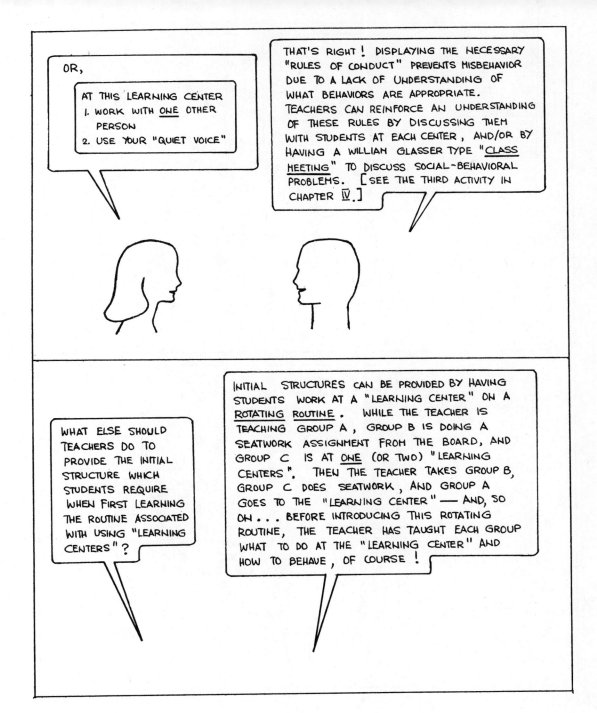

OR,

AT THIS LEARNING CENTER
1. WORK WITH <u>ONE</u> OTHER PERSON
2. USE YOUR "QUIET VOICE"

THAT'S RIGHT! DISPLAYING THE NECESSARY "RULES OF CONDUCT" PREVENTS MISBEHAVIOR DUE TO A LACK OF UNDERSTANDING OF WHAT BEHAVIORS ARE APPROPRIATE. TEACHERS CAN REINFORCE AN UNDERSTANDING OF THESE RULES BY DISCUSSING THEM WITH STUDENTS AT EACH CENTER, AND/OR BY HAVING A WILLIAM GLASSER TYPE "<u>CLASS MEETING</u>" TO DISCUSS SOCIAL-BEHAVIORAL PROBLEMS. [SEE THE THIRD ACTIVITY IN CHAPTER Ⅳ.]

WHAT ELSE SHOULD TEACHERS DO TO PROVIDE THE INITIAL STRUCTURE WHICH STUDENTS REQUIRE WHEN FIRST LEARNING THE ROUTINE ASSOCIATED WITH USING "LEARNING CENTERS"?

INITIAL STRUCTURES CAN BE PROVIDED BY HAVING STUDENTS WORK AT A "LEARNING CENTER" ON A <u>ROTATING ROUTINE</u>. WHILE THE TEACHER IS TEACHING GROUP A, GROUP B IS DOING A SEATWORK ASSIGNMENT FROM THE BOARD, AND GROUP C IS AT <u>ONE</u> (OR TWO) "LEARNING CENTERS". THEN THE TEACHER TAKES GROUP B, GROUP C DOES SEATWORK, AND GROUP A GOES TO THE "LEARNING CENTER" — AND, SO ON . . . BEFORE INTRODUCING THIS ROTATING ROUTINE, THE TEACHER HAS TAUGHT EACH GROUP WHAT TO DO AT THE "LEARNING CENTER" AND HOW TO BEHAVE, OF COURSE!

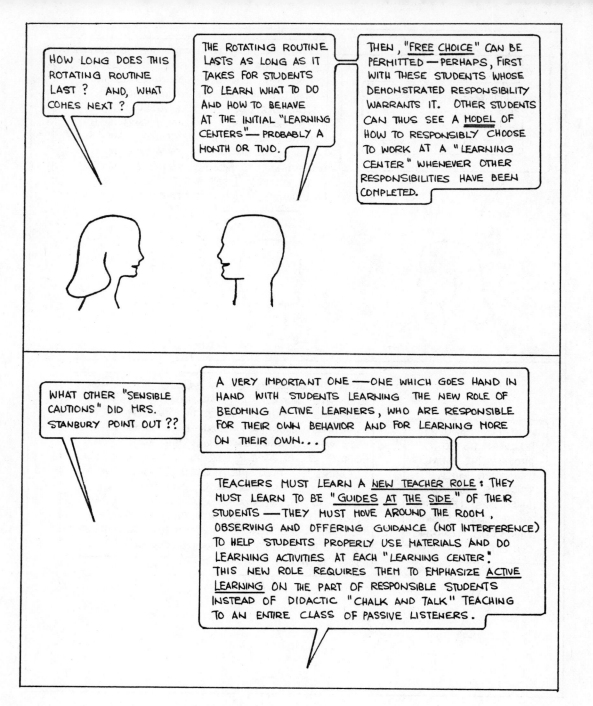

HOW LONG DOES THIS ROTATING ROUTINE LAST? AND, WHAT COMES NEXT?

THE ROTATING ROUTINE LASTS AS LONG AS IT TAKES FOR STUDENTS TO LEARN WHAT TO DO AND HOW TO BEHAVE AT THE INITIAL "LEARNING CENTERS" — PROBABLY A MONTH OR TWO.

THEN, "FREE CHOICE" CAN BE PERMITTED — PERHAPS, FIRST WITH THESE STUDENTS WHOSE DEMONSTRATED RESPONSIBILITY WARRANTS IT. OTHER STUDENTS CAN THUS SEE A MODEL OF HOW TO RESPONSIBLY CHOOSE TO WORK AT A "LEARNING CENTER" WHENEVER OTHER RESPONSIBILITIES HAVE BEEN COMPLETED.

WHAT OTHER "SENSIBLE CAUTIONS" DID MRS. STANBURY POINT OUT??

A VERY IMPORTANT ONE — ONE WHICH GOES HAND IN HAND WITH STUDENTS LEARNING THE NEW ROLE OF BECOMING ACTIVE LEARNERS, WHO ARE RESPONSIBLE FOR THEIR OWN BEHAVIOR AND FOR LEARNING MORE ON THEIR OWN...

TEACHERS MUST LEARN A NEW TEACHER ROLE: THEY MUST LEARN TO BE "GUIDES AT THE SIDE" OF THEIR STUDENTS — THEY MUST MOVE AROUND THE ROOM, OBSERVING AND OFFERING GUIDANCE (NOT INTERFERENCE) TO HELP STUDENTS PROPERLY USE MATERIALS AND DO LEARNING ACTIVITIES AT EACH "LEARNING CENTER." THIS NEW ROLE REQUIRES THEM TO EMPHASIZE ACTIVE LEARNING ON THE PART OF RESPONSIBLE STUDENTS INSTEAD OF DIDACTIC "CHALK AND TALK" TEACHING TO AN ENTIRE CLASS OF PASSIVE LISTENERS.

I DON'T KNOW IF I COULD MAKE A SUDDEN TRANSITION FROM PRESENTING LESSONS TO THE ENTIRE CLASS TO EMPHASIZING ACTIVE LEARNING ON THE PART OF EACH STUDENT ...WHAT DO YOU SUGGEST?

MRS. STANBURY ALSO REALIZED THE DIFFICULTY IN MAKING THIS TRANSITION . . . THAT'S WHY SHE SAID THAT SOME TEACHERS MIGHT WANT TO INITIATE THEMSELVES TO A "LEARNING CENTERS" APPROACH BY LETTING STUDENTS FIRST WORK AT A "LEARNING CENTER" ONLY IN THE AFTERNOON, AND ONLY AFTER THEY HAVE FINISHED THEIR SEATWORK FOLLOWING A TYPICAL LESSON PRESENTATION...

IN CONTRAST, THOSE TEACHERS WHO ARE ABLE TO LEARN THIS NEW ROLE MORE QUICKLY, MIGHT HAVE THEIR STUDENTS WORK AT "LEARNING CENTERS" MORE OFTEN INSTEAD OF AT THEIR DESKS — BUT ONLY IF THEIR STUDENTS CAN ALSO ADAPT QUICKLY TO THIS NEW ROUTINE AND LEARN THE REQUISITE RESPONSIBILITIES.

NOW THAT WE'VE DISCUSSED WHY TO USE "LEARNING CENTERS" AND SOME "SENSIBLE CAUTIONS" REGARDING THEIR USE, TELL ME MORE ABOUT WHAT THEY ARE.

A "LEARNING CENTER" IS A PHYSICALLY DESIGNATED AREA IN THE CLASSROOM (OR EVEN IN THE HALLWAYS OR OUT-OF-DOORS), WHICH CONTAINS A WIDE VARIETY OF MULTI-MEDIA RESOURCE MATERIALS THAT STUDENTS USE (ALONE OR WITH OTHER STUDENTS) AS THEY DO A "LEARNING ACTIVITY" DESCRIBED ON AN "ACTIVITY CARD".

293

THAT DEFINITION OF A "LEARNING CENTER" WAS QUITE A MOUTHFUL! COULD YOU BREAK IT DOWN FOR ME BY GIVING ME SOME EXAMPLES OF EACH PART?

THE <u>PHYSICAL</u> <u>ARRANGEMENT</u> OF MRS. STANBURY'S CLASSROOM IS ILLUSTRATED ON THE NEXT PAGE. NOTICE THAT "LEARNING CENTERS" ARE SET UP ON THE WALLS, ALONG THE WINDOW LEDGE, IN THE CLOAK ROOM, ON RECTANGULAR AND CIRCULAR TABLES, AND ON A SMALL RUG. ALSO, LOW BENCHES, T.V. TABLES, AND PICNIC TABLES CAN BE USED.

<u>RESOURCE</u> <u>LEARNING</u> <u>MATERIALS</u> FOR EACH "LEARNING CENTER" CAN BE OBTAINED BY A RESOURCEFUL TEACHER FROM A VARIETY OF SOURCES...

(1) A "PHOTOGRAPHY CENTER" CAN BE SET UP WITH EXPIRED FILM OBTAINED FROM A LOCAL PHOTOGRAPHER

(2) A LOCAL GARDEN OR LANDSCAPE SHOP MIGHT SUPPLY SAWED-OFF "TREE ROUNDS" SUITABLE FOR A "TREE CENTER".

(3) A LOCAL BAKERY MIGHT SUPPLY USED CUP-CAKE TINS, WHICH MAKE IDEAL PAINT CONTAINERS FOR PAINT AT THE ART CENTER, OR CAN BE USED AS COOKING UTENSILS AT A "COOKING CENTER".

(4) BUTTONS OF ALL SHAPES, SIZES AND COLORS CAN BE OBTAINED FROM STUDENTS' GRANDMOTHERS FOR USE IN A "CLASSIFYING CENTER".

(5) A FLOWER SHOP MIGHT SUPPLY RIBBONS, PIECES OF STYROFOAM, AND ARTIFICIAL FLOWERS FOR USE IN AN ART CENTER.

THE PHYSICAL ARRANGEMENT OF "LEARNING CENTERS" IN MRS. STANBURY'S PRIMARY CLASSROOM (GRADES 1 - 3)

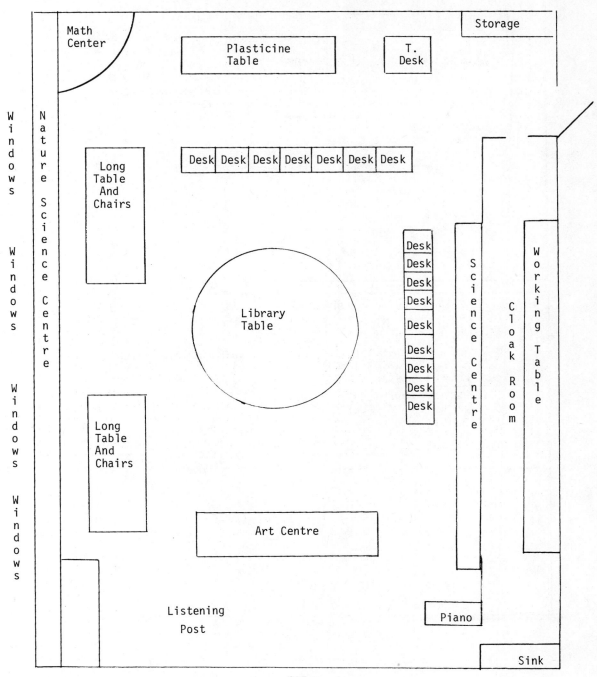

WHY ARE "ACTIVITY CARDS" IMPORTANT?

THESE "ACTIVITY CARDS" ARE EXTREMELY IMPORTANT FOR SPECIFYING WHAT STUDENTS ARE TO DO AT EACH "LEARNING CENTER"... WITHOUT THEM, "LEARNING CENTERS" LACK A DESIGNATED PURPOSE, AND STUDENTS TEND TO WANDER AIMLESSLY AROUND A "LEARNING CENTER", PERHAPS "PLAYING WITH" MATERIALS, BUT WITHOUT NECESSARILY LEARNING ANYTHING DEFINITE WHICH CAN BE ASSESSED AS LEARNING.

THERE ARE TWO TYPES OF ACTIVITY CARDS: (1) AN "ACTIVITY CARD MIGHT URGE STUDENTS TO "MESS AROUND" WITH MATERIALS IN AN OPEN-ENDED WAY TO CREATE OR DISCOVER SOMETHING. FOR EXAMPLE: "CREATE THE FASTEST SELF-PROPELLING 'MACHINE' YOU CAN OUT OF THE STICKS, RUBBER BANDS, AND THREAD SPOOLS PROVIDED. WHAT MAKES ONE OF YOUR 'MACHINES' MOVE FASTER THAN ANOTHER?"

OR, (2) AN "ACTIVITY CARD" MIGHT SPECIFY THE EXACT LEARNING OUTCOME EXPECTED, FOR EXAMPLE: "IN THIS PICTURE, THE MOUNTAINS REFLECT IN THE WATER. WHEN YOU LOOK AT A MIRROR, YOU CAN SEE YOUR REFLECTION, NAME TWO OTHER THINGS YOU CAN LOOK AT TO SEE YOUR REFLECTION."

IS THERE ANYTHING ELSE I SHOULD KNOW ABOUT "ACTIVITY CARDS"?

YES! THEY SHOULD SPECIFY AN "ORDERED INTERROGATION" —A SERIES OF QUESTIONS OR TASKS WHICH PROGRESSIVELY CHALLENGE THE STUDENT'S IMAGINATION AND HIGHER THINKING SKILLS. SOME EXAMPLES OF "ACTIVITY CARDS" FOR USE IN PROMOTING STUDENTS' THINKING SKILLS GIVEN IN THE FIRST ACTIVITY OF CHAPTER VII. BUT, I'LL GIVE YOU AN EXAMPLE HERE, ANYWAY.

1. Could the people in the picture be looking at a fish? Why or why not?

2. Could they be looking at a rocket?

3. Do the people look like your mom and dad? Do they look like anyone you know?

4. Compare the woman with your teacher. How are they the same and how are they different?

5. Write a story about this picture. Tell what the people are looking at. Does anything fall on their heads?

WHAT KINDS OF "LEARNING CENTERS" ARE POSSIBLE?

MRS. STANBURY HAS FIVE MAJOR "LEARNING CENTERS" IN HER PRIMARY CLASSROOM.

EXAMPLES OF LEARNING CENTERS IN A PRIMARY CLASSROOM

1. A <u>PLASTICINE CENTER</u> - where students have to complete two required assignments with plasticine before having "free play" with the plasticine. These assignments could be making letters of the alphabet or making numbers taught in an earlier class lesson. This activity could precede the making of words and number sets (or even equations) out of plasticine.

2. A <u>LIBRARY CENTER</u> - where students choose their own book or story, with an accompanying "activity card" telling them to write down the main character, the setting, or the plot in their "language workbooks". Open-ended questions can also be asked, such as "Which character in the story would you most like to be? Why? Would you have done the same things as that character did? Why not?"

3. A <u>LISTENING POST CENTER</u> - where many records and audio-tapes can be provided to meet the needs of those students whose preferred mode of learning is auditory. For example, the <u>talking alphabet</u> stresses a psycholinguistic approach to reading in which all the senses are used: Students are introduced to a new letter in a phonics lesson, then they <u>hear</u> the name of the letter and its sound on a record, they <u>see</u> it on the card in front of them, they <u>trace</u> the shape of the letter while repeating it along with the voice on the record, and, finally, they work on a stencil which reinforces the concept being taught.

4. A <u>CREATIVE WRITING CENTER</u> - where a buddy system is ideal for enabling a slower learner to dictate his story to a faster learner, who writes it down and then reads it to the class, giving credit to the younger author. A filmstrip projection and "story starters" can be provided to help those students who find this activity difficult.

5. A <u>SCIENCE AND NUMBER CENTER</u> - can be combined so that students observe and record something, such as the number of minutes that four fish go before breathing, which the students can then graph or compute to get an average. Emphasis should be on observing, recording, and showing conclusions — not on questions with Yes-No or Right-Wrong answers.

MRS. STANBURY'S FIVE "LEARNING CENTERS" SOUND INTERESTING !! ARE THERE OTHER TYPES AS WELL ?

YES ! MANY MORE. ROBERT VOIGHT HAS IDENTIFIED NINE OTHERS, WHICH I LIKE, IN HIS USEFUL BOOK, <u>INVITATION TO LEARNING: THE LEARNING CENTER HANDBOOK.</u>

1. <u>PROJECT-ORIENTED LEARNING CENTERS</u> - provide open-ended problem(s) to students, who work them out by means of multi-level activities. It is particularly in this area that Contracting is relevant.

2. <u>PROGRAMMED LEARNING CENTERS</u> - concentrate on cognitive and psychomotor skill development; employs the use of commercially prepared kits — e.g. S.R.A. Reading and Spelling Labs.

3. <u>PROGRAMMED-PROJECT LEARNING CENTERS</u> - are a combination of #1 and #2 above. That is, a commercial kit is adapted to meet the needs and interests of individual students.

4. <u>UNIT LEARNING CENTERS</u> - are based on a central theme. An exposition is set up to attract the attention of students and stimulate inquiry. This is followed by skill-building activities which help students to acquire information and use their knowledge to develop concepts and generalizations.

5. <u>COOPERATIVE LEARNING CENTERS</u> - result from teacher and students working together to set up a learning center. An agreement is reached between teacher and student as to subject matter, time limits, evaluation techniques, etc.

6. <u>STUDENT-DESIGNED LEARNING CENTERS</u> - are designed and set up by the student; emphasis is put on his own objectives and he carries the plan forth on his own.

7. <u>SKILL DEVELOPMENT LEARNING CENTERS</u> - usually consist of a graduated set of exercises or units, related but going from simple tasks to the more complex. Skills are developed through participation and practice by the learner.

8. <u>FUN LEARNING CENTERS</u> - include games, toys, listening centers, music, drama. The task is not necessarily stated as such and the learning process is achieved through interest and discovery on the part of the student.

9. <u>COMBINATION LEARNING CENTERS</u> - are combinations of two or more of the centers previously stated.

299

I'VE GOT TO SAY, BOB, THAT YOU HAVE GOTTEN ME INTERESTED IN DESIGNING MY OWN "LEARNING CENTER" FOR USE ON PRACTICUM OR FOR WHEN I HAVE MY OWN CLASS AS A BONA FIDE TEACHER.

I, TOO, AM EXCITED ABOUT DOING THIS — ESPECIALLY AFTER SEEING HOW WELL THEY WORK IN MRS. STANBURY'S CLASS. I BELIEVE I NOW UNDERSTAND WHY TO SET THEM UP AND HOW TO INTRODUCE THEM CAUTIOUSLY SO THAT BOTH MY STUDENTS AND I CAN ADAPT TO THE "LEARNING CENTERS" APPROACH.

NOW IT IS TIME FOR OUR READERS TO FIND OUT WHAT THEY HAVE LEARNED FROM BOB AND SUE'S DISCUSSION ABOUT
(1) THE BASIC PROCEDURES (INCLUDING CAUTIONS) FOR GETTING STUDENTS AND TEACHERS TO USE "LEARNING CENTERS" PROPERLY, AND
(2) THE MAIN CHARACTERISTICS OF A "LEARNING CENTER".

AFTER THIS, YOU WILL DESIGN YOUR OWN "LEARNING CENTER" FOR USE ON PRACTICUM.

BASIC PROCEDURES FOR USING LEARNING CENTERS PROPERLY

INSTRUCTIONS:

Students working in pairs, each write down on their own Worksheet #1, all of the basic procedures and "sensible cautions" for setting up "Learning Centers" and using them properly with your students, as presented in the Rationale.
Time: 10 minutes

A. BASIC PROCEDURES (CAUTIONS) REGARDING TEACHERS

B. BASIC PROCEDURES (CAUTIONS) REGARDING STUDENTS

C. BASIC PROCEDURES (CAUTIONS) REGARDING "LEARNING ACTIVITIES"

D. BASIC PROCEDURES (CAUTIONS) REGARDING MATERIALS

QUESTIONS FOR CONSIDERATION:

1. What new procedures (or cautions) can you think of?

2. Which set of procedures above (A, B, C, D) do you think you will find most troublesome or difficult?

MAIN CHARACTERISTICS OF A LEARNING CENTER

INSTRUCTIONS:

Students, working in pairs, each write down on their own Worksheet #2, the main characteristics of a Learning Center, as presented in the Rationale.
Time: 10 minutes

MAIN CHARACTERISTICS OF A LEARNING CENTER

QUESTIONS FOR CONSIDERATION:

1. Which characteristic(s) do you consider to be most important? Did you list it (them) first?

2. What new essential characteristics did you think of?

CHAPTER 6

DEVELOPING SKILLS FOR PROMOTING YOUR STUDENTS' PERSONALITY AND SOCIAL DEVELOPMENT

A PROMOTING THE DEVELOPMENT OF NORMAL, MENTALLY HEALTHY PEOPLE

AIMS:
1. To understand nine different viewpoints about the concepts of mental health, normality and abnormality.

2. To agree on a definition for these three concepts.

3. To propose specific ways for teachers to promote the development of normal, mentally healthy people based on their understanding of what these concepts mean.

RATIONALE FOR DOING THIS ACTIVITY:

304

1. STATISTICAL POINT OF VIEW

From a statistical point of view, normality refers to what is typical of the <u>average</u> person while abnormality refers to any <u>deviation</u> from this average or norm. The bell-shaped curve below illustrates how human characteristics deviate from the norm or average for a large population of people. Normal refers to the range of deviations on either side of the norm. Thus, normal could refer to the 68% of people whose characteristics deviate 1 standard deviation on both sides of the norm (=34% + 34%), or to the 98% of the people whose characteristics deviate 2 standard deviations on both sides of the norm (=15% + 34% + 34% + 15%).

In this statistical view of normality, abnormality occurs at both extreme ends of the curve. For example, if you had all your classmates tap their index finger on their desk top as many times as each person could in one minute, a few people would tap a lot and a few would tap a little, while most people would tap with a frequency somewhere between these two extremes. A bar graph of the number of people who tapped at each frequency would look like the bell-shaped curve. Those people whose finger tapping frequency is plotted at either end of the curve would be called "abnormal finger tappers", whereas those persons in the middle range around the average or norm would be called "normal finger tappers".

If a large population of people are asked to make responses of almost any kind, the number of people who make responses at each frequency will look like the bar graph for finger tapping. That is, the population of people will be distributed in the shape of the bell-shaped curve. For example, on personality tests, on intelligence tests, and on tests of almost any human characteristic, the majority (=68%) of the people will fall in the middle range (±1 standard deviation above and below the average or norm). These people could be said to be normal on that characteristic from a statistical point of view. The people whose test scores fall at either extreme could be said to be abnormal with regard to the characteristic being measured since they have less of it compared to everyone else.

There is a problem here, however, when we talk about mental health because people who score <u>low</u> on a characteristic related to it can be said to be mentally unhealthy, but what about people who score <u>high</u> on this characteristic? They are certainly abnormal from a statistical point of view in that their score is "away from the norm" (a<u>b</u> = away from). But we would not say a person who scored extremely <u>high</u> on a measurement of self-concept or self-esteem is mentally <u>un</u>healthy. Indeed, we would expect them to be more mentally healthy than those who scored below them, even around the normal range of scores. And, we would expect those who score <u>lowest</u> to be the least mentally healthy. Thus, there is a difference between what the concepts of normal/abnormal and mental health mean from a statistical point of view.

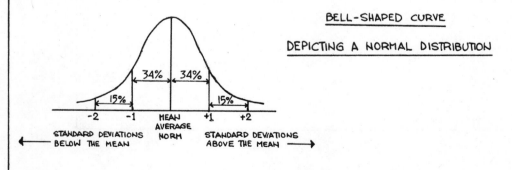

BELL-SHAPED CURVE

DEPICTING A NORMAL DISTRIBUTION

2. SOCIOLOGICAL POINT OF VIEW

Normality is not so much a matter of being around the average or norm as it is a matter of social conformity to accepted social standards. An example will illustrate this important difference. If there is no stop sign at an intersection, motorist's behavior will look like the statistician's bell-shaped curve in Figure 1 below. Some will come to a full stop, and some will continue through the intersection at the same speed. But most motorists will do neither of these extreme things—most motorists will slow down at the intersection. Without a stop sign, there is no social pressure to behave in a socially conforming manner.

But with a stop sign present to tell motorists how they ought to behave, the bell-shaped curve gets "pushed out of shape" as motorists behave in a socially acceptable manner because of the "social pressure" exerted by the stop sign. (See Figure 2). For example, 75% of the motorists will come to a full stop, while only 1% will show no social conformity at all by continuing at the same speed. This 1% could be called abnormal from a sociological view point because they do not conform to social standards at all. The two middle groups would be less normal than the 75% who displayed full social conformity by coming to a full stop. These 75% are socially normal because of their conformity to social standards.

The 1% who continue at the same speed through the intersection could be said to be mentally unhealthy in that their disobedience of social standards reflects a disregard for the well-being of other people and of themselves. These people could be said to lack a social regard for accepted social standards. In contrast, the 75% who came to a full stop would be considered by society to be socially normal and therefore, mentally healthy because they conformed to social standards or expectations. The two groups of motorists who drove very slowly or slowed down slightly could be said to fall somewhere in between the socially normal (=mentally healthy) drivers who came to a full stop and the socially abnormal (=mentally unhealthy) drivers who continued at the same speed.

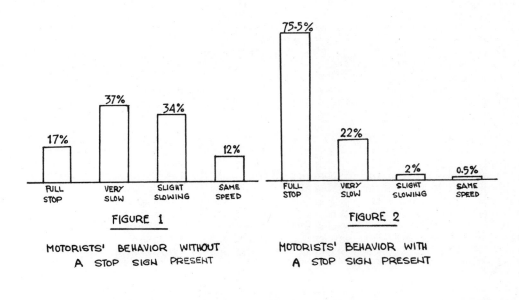

FIGURE 1

MOTORISTS' BEHAVIOR WITHOUT A STOP SIGN PRESENT

FIGURE 2

MOTORISTS' BEHAVIOR WITH A STOP SIGN PRESENT

3. <u>ANTHOPOLOGICAL POINT OF VIEW</u>

Mental health, normality, and abnormality vary enormously from one culture to another, and within the same culture from one point in time to another. This is a <u>pluralistic</u> world containing people who differ from one culture to another and even within the same culture. Therefore, there cannot be a single or universal set of human standards for all peoples everywhere. Witness the fact that when western man has imposed his values and standards on simpler societies, which were functioning alright in accordance with their cultural expectations and standards, the result has been an upsetting of their normal way of doing things.

There are cultures where it is normal (that is, culturally expected) for people to steal from one another, or to take advantage of their neighbors in order to gain esteem from other people. These examples show that what is mentally healthy differs from one culture to another according to what behavior, values, or beliefs each culture expects and encourages.

This does not mean that slavish conformity either to cultural customs and laws or to culturally derived religious moral codes results in mental health. Why not? Because man-made laws can be stupid (such as putting someone in prison for life for stealing a loaf of bread), and cultural customs can be mentally unhealthy for some people (such as enslaving other people because they are viewed as inferior or subhuman).

Even so-called God-given moral codes operating in one culture can be seen to be narrowly conceived when viewed in terms of the values and beliefs of other cultures. For example, in our Judaeo-Christian culture, we have historically believed that marriage should not be dissolved by divorce because "what God has joined together let no man put assunder." We have believed that unwanted pregnancies should not be aborted even in their early stages and that terminally ill persons should not be allowed to die naturally even if they want to because "Thou shalt not kill."

Imagine what would happen if a given culture required slavish conformity to its laws, to its customs, or to its moral (religious) codes and did not tolerate different views on these matters. There would be no changes in laws, customs, or moral codes which reflect broader viewpoints. There would be no equal rights under the law for those persons who fall outside of the normal (=cultural) mainstream, such as women and minority groups. There would be no enlightened cultural customs emerging, such as trying to end racial, religious, and sexual discrimination in people's daily relations with one another. There would be no "new morality" where people act—not simply on the basis of categorical black-or-white, right-or-wrong beliefs—but on the basis of reasoned decisions about what to do in that particular situation so that everyone benefits.

From an anthropological point of view, slavish conformity to stupid laws, to outdated cultural customs, or to unquestioned moral codes might make people culturally normal, but this does not mean that these people are necessarily mentally healthy. A person may be more mentally healthy for disobeying stupid laws, or for not adhering to harmful cultural customs, or for acting ethically as the situation warrants rather than morally on the basis of some pre-established moral code of right-and-wrong. The mentally healthy person in any culture is part of the solution to problems in that culture, while culturally normal persons simply remain a part of the problem by perpetuating what is already established. In this sense, the mentally healthy person innovates to improve the situation whereas the normal person perpetuates the cultural norm and his place in it.

4. PSYCHO-BIOLOGICAL POINT OF VIEW

There are three biological perspectives having corresponding psychological correlates from which to consider the concepts of mental health, normality, and abnormality.

First, normality is evident when an individual <u>functions efficiently psycho-biologically</u> -- i.e., when the whole human body functions in a natural, healthy way as it was designed to do, both at the physiological level and at the psychological level. There are no physical deficiencies that cause impaired mental functioning (such as happens when there is damage to cortical brain cells). And, there are no psychological impairments that cause corresponding physiological impairment (such as happens when psychological stress produces psychosomatic changes in bodily functions—e.g. ulcers). The mentally healthy person is one who functions in a healthy, natural, efficient manner, both biologically and psychologically.

Second, normality is evident when an individual makes <u>adaptations</u> which insure his survival, or the survival of the species as a whole. Darwin proposed biological adaptation—i.e., changes in biological structure and capabilities—to explain both the evolution of increasingly superior generations within a species and even the generation of new species via mutations that were superior to the existing species. Psychological adaptation occurs as an individual is acting on his environment to cope with conflicts and danger. The adaptation is psychological in that the individual is <u>learning how</u> to cope or adapt—i.e., he is "learning by adapting" (or "learning by doing" as John Dewey would say). Jean Piaget has researched the nature of this psycho-biological adaptation for almost 50 years and contends that increasingly higher levels of cognitive development result from the individual's interactions with his environment—i.e., the environment forces improvements in cognitive structures so that the individual becomes capable of higher levels of thinking. He becomes capable of considering many possible behaviors and their consequences "in his head" rather than having to actually act them out and thus becomes capable of <u>better psychological adaptations</u> than his lower animal cousins, which must act out each adaptation in a more or less trial-and-error behavioral manner. Thus, the mentally healthy person is one who is capable of considering the best plan of action at a higher psychological level and then act it out.

Third, normality also involves <u>equilibrium or balance</u>. The biological and psychological views of equilibrium are not exactly in agreement, however, and some psychologists would say they disagree drastically. For example, biological equilibrium—called <u>homeostatis</u>—involves a bodily mechanism over which a person has no control, which tries to maintain a "physiological steady state" of <u>comfort</u> (e.g. 98.6°F temperature) and <u>safety</u> (e.g. white blood cells attacking germs entering the body at a cut). Psychological research by Donald Hebb indicates that an individual cannot remain psychologically stable for long without stimulation from the environment, so perhaps there is also a "psychological steady state" of a required amount of psychological stimulation. Another psychological consideration is that a person tries to maintain a "psychological consistency" in his attitudes, in his beliefs, in his habits, and in his approach to solving problems. Sometimes, however, an inconsistency occurs between these personal characteristics—e.g. when people believe in equality yet treat some people in an inferior manner, or when they like a democratic style of leadership but cannot use it to solve problems with employees. People with many such severe "psychological inconsistencies" might be considered to be mentally unhealthy.

5. THEOLOGICAL POINT OF VIEW

Historically, it was believed that <u>neurosis</u> (which Sigmund Freud equates with abnormality) resulted from being "possessed by demons". Recovery back to normality occurred when the demon was driven out—and the demon's evil with it. Being possessed by a demon was believed to lead to "moral failure" or "wrong-doing", whereas being possessed with "Godliness" was believed to result in virtue or "right-doing".

Even today, morally good and virtuous people generally seem to be happy people because they have learned a certain degree of conformity to the Laws of God, which keeps them from becoming a "moral failure". From a traditional theological viewpoint, the question of normality has to do with being good and virtuous in accordance with God's Laws while the question of abnormality has to do with being evil, being a "moral failure" in not conforming to God's Laws.

Some contemporary theologians, however, do not subscribe to this view that normality is equated with moral conformity to God's Laws while abnormality is equated with "moral failure" and "wrong-doing" because this view is too black-or-white in categorizing people. Instead, these theologians talk about a "new morality" called "situational ethics"—which means to act in each situation on the basis of what seems <u>reasonably best</u> for everyone concerned rather than doing just what is moralistically right according to God's Law. To act in an ethical way requires the individual to think about what he is doing in each situation—to reason through the consequences of doing this or that—rather than just doing what he has always done because he was taught that it was the "right thing to do".

According to the "new morality" point of view, the mentally healthy person is someone who can analyze the traditional moral codes of right and wrong he has previously been taught in order to determine whether they are applicable to a new situation or whether he must act in a new (perhaps unconventional) way to do what is best for everyone concerned.

6. PHILOSOPHICAL POINT OF VIEW

There are too many different philosophic "schools of thought" to consider in detail here how each has relevance for understanding the concepts of mental health, normality, and abnormality. Instead, emphasis will be given to how a mentally healthy, normal individual resolves the "ethical struggle" of gaining rational control over his emotions so that an "ethical character" develops, which brings "better long-term happiness" than would result if his emotions were in control of his personality to bring about "immediate gratification".

There are three value systems from which to consider whether one's behavior is valuable in bringing about an "ethical character" and "better long-term happiness" based on rationality rather than emotionality:

1. A behavior is valuable if it is adaptive—i.e., if it enables a person or his species to survive. Three philosophical "schools of thought" are relevant here: according to Pragmatism, if a behavior works effectively, it is valuable; according to Experimentalism, there are no singularly (absolute) best ways of doing things, and thus the person will survive who tries out different behaviors; according to Utilitarianism, the behavior that results in the "greatest good for the greatest number" is valuable. All three of these philosophies emphasize the value of a behavior in ensuring survival.

2. A behavior is valuable if it is adjustive—i.e., if it increases a person's physical comfort or satisfies a basic need (e.g. hunger, thirst, sex). Philosophic Hedonism emphasizes the immediate gratification of needs ("I want what I want when I want it"), and the striving for pleasure for its own sake ("it feels good"). An important part of the "ethical struggle" is to control the emotional urge to seek immediate gratification and pleasure in order to insure that a "better happiness" occurs in the long run (i.e., in the future).

3. A behavior is valuable if it is integrative—i.e., if it enables a person to reconcile, or harmonize, or unify the conflicting demands placed upon him. This requires the highest kind of mental activity —gaining rational control over emotions—which is emphasized in the philosophic "school of thought" called Rationalism.

In sum, the mentally healthy person is the one who develops an "ethical character" in which his behavior is adaptive, adjustive, and integrative (as explained above), in bringing about happiness through the rational control of his emotions. It is normal for a person to strive for such an "ethical character" and abnormal for him not to.

7. PSYCHOANALYTICAL POINT OF VIEW

According to Freud, the two distinguishing characteristics of a normal (=mentally healthy) person is that (a) he has very little <u>general anxiety</u>, and (b) he behaves maturely in accordance with the realities of the situation (=the "reality principle") rather than immaturely in accordance with his own self-centered urge to seek immediate gratification of his needs (=the "pleasure principle").

In contrast, the abnormal (=mentally unhealthy) person is generally anxious because of a <u>repressed fear</u> acquired in his youth when he behaved so as to gain immediate gratification of his needs and was punished for doing this. This type of person Freud called <u>neurotic</u>. (He did not deal with psychotics or criminals, so his theory applies only to neurotics). According to Freud, young children have certain basic impulses (usually of a sexual or hostile nature), which cause him to engage in exploratory behavior in an effort to satisfy them (this is called the "pleasure principle"). The behavior which brings pleasure (by satisfying the basic impulse) becomes established as a "habit". However, this "habit" is often socially disapproved, and thus representatives of the child's society (e.g. parents, teachers, Scout masters) punish him so that he will learn that his behavior is socially disapproved. This results in the child becoming <u>conditioned</u> so that when he starts to do the forbidden act, the <u>fear of punishment</u> is aroused. All of this places the child in a dilemma of wanting to satisfy the original impulse, to feel physically comfortable, but hesitating to do this because of the <u>stronger</u> fear of being punished. As a means of escaping from the fear that the impulse always arouses, the child repudiates the impulse, <u>represses it</u>, denies it access to consciousness. Whenever the repression is weakened, there occurs a return of the repressed impulse, which causes the person to experience <u>general anxiety</u>. It is this general anxiety—caused by a repressed fear—which starts people behaving in a neurotic way.

According to Freud, we are never anxious about something specific, but rather we become <u>generally anxious</u> when we become conditioned to fear something specific, such as the power and authority of social agents (parents, teachers, etc.), who punish us so that we will learn not to do those forbidden acts that bring gratification of the basic impulses.

The aim of psychoanalysis is to help the neurotic person "gain insight" into those repressed impulses or motives which are causing him to experience general anxiety. "Gaining insight" means that the person becomes consciously aware of the impulses or motives he has previously repressed into unconsciousness, and thus becomes able to see that the conditioned fear associated with satisfying his impulse is no longer valid because this fear was part of his immature growth, or that there are now available to him, more mature ways of satisfying his needs while taking into account the "realities of the situation".

In sum, the normal (=mentally healthy) person has learned to overcome the urge to function in accordance with the "pleasure principle" and to function in accordance with the "reality principle" while the mentally unhealthy, abnormal neurotic has not. These two principles roughly translate as follows:

    The "Pleasure Principle"—— I want what I want when I want it.
                               (= immediate gratification)
    The "Reality Principle" —— You'll get what you get when you get it.
                               (= delayed gratification)

8. EXPERIMENTAL PSYCHOLOGIST'S POINT OF VIEW

Two aspects of experimental psychology have relevance for defining the concepts of mental health, normality, and abnormality: (1) the psychometric measurement of personality characteristics and (2) a behavioristic explanation of how people learn.

Psychometricians view mental health not as a single entity, but as a complex of personality characteristics, which can be measured to give a personality profile of a particular individual. We know that different people have different personalities. A personality profile reflects, or indicates these differences.

It is important to point out that while a personality profile is based on a quantitative measurement of each personality characteristic, the profile that results actually provides a qualitative description of how people differ from each other in the kind of personality each has (i.e., the profile describes the "qualities" constituting a person's personality). We can talk about extreme kinds of personality profiles, extreme variations on the characteristics in relation to each other, as being less mentally healthy than a profile in which the scores make sense in relation to each other.

Behavioral psychologists have demonstrated that as much as 60-70% of human learning occurs in accordance with the principle of reinforcement. As people act on (operate on) their environment to satisfy basic drives (hunger, thirst, safety), and secondary drives related to them (attention, power, earning money), the specific behavior that is effective in satisfying a drive becomes reinforced (strengthened) so that it is more likely to occur again the next time the drive requires satisfying.

Edward Thorndike called this the Law of Effect because the effects (consequences) of a behavior reinforce it; and B. F. Skinner called it operant conditioning because the operants (= behaviors operating on the environment) which satisfy basic drives become reinforced (strengthened or conditioned).

According to the principle of reinforcement, a person will learn those behaviors (bizarre or conventional or innovative) which are effective in bringing him satisfaction, comfort, or pleasure. For example, a person will learn to "clown around" if this behavior brings him attention, or he will produce high achievement in school if this behavior brings him attention. A person will throw "temper tantrums" if this behavior enables him to control others (who try to reconcile him by giving in to his demands), or he might "withdraw into himself" altogether if this behavior proves to bring him more satisfaction.

In summary, a behavioral psychologist does not really look at non-observable concepts such as mental health, normality or abnormality, but rather he looks at the behaviors which are learned as a result of the reinforcement they have received, and he looks at the reinforcers that result in these behaviors being learned because he knows that if you control the reinforcers, you can produce any kind of behavior you desire. (Skinner calls this "behavioral engineering".)

313

9. HUMANISTIC PSYCHOLOGIST'S POINT OF VIEW

It makes sense to talk about a normal, mentally healthy person not as a finished product, but rather in terms of becoming that kind of person by means of certain main capabilities which the person develops in order to actualize all of his potentialities.

To become this kind of self-actualizing person requires (a) an internal kind of motivation where you take responsibility for your own behavior and for developing your own potential through your own efforts; (b) it requires an attitude that allows you to be "open to your experiences", which means to seek out and accept new experiences which might even be discrepant with the values and viewpoints you already hold; (c) it requires the intellectual ability to question what you have previously been taught to accept as truth or fact and to propose novel alternatives which seem better suited to each situation; and (d) it requires an awareness of your feelings so that you can behave in ways that are congruent (consistent) with how you feel.

From a humanistic viewpoint, this kind of self-actualizing person is on the path to becoming mentally healthy. But this cannot be said to be normal from a statistical viewpoint in that it is not commonly done. It is normal, however, in that everyone has the potential to develop the main capabilities described above (although to different degrees), which can then help the individual strive towards actualizing all of his or her potentialities.

A person cannot become all he is capable of becoming (a) if he blames his environment for what he is rather than taking responsibility to alter his own circumstances, (b) if he rejects all values and viewpoints which are different from his own rather than trying to understand these different viewpoints and trying to accept that there will be different viewpoints, (c) if he totally accepts all he has been taught without questioning its basis or validity in fact, and if he thinks in narrow, conventional ways rather than in broader, novel ways, and (d) if he disregards his feelings and behaves in ways that result in emotional upset rather than "doing what feels right".

The self-actualizing person is in a continuous process of becoming all he or she is capable of becoming, which means that there will be continuous motivational, attitudinal, intellectual, and emotional changes in this kind of person—changes in the direction of becoming more and more mentally healthy.

BASIC DEFINITIONS PRESENTED FOR:

POINT OF VIEW	MENTAL HEALTH	NORMALITY	ABNORMALITY
1. STATISTICAL			
2. SOCIOLOGICAL			
3. ANTHROPOLOGICAL			
4. BIOLOGICAL			
5. THEOLOGICAL			
6. PHILOSOPHICAL			
7. PSYCHOANALYTICAL			
8. EXPERIMENTAL PSYCHOLOGIST'S			
9. HUMANISTIC PSYCHOLOGIST'S			
GROUP CONSENSUS DEFINITIONS (Can your Group reach Consensus?)			

WAYS OF PROMOTING THE DEVELOPMENT OF NORMAL, MENTALLY HEALTHY PEOPLE
IN SCHOOL

INSTRUCTIONS: 1. The Discussion Moderator will prepare a list of the best proposals made by his/her group (after the group has evaluated the proposals initially made). 2. The capital letters indicate Major Categories into which the proposals can be grouped which are listed beneath the heading.

A. THROUGH TEACHING METHODS

1.

2.

3.

4.

5.

B. THROUGH TEACHING/LEARNING MATERIALS

1.

2.

3.

4.

5.

C. THROUGH INTERPERSONAL RELATIONSHIPS WITH STUDENTS

1.

2.

3.

4.

5.

D. THROUGH SPECIAL LEARNING EXPERIENCES

1.

2.

3.

4.

5.

AIMS: 1. To identify the Ego States through which you express
your personality.

2. To develop skills in identifying Ego States.

3. To develop skills in analyzing transactions between
Ego States.

4. To develop skills in identifying Life Positions.

5. To learn ways of promoting constructive personality
growth in your own students.

RATIONALE FOR DOING THIS ACTIVITY:

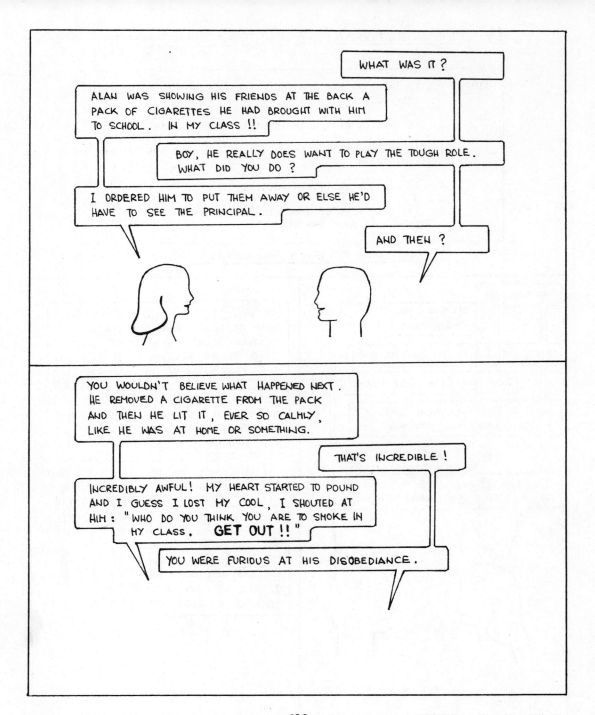

WAS I EVER. AND YOU KNOW WHAT HE DID— HE JUST SAT THERE EVER SO COOLLY AND SAID: "MAKE ME".

HE CHALLENGED YOU OPENLY.

I GUESS THAT'S WHAT IT WAS. MAN, I WAS BEGINING TO WONDER WHO WAS RUNNING THE CLASS: HIM OR ME.

UNDER THE CIRCUMSTANCES, I'M NOT SURPRISED. WHAT DID YOU DO ABOUT IT?

I SENT FOR THE PRINCIPAL AND HE CAME DOWN AND TOOK ALAN OUT. A LETTER WAS SENT TO HIS PARENTS AND IT LOOKS LIKE HE MAY GET SUSPENDED.

BUT WHAT REALLY BOTHERS ME IS I DON'T REALLY UNDERSTAND WHY HE ACTS LIKE THIS. AND I GUESS I'M A LITTLE EMBARRASSED THAT I LOST MY COOL IN FRONT OF MY CLASS. THAT'S JUST NOT ME. WHAT THE HECK WAS HE TRYING TO PROVE? WHAT DO YOU THINK ABOUT ALL THIS?

I'VE BEEN READING A BOOK CALLED GAMES STUDENTS PLAY BY KEN ERNST WHICH MIGHT EXPLAIN WHAT HAPPENED BETWEEN YOU AND ALAN. IT'S BASED ON AN APPROACH TO UNDERSTANDING PERSONALITY CALLED TRANSACTIONAL ANALYSIS (OR T.A. FOR SHORT).

WHAT IS T.A.?

TRANSACTIONAL ANALYSIS IS THE STUDY OF THE TRANSACTIONS THAT GO ON BETWEEN PEOPLE. THE FOUNDER OF THIS APPROACH TO INTERPERSONAL BEHAVIOR IS ERIC BERNE.
YOU MAY HAVE HEARD OF HIS BOOK GAMES PEOPLE PLAY OR SOME OF THE MORE RECENT BOOKS SUMMARIZING HIS THEORY: THOMAS HARRIS' I'M O.K., YOU'RE O.K. AND MURIEL JAMES' BORN TO WIN.

YES, I'VE SEEN SOME OF THEM IN THE BOOKSTORES, BUT WHAT EXACTLY IS THIS T.A. THEORY ALL ABOUT AND HOW DOES IT APPLY TO ALAN AND ME?

319

YOUR PARENT EGO STATE CONTAINS ATTITUDES AND BEHAVIORS LEARNED FROM YOUR PARENTS AND OTHER SIGNIFICANT ADULTS WHEN YOU WERE A CHILD.

THERE ARE TWO PARTS TO THE PARENT EGO STATE. WHEN YOU ARE CRITICAL, PREJUDICED OR ACT AUTHORITARIAN, THAT'S YOUR CRITICAL PARENT.

HMMM... WHEN I YELLED AT ALAN TO GET OUT OF THE ROOM, I GUESS I WAS ACTING LIKE A CRITICAL PARENT!

WE ALL DO NOW AND THEN BECAUSE EVERYBODY'S GOT A CRITICAL PARENT — THE DIFFERENCE BETWEEN PEOPLE IS ONLY ONE OF DEGREE.

I HAVE AN UNCLE YOU WOULDN'T BELIEVE. HE HAS TOO MUCH CRITICAL PARENT AS FAR AS I'M CONCERNED. HE CRITICIZES EVERYBODY ABOUT EVERYTHING — HE DRIVES MY AUNT AND EVERYONE ELSE CRAZY!

SOUNDS LIKE THE PRINCIPAL AT MY OLD SCHOOL. THE TEACHERS AND STUDENTS AVOIDED HIM LIKE THE PLAGUE. IF YOU HAVE TOO MUCH CRITICAL PARENT YOU TEND TO PLAY THE ROLE OF PERSECUTOR WITH OTHERS — A PERSECUTOR IS SOMEONE WHO FREQUENTLY BLAMES, CRITICIZES, PUNISHES, HURTS, OR IS AGGRESSIVE TOWARDS OTHERS.

I CAN SEE HOW HAVING TOO MUCH CRITICAL PARENT ISN'T GOOD. HOW ABOUT HAVING TOO LITTLE?

THAT'S A GOOD POINT. AS I SEE IT, THE CRITICAL PARENT ISN'T ALL BAD. IF ONE OF YOUR STUDENTS RUNS AFTER HIS BALL TOWARDS THE ROAD AND A CAR IS COMING, YOU YELL AT HIM. THAT'S YOUR CRITICAL PARENT. THERE JUST ISN'T TIME TO SIT DOWN AND HAVE A RATIONAL ADULT DISCUSSION ABOUT STREET SAFETY.

SOMETIMES YOUR CRITICAL PARENT CAN BE REALLY VALUABLE.

YES, IT IS NOT AN ALL OR NOTHING KIND OF THING. IN CERTAIN SITUATIONS IT IS APPROPRIATE TO USE YOUR CRITICAL PARENT, IN OTHER SITUATIONS, IT HAS A DESTRUCTIVE EFFECT ON OTHERS.

THAT'S THE CASE WITH MY UNCLE. HE'S IN HIS CRITICAL PARENT IN *EVERY* KIND OF SITUATION.

YOU MENTIONED THAT THERE WAS A SECOND PART TO THE PARENT EGO STATE?

WHEN SOMEONE IS UPSET OR NEEDS YOUR HELP AND YOU COMFORT THEM, THAT'S YOUR NURTURING PARENT. IF YOU HAVE TOO MUCH NURTURING PARENT YOU TEND TO PLAY THE ROLE OF RESCUER AND GO AROUND "SAVING" PEOPLE WHO DON'T REALLY NEED YOUR "HELP".

I KNOW SOMEONE LIKE THAT. SHE DOES EVERYTHING FOR HER DAUGHTER AND IS SO MUCH OF A "SMOTHER MOTHER" THAT IT'S JUST ENCOURAGING DEPENDENCY IN THE DAUGHTER.

PEOPLE WHO HAVE A COMPULSION TO HELP OTHERS WITH THEIR EMOTIONAL OR OTHER PROBLEMS ARE LIKE THAT TOO. IT'S NOT SO MUCH THAT THEY WANT TO HELP, THEY HAVE A COMPULSIVE NEED TO HELP, AND IT DOESN'T MATTER IF THE OTHER PERSON WANTS THE HELP OR NOT.

I THINK THERE'S A POSITIVE SIDE TO THE NURTURING PARENT THOUGH. A MOTHER LOOKING AFTER HER BABY — THAT'S THE NURTURING PARENT. AND SOME PEOPLE REALLY DO NEED COMFORTING.

I AGREE. WHETHER THE NURTURING PARENT IS USED CONSTRUCTIVELY OR DESTRUCTIVELY DEPENDS ON THE APPROPRIATENESS OF THE SITUATION. AND THAT GOES FOR ALL THE EGO STATES.

WHAT'S THE ADULT EGO STATE?

THE ADULT EGO STATE

A   ADULT

THE ADULT IS THE PART OF YOUR PERSONALITY THAT IS LIKE A COMPUTER. IT IS RATIONAL, EMOTIONLESS, AND EXPERT AT PROCESSING DATA AND SOLVING PROBLEMS. WHEN YOU PREPARE A MATH LESSON, CALCULATE THE COST OF YOUR GROCERIES, OR EXCHANGE INFORMATION WITH SOMEONE, THAT'S USING YOUR ADULT.

LET'S SEE... WHEN I WAS MORE OR LESS CALMLY GIVING INFORMATION TO YOU ABOUT MY INCIDENT WITH ALAN THAT WAS MY ADULT, RIGHT?

RIGHT! AND AS I'M GIVING INFORMATION TO YOU ON WHAT I KNOW ABOUT TA, THAT'S MY ADULT.

WHAT ARE THE POSITIVE AND NEGATIVE FEATURES OF HAVING TOO MUCH OR TOO LITTLE ADULT?

WELL, IF YOU SPEND ALL YOUR TIME IN YOUR ADULT YOU CAN REALLY BORE EVERYONE TO TEARS BECAUSE YOU NEVER LAUGH OR EXPRESS FEELINGS. HOW'D YOU LIKE TO HAVE A COMPUTER FOR A BOYFRIEND?

NO WAY! EXPRESSING FEELINGS IS A PART OF BEING ALIVE. IF YOU'VE GOT A FIXED ADULT YOU'RE NOT REALLY LIVING. ON THE OTHER HAND, IF YOU'VE GOT NO ADULT AT ALL YOU WOULDN'T KNOW HOW TO LOOK AFTER YOURSELF, TO SOLVE PROBLEMS... YOU'D BE A REAL DUMMY.

323

YOU SURE WOULD. THE ADULT IS THE "INTELLIGENT", NATURAL THINKING PART OF THE PERSONALITY. EVERYBODY NEEDS SOME OF THAT TO GET AROUND!

THAT'S FOR SURE! TELL ME ABOUT THE CHILD EGO STATE.

THERE ARE THREE PARTS TO THE CHILD EGO STATE. WHEN YOU SPONTANEOUSLY EXPRESS YOUR FEELINGS OF HAPPINESS, LOVE AND JOY, OR ACT LIKE A "BIG KID" WHO IS HAVING A GOOD TIME, THAT IS YOUR NATURAL CHILD.

THE CHILD EGO STATE

ADAPTED CHILD

AC

RC   NC

REBELLIOUS CHILD

NATURAL CHILD

THAT'S A PART OF ME THAT I REALLY VALUE. WHEN I'M WITH SOMEONE I REALLY LIKE I FEEL GOOD, AND JOKE AND FOOL AROUND JUST LIKE A KID.

THOSE GOOD FEELINGS, THAT MAKE LIFE SO WORTHWHILE, ARE LACKING IN THE PERSON WITH A VERY SMALL NATURAL CHILD.

I CAN SEE THE PROBLEM WITH SOMEONE WHO HAS TOO MUCH NATURAL CHILD — IT'S FUN BEING A BUBBLY KID, BUT NOT ALL THE TIME. IT'S IMPORTANT TO EXPRESS YOUR NATURAL CHILD IN APPROPRIATE SITUATIONS. WHAT'S THE ADAPTED CHILD?

THE ADAPTED CHILD IS THE PART OF YOU THAT COLLECTS BAD FEELINGS SUCH AS ANXIETY, OR DEPRESSION. PEOPLE WHO HAVE TOO STRONG AN ADAPTED CHILD TEND TO PLAY THE ROLE OF VICTIM WITH OTHERS. A VICTIM IS SOMEONE WHO ALWAYS GETS PERSECUTED OR NEEDS RESCUING. IF OTHERS ARE ALWAYS PUTTING YOU DOWN OR TRYING TO COMFORT YOU AND YOU FEEL DEPRESSED AND BLAME YOURSELF A LOT, YOU'RE PROBABLY PLAYING A VICTIM ROLE.

THE ADAPTED CHILD IS ALSO THE PART OF YOU THAT MANIPULATES OTHERS TO GET WHAT YOU WANT, LIKE A STUDENT WHO ACTS LIKE A "GOODY-GOODY" TO GET SPECIAL APPROVAL FROM HIS TEACHER.

I CAN SEE HOW THIS APPLIES TO ME. AFTER THE CONFLICT WITH ALAN I FELT BAD BECAUSE I LOST MY COOL IN FRONT OF THE CLASS. THAT WAS MY ADAPTED CHILD. I FELT JUST LIKE A LITTLE KID WHO HAD DONE SOMETHING BAD.

IT'S NO FUN WHEN YOUR ADAPTED CHILD IS TURNED ON. YOU FEEL LOUSY JUST LIKE YOU DID WHEN YOU WERE A LITTLE KID IN A SIMILAR KIND OF SITUATION. THE BAD FEELINGS ARE STORED UP IN THE BRAIN, LIKE ON A TAPE RECORDER. IN CERTAIN KINDS OF SITUATIONS — LIKE WHEN SOMEONE ZAPS US WITH HIS CRITICAL PARENT OR WHEN WE PUT OURSELVES DOWN WITH OUR OWN CRITICAL PARENT — THE ADAPTED CHILD BUTTON IS PUSHED AND THOSE OLD BAD FEELINGS ARE REPLAYED.

I THINK THAT'S WHAT HAPPENED TO ME. IT WAS LIKE AN INTERNAL DIALOGUE BETWEEN MY PARENT AND MY CHILD.

MY CRITICAL PARENT WAS SAYING "YOU BLEW IT" AND MY ADAPTED CHILD WAS RESPONDING "IT'S ALL MY FAULT, I'M NO GOOD".

YOU KNOW, WHEN I WAS A KID, MY PARENTS USED TO REALLY CRITICIZE ME WHENEVER I MADE A MISTAKE. AND NOW I'M SILENTLY CRITICIZING MYSELF JUST LIKE THEY USED TO!

THIS DIAGRAM SHOWS WHAT WAS HAPPENING INSIDE ME:

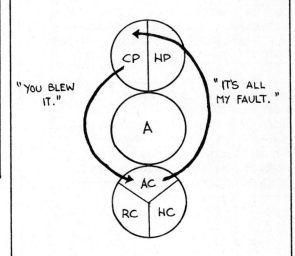

"YOU BLEW IT."

"IT'S ALL MY FAULT."

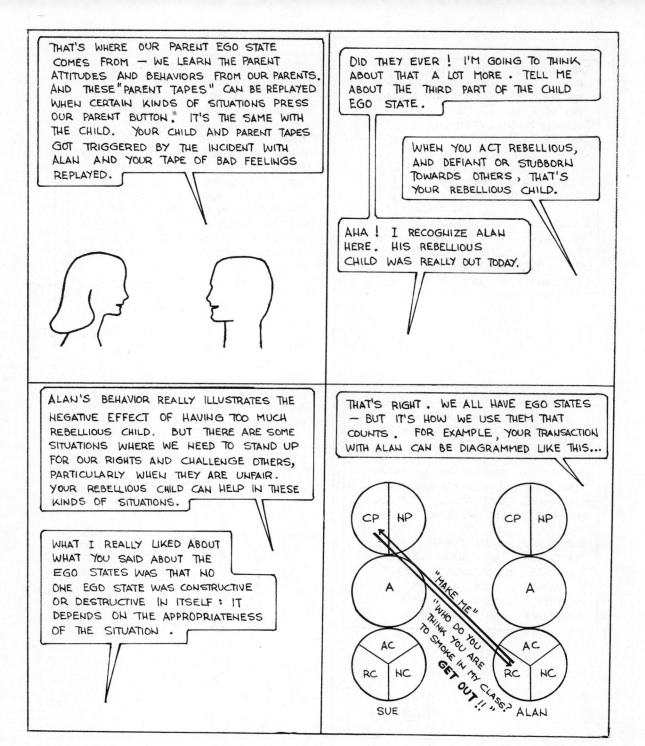

THAT'S WHERE OUR PARENT EGO STATE COMES FROM — WE LEARN THE PARENT ATTITUDES AND BEHAVIORS FROM OUR PARENTS. AND THESE "PARENT TAPES" CAN BE REPLAYED WHEN CERTAIN KINDS OF SITUATIONS PRESS OUR PARENT BUTTON. IT'S THE SAME WITH THE CHILD. YOUR CHILD AND PARENT TAPES GOT TRIGGERED BY THE INCIDENT WITH ALAN AND YOUR TAPE OF BAD FEELINGS REPLAYED.

DID THEY EVER! I'M GOING TO THINK ABOUT THAT A LOT MORE. TELL ME ABOUT THE THIRD PART OF THE CHILD EGO STATE.

WHEN YOU ACT REBELLIOUS, AND DEFIANT OR STUBBORN TOWARDS OTHERS, THAT'S YOUR REBELLIOUS CHILD.

AHA! I RECOGNIZE ALAN HERE. HIS REBELLIOUS CHILD WAS REALLY OUT TODAY.

ALAN'S BEHAVIOR REALLY ILLUSTRATES THE NEGATIVE EFFECT OF HAVING TOO MUCH REBELLIOUS CHILD. BUT THERE ARE SOME SITUATIONS WHERE WE NEED TO STAND UP FOR OUR RIGHTS AND CHALLENGE OTHERS, PARTICULARLY WHEN THEY ARE UNFAIR. YOUR REBELLIOUS CHILD CAN HELP IN THESE KINDS OF SITUATIONS.

WHAT I REALLY LIKED ABOUT WHAT YOU SAID ABOUT THE EGO STATES WAS THAT NO ONE EGO STATE WAS CONSTRUCTIVE OR DESTRUCTIVE IN ITSELF: IT DEPENDS ON THE APPROPRIATENESS OF THE SITUATION.

THAT'S RIGHT. WE ALL HAVE EGO STATES — BUT IT'S HOW WE USE THEM THAT COUNTS. FOR EXAMPLE, YOUR TRANSACTION WITH ALAN CAN BE DIAGRAMMED LIKE THIS...

CP HP / A / AC / RC NC — SUE
CP HP / A / AC RC NC — ALAN

"MAKE ME" "WHO DO YOU THINK YOU ARE TO SMOKE IN MY CLASS? GET OUT!!"

ANOTHER WAY OF LOOKING AT ALAN'S BEHAVIOR IS FROM THE POINT OF VIEW OF HIS LIFE POSITION.

LIFE POSITION? WHAT'S THAT??

YOU LIFE POSITION IS YOUR GENERAL ATTITUDE TOWARDS YOUR SELF-WORTH AND THE WORTH OF OTHERS. THERE ARE 4 BASIC LIFE POSITIONS...

THEY ARE: (1) I'M O.K. , YOU'RE O.K.
(2) I'M O.K. , YOU'RE NOT O.K.
(3) I'M NOT O.K. , YOU'RE O.K.
(4) I'M NOT O.K. , YOU'RE NOT O.K.

SO THE PERSON WHO BELIEVES "I'M O.K. , YOU'RE O.K." THINKS THAT HE IS A WORTHWHILE PERSON, AND THAT OTHERS ARE WORTHWHILE TOO?

EXACTLY. THE "I'M O.K., YOU'RE O.K." PERSON KNOWS THAT HE AND OTHERS HAVE LOTS OF FAULTS BUT HE ACCEPTS HIMSELF AND OTHERS AS HAVING WORTH...

...BEING LOVABLE!

...DESPITE HIS OR THEIR IMPERFECTIONS. THIS IS THE MOST MENTALLY HEALTHY POSITION.

THE PERSON WHO BELIEVES "I'M O.K., YOU'RE NOT O.K." THINKS THAT HE IS FAULTLESS AND THAT OTHERS ARE OF LITTLE WORTH...

...SO HE BLAMES THEM AND PUTS THEM DOWN!

THIS IS A PARANOID POSITION TAKEN BY PEOPLE WHO FEEL THAT OTHERS ARE UNFAIR AND OUT TO "GET" THEM.

BECAUSE THE "I'M O.K., YOU'RE NOT O.K." PERSON SEES OTHERS AS BEING SO UNPLEASANT AND UNWORTHY, AND HIMSELF AS BEING VIRTUOUS, HE FEELS HE HAS THE RIGHT TO BLAME AND CRITICIZE OTHERS. IN EXTREME FORM, THIS IS THE POSITION ADOPTED BY DELINQUENTS AND CRIMINALS...

...WHO FEEL THEY HAVE THE RIGHT TO PUNISH AND GET EVEN! THAT REMINDS ME A BIT OF ALAN.

THE "I'M NOT O.K., YOU'RE O.K." POSITION IS THAT TAKEN BY THE PERSON WHO THINKS HE IS "NO GOOD", "WORTHLESS", OR "BAD", COMPARED TO OTHERS WHO ARE "WORTHWHILE", "GOOD", AND "O.K."

INSTEAD OF BLAMING OTHERS, HE BLAMES HIMSELF!

329

THE "I'M NOT O.K., YOU'RE O.K." PERSON HAS VERY LOW SELF-ESTEEM, DOESN'T REALLY LIKE HIMSELF, AND IS VERY NON-ASSERTIVE.

THAT SOUNDS LIKE A VERY PASSIVE, "LOSER" POSITION.

IT IS, BUT NOT SO MUCH AS THE NEXT POSITION WHICH IS THE "I'M NOT O.K., YOU'RE NOT O.K." LIFE POSITION.

THE PERSON WHO BELIEVES THIS THINKS THAT HE IS WORTHLESS AND THAT OTHERS ARE WORTHLESS TOO.

GEE, IF I EVER FELT LIKE THAT, I'D JUST GIVE UP LIVING!

THE PEOPLE WHO THINK "I'M NOT O.K., YOU'RE NOT O.K." OFTEN DO JUST THAT. THEY FEEL THEY HAVE NO HOPE, NOTHING TO LIVE FOR, AND SOME, IN EXTREME CASES, COMMIT SUICIDE...

...OR HOMICIDE TOO, BECAUSE AFTER ALL, THEY THINK OTHERS ARE WORTHLESS TOO.

THIS SOUNDS LIKE THE MOST DISCOURAGING LIFE POSITION OF ALL.

IT IS. AND IT'S A SAD FACT OF LIFE THAT SOCIETY TENDS TO BRING PEOPLE TO THE POINT WHERE THEY DO GET SO DISCOURAGED.

ARE YOU SAYING THAT SOCIETY TEACHES PEOPLE TO TAKE THESE POSITIONS, THAT PEOPLE LEARN TO TAKE ON THESE "O.K., NOT O.K." ATTITUDES?

THAT'S RIGHT. AND IT'S MOSTLY OUR PARENTS THAT REINFORCE IN US THESE DIFFERENT LIFE POSITIONS OR ATTITUDES TOWARDS OURSELVES AND OTHERS.

330

AND IT WOULDN'T REINFORCE HIS MISTAKEN ATTITUDE — HIS LIFE POSITION THAT GUIDES MOST OF HIS ANTI-SOCIAL CLASSROOM BEHAVIOR. I THINK I'LL TRY IT!

SOUNDS GOOD! LET ME KNOW HOW IT WORKS OUT.

IN TALKING WITH BOB ABOUT T.A., SUE HAS LEARNED A USEFUL APPROACH TO UNDERSTANDING HER PERSONALITY AND HOW SHE INTERACTS WITH OTHER PEOPLE. T.A. HAS BECOME A POPULAR THEORY DUE IN LARGE PART TO THE EASE WITH WHICH PEOPLE CAN UNDERSTAND THE BASIC CONCEPTS OF PARENT, ADULT, CHILD.

IN THE FOLLOWING EXERCISES YOU WILL LEARN TO RECOGNIZE YOUR OWN AND OTHER'S EGO STATES AND YOU WILL DEVELOP AN UNDERSTANDING OF HOW THE EGO STATES AND LIFE POSITION ASPECTS OF PERSONALITY ARE FORMED AND CAN BE MODIFIED TO PROMOTE THE PERSONAL GROWTH OF YOUR STUDENTS.

EXERCISES IN SECTION "B"   WORKSHEETS

1. Identifying Ego States   Ego State Inventory

2. My Ego State   Ego State Behavior Worksheet

3. Ego State Collage

4. Analyzing Transactions Between Ego States   Transactional Analysis
                                                  Worksheet
                                                  T.A. Role Play Situation
                                                  Worksheet

5. Identifying Life Positions   Life Positions Analysis
                                              Worksheet

6. Promoting Constructive Personality Growth   Promoting Constructive
    In Your Students   Personality Growth In
                                                  Students Worksheet

EGO STATE INVENTORY

NAME OF PERSON RATED: ___YOURSELF_____

RATED BY: ___YOURSELF_____

INSTRUCTIONS: Show the extent to which you feel the person you are rating displays
each of the following characteristics by placing a check (✓) in the
appropriate column to the right.

CHARACTERISTIC	A GREAT DEAL	MODER-ATELY	MILDLY	NOT AT ALL
1. Comforts others.				
2. Does not react emotionally.				
3. Uses expressions like "Wow!", "Gosh!", "Golly!", "Gee!".				
4. Ignores the leader.				
5. Disapproves of the way others behave.				
6. Shows sympathy for others.				
7. Always disagrees.				
8. Is spontaneous with his (her) feelings.				
9. Acts shy.				
10. Likes to talk about "intellectual" things: e.g. politics, economics, current affairs.				
11. Tries to please others.				
12. Stands up for others.				
13. Is good at solving problems.				
14. Is mean to others.				
15. Always conforms to the rules.				
16. Argues with others.				
17. Laughs and jokes a lot.				
18. Gets upset easily.				
19. Is critical of others.				
20. Protects the weak.				
21. Is a clear thinker.				

334

Continued

CHARACTERISTIC	A GREAT DEAL	MODER-ATELY	MILDLY	NOT AT ALL
22. Often acts like a "big" kid.				
23. Tells others what they should, or ought to do.				
24. Acts helpless.				
25. Trusts others.				
26. Is stubborn.				
27. Often says or does silly things.				
28. Acts superior to others.				
29. Looks at the facts realistically.				
30. Is excessively polite.				
31. Likes to help others with their problems.				
32. Acts nervous.				
33. Withholds his (her) cooperation passively.				
34. Is able to see both sides of the situation.				
35. Is fun to be with.				
36. Will not do what he (she) is told.				
37. Tries to dominate others.				
38. Is very rational.				
39. Is a good person to talk to about one's personal problems.				
40. Refuses to do assigned work.				
41. Is considerate of other people's feelings.				
42. Points out others' mistakes to them.				

EGO STATE INVENTORY

NAME OF PERSON RATED: _____

RATED BY: _____

INSTRUCTIONS: Show the extent to which you feel the person you are rating displays each of the following characteristics by placing a check (✓) in the appropriate column to the right.

CHARACTERISTIC	A GREAT DEAL	MODER- ATELY	MILDLY	NOT AT ALL
1. Comforts others.				
2. Does not react emotionally.				
3. Uses expressions like "Wow!", "Gosh!", "Golly!", "Gee!".				
4. Ignores the leader.				
5. Disapproves of the way others behave.				
6. Shows sympathy for others.				
7. Always disagrees.				
8. Is spontaneous with his (her) feelings.				
9. Acts shy.				
10. Likes to talk about "intellectual" things: e.g. politics, economics, current affairs.				
11. Tries to please others.				
12. Stands up for others.				
13. Is good at solving problems.				
14. Is mean to others.				
15. Always conforms to the rules.				
16. Argues with others.				
17. Laughs and jokes a lot.				
18. Gets upset easily.				
19. Is critical of others.				
20. Protects the weak.				
21. Is a clear thinker.				

Continued

CHARACTERISTIC	A GREAT DEAL	MODER-ATELY	MILDLY	NOT AT ALL
22. Often acts like a "big" kid.				
23. Tells others what they should, or ought to do.				
24. Acts helpless.				
25. Trusts others.				
26. Is stubborn.				
27. Often says or does silly things.				
28. Acts superior to others.				
29. Looks at the facts realistically.				
30. Is excessively polite.				
31. Likes to help others with their problems.				
32. Acts nervous.				
33. Withholds his (her) cooperation passively.				
34. Is able to see both sides of the situation.				
35. Is fun to be with.				
36. Will not do what he (she) is told.				
37. Tries to dominate others.				
38. Is very rational.				
39. Is a good person to talk to about one's personal problems.				
40. Refuses to do assigned work.				
41. Is considerate of other people's feelings.				
42. Points out others' mistakes to them.				

EGO STATE INVENTORY

NAME OF PERSON RATED: _____

RATED BY: _____

INSTRUCTIONS: Show the extent to which you feel the person you are rating displays each of the following characteristics by placing a check (✓) in the appropriate column to the right.

CHARACTERISTIC	A GREAT DEAL	MODER-ATELY	MILDLY	NOT AT ALL
1. Comforts others.				
2. Does not react emotionally.				
3. Uses expressions like "Wow!", "Gosh!", "Golly!", "Gee!".				
4. Ignores the leader.				
5. Disapproves of the way others behave.				
6. Shows sympathy for others.				
7. Always disagrees.				
8. Is spontaneous with his (her) feelings.				
9. Acts shy.				
10. Likes to talk about "intellectual" things: e.g. politics, economics, current affairs.				
11. Tries to please others.				
12. Stands up for others.				
13. Is good at solving problems.				
14. Is mean to others.				
15. Always conforms to the rules.				
16. Argues with others.				
17. Laughs and jokes a lot.				
18. Gets upset easily.				
19. Is critical of others.				
20. Protects the weak.				
21. Is a clear thinker.				

Continued

CHARACTERISTIC	A GREAT DEAL	MODER- ATELY	MILDLY	NOT AT ALL
22. Often acts like a "big" kid.				
23. Tells others what they should, or ought to do.				
24. Acts helpless.				
25. Trusts others.				
26. Is stubborn.				
27. Often says or does silly things.				
28. Acts superior to others.				
29. Looks at the facts realistically.				
30. Is excessively polite.				
31. Likes to help others with their problems.				
32. Acts nervous.				
33. Withholds his (her) cooperation passively.				
34. Is able to see both sides of the situation.				
35. Is fun to be with.				
36. Will not do what he (she) is told.				
37. Tries to dominate others.				
38. Is very rational.				
39. Is a good person to talk to about one's personal problems.				
40. Refuses to do assigned work.				
41. Is considerate of other people's feelings.				
42. Points out others' mistakes to them.				

SCORING KEY FOR EGO STATE INVENTORY   <u>A</u>

<u>INSTRUCTIONS:</u>

1. For each check you have placed in the inventory, <u>circle</u> the number in the corresponding space shown on the scoring key: e.g. for item 1, if you checked "A GREAT DEAL", then circle 3 for item 1 on this sheet.

2. Total the scores for each Ego State (CP, NP, A, AC, RC, NC), and transfer these scores to the Results Sheet (on the next page).

ITEM	A GREAT DEAL	MODER-ATELY	MILDLY	NOT AT ALL	EGO STATE	ITEM	A GREAT DEAL	MODER-ATELY	MILDLY	NOT AT ALL	EGO STATE
1	3	2	1	0	NP	22	3	2	1	0	NC
2	3	2	1	0	A	23	3	2	1	0	CP
3	3	2	1	0	NC	24	3	2	1	0	AC
4	3	2	1	0	RC	25	3	2	1	0	NC
5	3	2	1	0	CP	26	3	2	1	0	RC
6	3	2	1	0	NP	27	3	2	1	0	CP
7	3	2	1	0	RC	28	3	2	1	0	CP
8	3	2	1	0	NC	29	3	2	1	0	A
9	3	2	1	0	AC	30	3	2	1	0	AC
10	3	2	1	0	A	31	3	2	1	0	NP
11	3	2	1	0	AC	32	3	2	1	0	AC
12	3	2	1	0	NP	33	3	2	1	0	RC
13	3	2	1	0	A	34	3	2	1	0	A
14	3	2	1	0	CP	35	3	2	1	0	NC
15	3	2	1	0	AC	36	3	2	1	0	RC
16	3	2	1	0	RC	37	3	2	1	0	CP
17	3	2	1	0	NC	38	3	2	1	0	A
18	3	2	1	0	AC	39	3	2	1	0	NP
19	3	2	1	0	CP	40	3	2	1	0	RC
20	3	2	1	0	NP	41	3	2	1	0	NP
21	3	2	1	0	A	42	3	2	1	0	CP

INSTRUCTIONS:

1. For each check you have placed in the inventory, circle the number in the corresponding space shown on the scoring key: e.g. for item 1, if you checked "A GREAT DEAL", then circle 3 for item 1 on this sheet.

2. Total the scores for each Ego State (CP, NP, A, AC, RC, NC), and transfer these scores to the Results Sheet (on the next page).

ITEM	A GREAT DEAL	MODER- ATELY	MILDLY	NOT AT ALL	EGO STATE	ITEM	A GREAT DEAL	MODER- ATELY	MILDLY	NOT AT ALL	EGO STATE
1	3	2	1	0	NP	22	3	2	1	0	NC
2	3	2	1	0	A	23	3	2	1	0	CP
3	3	2	1	0	NC	24	3	2	1	0	AC
4	3	2	1	0	RC	25	3	2	1	0	NC
5	3	2	1	0	CP	26	3	2	1	0	RC
6	3	2	1	0	NP	27	3	2	1	0	CP
7	3	2	1	0	RC	28	3	2	1	0	CP
8	3	2	1	0	NC	29	3	2	1	0	A
9	3	2	1	0	AC	30	3	2	1	0	AC
10	3	2	1	0	A	31	3	2	1	0	NP
11	3	2	1	0	AC	32	3	2	1	0	AC
12	3	2	1	0	NP	33	3	2	1	0	RC
13	3	2	1	0	A	34	3	2	1	0	A
14	3	2	1	0	CP	35	3	2	1	0	NC
15	3	2	1	0	AC	36	3	2	1	0	RC
16	3	2	1	0	RC	37	3	2	1	0	CP
17	3	2	1	0	NC	38	3	2	1	0	A
18	3	2	1	0	AC	39	3	2	1	0	NP
19	3	2	1	0	CP	40	3	2	1	0	RC
20	3	2	1	0	NP	41	3	2	1	0	NP
21	3	2	1	0	A	42	3	2	1	0	CP

RESULTS SHEET FOR EGO STATE INVENTORY

EGO STATE	SELF SCORE	A SCORE	B SCORE
1. Critical Parent (CP)	21	21	21
2. Nurturing Parent (NP)	21	21	21
3. Adult (A)	21	21	21
4. Adapted Child (AC)	21	21	21
5. Rebellious Child (RC)	21	21	21
6. Natural Child (NC)	21	21	21

* *

	SELF SCORE	A SCORE	B SCORE
7. Total Parent (add 1 + 2)	42	42	42
8. Total Adult (3)	21	21	21
9. Total Child (add 4 + 5 + 6)	63	63	63
10. Anger-related Ego States (add 1 + 5)	42	42	42
11. Loving-related Ego States (add 2 + 6)	42	42	42

342

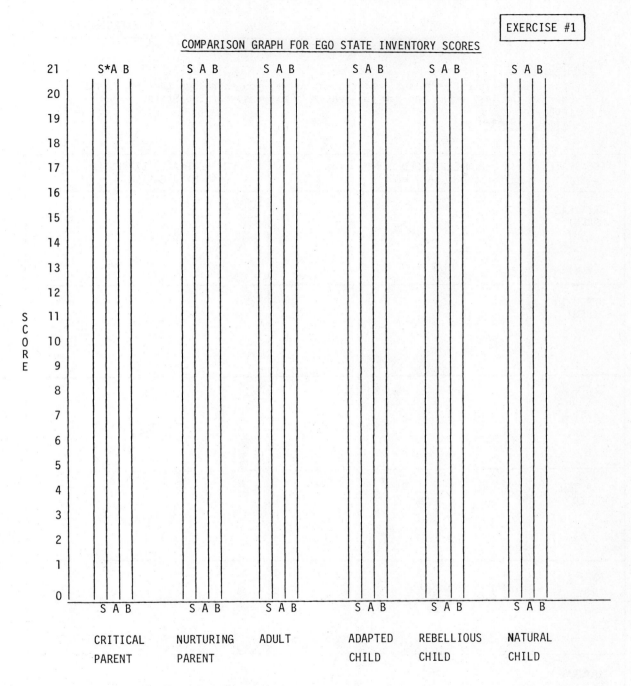

COMPARISON GRAPH FOR EGO STATE INVENTORY SCORES

EXERCISE #1

S* = Scores for yourself

343

EGO STATE BEHAVIOR WORKSHEET

INSTRUCTIONS:

For each of your Ego States, write down one way you expressed that Ego State during the last week, and how you generally express your Ego States in your behavior.
Time: 15 minutes

EGO STATE	HOW EXPRESSED DURING THE LAST WEEK	HOW GENERALLY EXPRESSED IN MY BEHAVIOR
CRITICAL PARENT		
NURTURING PARENT		
ADULT		
ADAPTED CHILD		
REBELLIOUS CHILD		
NATURAL CHILD		

344

TRANSACTIONAL ANALYSIS WORKSHEET

INSTRUCTIONS:

1. Together with your partner, discuss the dialogue in each example and try to get consensus on what transactions are occurring between the Ego States of the persons in the example.

2. When you achieve consensus, diagram the agreed upon transactions, using the Ego State diagrams provided. Example 1 has been done for you.
    Time: 15 minutes

EXAMPLE 1

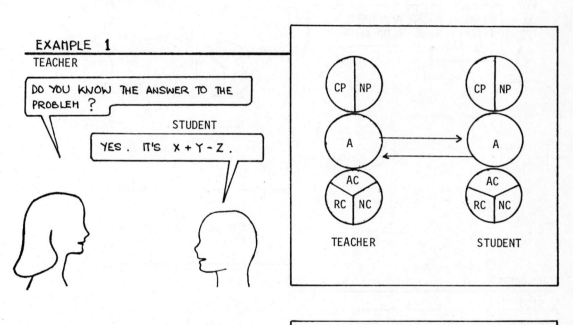

TEACHER

DO YOU KNOW THE ANSWER TO THE PROBLEM ?

STUDENT

YES. IT'S X + Y - Z.

TEACHER   STUDENT

EXAMPLE 2

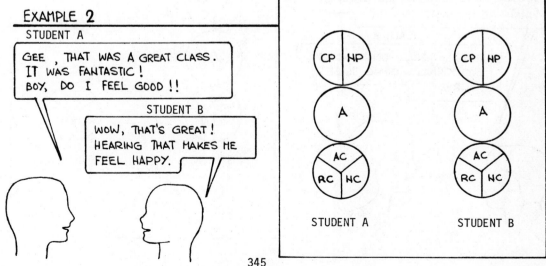

STUDENT A

GEE , THAT WAS A GREAT CLASS. IT WAS FANTASTIC! BOY, DO I FEEL GOOD !!

STUDENT B

WOW, THAT'S GREAT! HEARING THAT MAKES ME FEEL HAPPY.

STUDENT A   STUDENT B

345

EXAMPLE 3

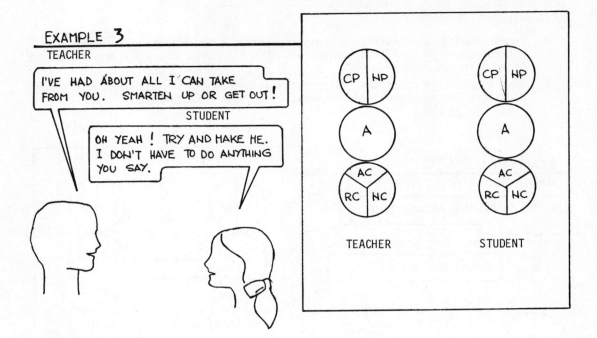

EXAMPLE 4

346

EXAMPLE 5

EXAMPLE 6

347

TA ROLE PLAY SITUATION WORKSHEET

INSTRUCTIONS:

Each pair will be assigned one of the role play situations shown below. Prepare a 1 minute role play in which you and your partner portray the roles and Ego States shown for the specified situation.

SITUATION	ROLES	EGO STATES TO BE DEMONSTRATED
1. Teacher and student discuss plans for extra-curricular activity they are all involved in (e.g. school play, track meet, etc.)	Teacher....... Student.......	Adult Adult
2. Students are planning a fun activity for the weekend; talk enthusiastically.	Student....... Student.......	Natural Child Natural Child
3. Teachers share prejudiced opinions about how irresponsible students are today.	Teacher....... Teacher.......	Critical Parent Critical Parent
4. Student A is happy, excited, wants to have fun. Student B is critical, shows disapproval of such "childishness".	Student A..... Student B.....	Natural Child Critical Parent
5. Student has lost a textbook, is upset. Teacher is consoling.	Student....... Teacher.......	Adapted Child Nurturing Parent
6. Parent is angry about son being suspended. Teacher calmly explains why.	Parent........ Teacher.......	Critical Parent Adult
7. Sponsor Teacher criticizes Student Teacher for Student Teacher's poor control during a lesson. Student Teacher is apologetic, submissive, puts self down.	Sponsor Teacher....... Student Teacher.......	Critical Parent Adapted Child
8. Student hands essay in late. Teacher is critical; student is argumentative.	Teacher....... Student.......	Critical Parent Rebellious Child
9. Student hands essay in late. Teacher is critical; student is apologetic.	Teacher....... Student.......	Critical Parent Adapted Child
10. Teacher and student both talk enthusiastically about a hobby (or activity) they both have an interest in.	Teacher....... Student.......	Natural Child Natural Child
11. Teacher and student quietly share information about a hobby (or activity) they both have an interest in.	Teacher....... Student.......	Adult Adult
12. Teacher is giving lecture on migration/minority groups. Student makes prejudiced statement.	Teacher....... Student.......	Adult Critical Parent

Continued

SITUATION	ROLES	EGO STATES TO BE DEMONSTRATED
13. Parent accuses teacher of being unfair to his/ her son (or daughter). Teacher counter-attacks by accusing the parent of being a "poor" parent.	Parent........	Critical Parent
	Teacher.......	Critical Parent
14. Teacher asks for suggestions on how to improve appearance of classroom. Student gives suggestions.	Teacher.......	Adult
	Student.......	Adult
15. Student refuses to work. Teacher criticizes student, using lots of "shoulds" and "you ought's". An argument begins.	Student.......	Rebellious Child
	Teacher.......	Critical Parent
16. University instructor is giving a lecture. Student interrupts instructor with a "question" aimed at tripping up the instructor.	Instructor....	Adult
	Student.......	Rebellious Child
17. University instructor is giving a lecture. Student puts hand up and asks a relevant question.	Instructor....	Adult
	Student.......	Adult
18. Student A and Student B are discussing politics. Student A gives Student B a put-down. Student B has a hurt look on his/her face.	Student A.....	Critical Parent
	Student B.....	Adapted child
19. Student A and Student B are discussing politics. Student A gives Student B a put-down. Student B gives Student A a put-down in return.	Student A.....	Critical Parent
	Student B.....	Critical Parent
20. Student A and Student B are discussing politics. Student A gives Student B a put-down. Student B replies: "That was a put down", or "I didn't like it when you put me down".	Student A.....	Critical Parent
	Student B.....	Adult

LIFE POSITIONS ANALYSIS WORKSHEET

EXERCISE #5

INSTRUCTIONS:

Obtain group consensus on the "answers" to the Five Questions (on the left) as they pertain to each of the Four Life Positions below. The answers for each question should apply to a student in a school situation. One person in the group should record the group's "answers" to the Five Questions on his/her Life Positions Analysis Worksheet.
Time: 35 minutes

FIVE QUESTIONS	FOUR LIFE POSITIONS			
	I'M OK YOU'RE NOT OK	I'M NOT OK YOU'RE OK	I'M NOT OK YOU'RE NOT OK	I'M OK YOU'RE OK
1. What is the student's dominant Ego State?				
2. What is the student's dominant psychological role? (Persecutor, Rescuer, Victim)				
3. What are the student's characteristic feelings? (Happy, sad, angry, etc.)				
4. What is the student's typical class-room behavior?				
5. How is the student probably treated by his parents or teachers?				

PROMOTING CONSTRUCTIVE PERSONALITY GROWTH IN STUDENTS WORKSHEET

INSTRUCTIONS:

1. In your group, "brainstorm" as many suggestions as you can to help a student with each of the three less productive Life Positions on the left change to a more productive, mentally healthy "I'm OK, You're OK" Life Position (on the right). Do not make value judgments at this time about whether the suggestions being made are "good" or "bad". One member of the group (the Recorder) should record all suggestions on his/her Worksheet.

2. Then, using the group consensus method, decide on which two suggestions are best for helping a student change from each less productive Life Position. The Recorder writes these best suggestions down.
   Time: 35 minutes

LESS PRODUCTIVE LIFE POSITIONS	WAYS A TEACHER COULD PROMOTE A MORE MENTALLY HEALTHY "I'M OK, YOU'RE OK" LIFE POSITION
I'M OK, YOU'RE NOT OK	
I'M NOT OK, YOU'RE OK	
I'M NOT OK, YOU'RE NOT OK	

AIMS: 1. To distinguish between three levels of teaching and learning.

2. To design an assignment with an emphasis on clarifying students' personal values.

RATIONALE FOR DOING THIS ACTIVITY:

353

I GOT THE IDEA FOR USING THESE THREE LEVELS IN MY TEACHING FROM A USEFUL BOOK CALLED <u>CLARIFYING VALUES THROUGH SUBJECT MATTER</u> BY HARMIN, KIRSCHENBAUM AND SIMON. THIS BOOK GIVES EXAMPLES OF HOW TO USE THESE THREE LEVELS IN EACH SUBJECT AREA AS A MEANS OF CLARIFYING STUDENTS' VALUES.

COULD YOU GIVE ME AN EXAMPLE OF HOW YOU CLARIFIED STUDENTS' VALUES?

CERTAINLY!... WE WERE STUDYING POETRY, WHICH I KNEW WAS NOT VERY WELL LIKED BY A NUMBER OF MY STUDENTS. SO, TO GET THEM INTERESTED IN STUDYING POETRY, I EMPHASIZED THE VALUES LEVEL IN SEVERAL POEMS, SUCH AS ROBERT FROST'S "THE ROAD NOT TAKEN"

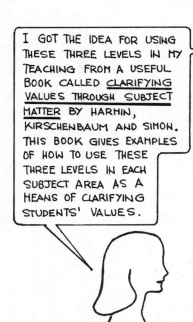

THE ROAD NOT TAKEN

Two roads diverged in a yellow wood,
And sorry I could not travel both
And be one traveler, long I stood
And looked down one as far as I could
To where it bent in the undergrowth;

Then took the other, as just as fair,
And having perhaps the better claim,
Because it was grassy and wanted wear;
Though as for that, the passing there
Had worn them really about the same,

And both that morning equally lay
In leaves no step had trodden black.
Oh, I kept the first for another day!
Yet knowing how way leads on to way,
I doubted if I should ever come back.

I shall be telling this with a sigh
Somewhere ages and ages hence:
Two roads diverged in a wood, and I —
I took the one less traveled by,
And that has made all the difference.

BOB, WHAT KIND OF FACTUAL INFORMATION QUESTIONS OR ASSIGNMENTS COULD YOU HAVE STUDENTS DO WITH FROST'S POEM?

(1) WHEN WAS THE POEM WRITTEN?
(2) MEMORIZE THE POEM.

Reprinted by permission.

From: THE POETRY OF ROBERT FROST edited by Edward Connery Lathem. Copyright 1916, © 1969 by Holt, Rinehart and Winston. Copyright 1944 by Robert Frost. Reprinted by permission of Holt, Rinehart and Winston, Publishers.

WHAT KIND OF CONCEPT OR MAIN IDEA LEVEL QUESTIONS COULD YOU ASK STUDENTS TO ANSWER?

(1) WHAT IS FROST SAYING?
(2) HOW DOES FROST'S PHILOSOPHY OF LIFE COMPARE WITH THAT OF EMERSON OR THOREAU?
(3) WHAT CONCEPTS OR IDEAS DO THESE THREE MEN SHARE IN COMMON?

BOTH THE FACTUAL AND CONCEPTUAL LEVELS ARE VERY FAMILIAR TO ME BECAUSE MY TEACHERS HAD ME ANSWER QUESTIONS AND DO ASSIGNMENTS AT THESE TWO LEVELS... BUT, TELL ME WHAT YOU HAD YOUR STUDENTS DO AT THE VALUES LEVEL.

I PUT SIX VALUES LEVEL QUESTIONS ON THE CHALKBOARD AND TOLD MY STUDENTS THAT FROST'S POEM HAS A LOT OF PERSONAL MEANING FOR THE HUMAN DILEMMA PEOPLE FACE EACH TIME THEY MUST MAKE A PERSONAL CHOICE TO DO ONE THING OR ANOTHER. I TOLD THEM THAT WE WOULD DISCUSS HOW THIS HUMAN DILEMMA PERTAINS TO US PERSONALLY... AND THAT THESE SIX QUESTIONS WOULD HELP US UNDERSTAND THIS HUMAN DILEMMA.

VALUES LEVEL QUESTIONS:

1. What was the most important choice you had to make in your life?

2. Have you ever faced a "grassy" road that wanted wear?

3. In what way(s) has one of your choices made a difference in your life?

4. Which of your choices are you most proud of? Do you have reasons?

5. Is there someone close to you who can help you make choices?

6. What forces have or do effect your decisions concerning such choices?

355

GUIDELINES FOR LEADING A
VALUES-ORIENTED DISCUSSION

1. Be accepting of what students say and don't make value judgments about it.

2. Encourage diversity of opinion.

3. Respect students' right not to participate.

4. Encourage honest/open student responses.

5. Avoid questions that require "yes-no" or "either-or" answer.

6. LISTEN!

THANK YOU, SUE FOR YOUR EXAMPLE OF HOW YOU CLARIFIED STUDENTS' PERSONAL VALUES THROUGH POETRY AND USED THE VALUES LEVEL OF TEACHING TO MOTIVATE YOUR STUDENTS TO LEARN . . . I WOULD JUST LIKE TO ADD A COMMENT ABOUT WHY IT IS IMPORTANT FOR TEACHERS TO HELP STUDENTS UNDERSTAND THEIR PERSONAL VALUES. THERE ARE THREE TRADITIONAL WAYS IN WHICH ADULTS HAVE TYPICALLY INFLUENCED THE DEVELOPMENT OF VALUES IN YOUNGER PERSONS . . .

(1) ADULTS HAVE DIRECTLY TOLD YOUNGER PERSONS WHAT VALUES THEY SHOULD HAVE BY MORALIZING, PREACHING, AND EVEN BY TEACHING . . . HOWEVER, THIS DOES NOT ALLOW A YOUNGER PERSON TO DEVELOP A PROCESS OR STRATEGY THAT CAN BE USED TO SELECT THE BEST AND TO REJECT THE WORST ELEMENTS CONTAINED IN THE VARIOUS VALUE SYSTEMS WHICH MORALIZING ADULTS HAVE URGED UPON THEM.

(2) ADULTS HAVE HAD YOUNGER PERSONS EMULATE "ACCEPTABLE" ADULT MODELS, WHOSE VALUES AND BEHAVIOR "SETS A GOOD EXAMPLE" FOR YOUNGER PERSONS TO FOLLOW . . . TODAY, HOWEVER, THERE IS LESS PUBLIC AGREEMENT ON WHICH MODEL IS A "GOOD" ONE TO EMULATE BECAUSE THERE ARE SO MANY DIFFERENT MODELS, PRESENTING CONFLICTING VALUE SYSTEMS.

(3) ADULTS HAVE ALSO INFLUENCED THE VALUES YOUNGER PERSONS ACQUIRE BY "DOING NOTHING" — THAT IS, LAISSEZ-FAIRE ADULTS HAVE SUPPLIED NO GUIDANCE AT ALL, BASED ON THE BELIEF THAT "BASICALLY GOOD" YOUNG PEOPLE COULD FORGE THEIR OWN SET OF "RIGHT VALUES" IF NOT INTERFERED WITH BY ADULTS... BUT, THIS VIEW WAS ESPOUSED BY ROUSSEAU, THE FRENCH PHILOSOPHER, AT A TIME WHEN IT MIGHT HAVE WORKED — AT A TIME WHEN THERE WAS MORE PUBLIC AGREEMENT ON "RIGHT VALUES" AND THUS FEW CONFLICTING ADULT MODELS TO CONFUSE YOUNG PEOPLE.

IN CONTRAST, WHEN ADULTS USE "VALUES CLARIFICATION" TECHNIQES, SUCH AS SUE DESCRIBED, THEY HELP YOUNG PEOPLE DEVELOP A PROCESS OR STRATEGY FOR UNDERSTANDING (1) HOW THEY LEARNED THEIR VALUES, (2) WHETHER OR NOT THEY ARE PROUD OF THEIR VALUES, AND (3) WHETHER OR NOT THEY ACT IN A WAY THAT IS CONSISTENT WITH THEIR VALUES.

IN SUM, "VALUES CLARIFICATION" TECHNIQUES ENABLE ADULTS TO AVOID THE LESS EFFECTIVE EXTREMES ADULTS HAVE TRADITIONALLY USED — THE EXTREMES OF "IMPOSING" VALUES OR "DOING NOTHING" TO GUIDE THE DEVELOPMENT OF VALUES IN YOUNG PEOPLE.

IF YOU — LIKE SUE AND BOB — WANT TO TAKE RESPONSIBILITY FOR HELPING YOUR STUDENTS DEVELOP A STRATEGY FOR UNDERSTANDING AND ACQUIRING VALUES, FOLLOW THE PROCEDURE BELOW. YOU MIGHT REFER TO <u>CLARIFYING VALUES THROUGH SUBJECT MATTER</u>, AS SUE DID — ALSO TO <u>VALUES CLARIFICATION</u> BY THE SAME AUTHORS (SIMON, HOWE, KIRCHENBAUM).

* *

<u>PROCEDURE FOR CLARIFYING STUDENTS' VALUES THROUGH SUBJECT MATTER:</u>

I. Pick a topic in a subject area in which your students seem especially <u>disinterested</u>.

II. In studying this topic, at first de-emphasize the Factual and Concept/ Main Idea levels of teaching and learning in favour of <u>initially</u> emphasizing the Values Level. (Refer to the kinds of Values Level questions Sue used). That is, use the Values Level to motivate students to learn at a Factual and Concepts/Main Idea levels.

III. Employ the "Guidelines for Leading a Values-Oriented Discussion" used by Sue to solicit student participation in the first place and then keep it at a high level.

* *

A CLASS PERIOD MIGHT BE SCHEDULED TO HELP YOU BEGIN PREPARING THIS VALUES-LEVEL ASSIGNMENT TO BE USED BY YOUR STUDENTS DURING PRACTICUM. ALSO, A CLASS PERIOD AFTER PRACTICUM MIGHT BE SCHEDULED SO THAT YOU CAN REPORT ON HOW WELL IT WORKED.

359

D   IDENTIFYING AND ELIMINATING PREJUDICE

AIMS: 1. To identify different types of prejudice.

2. To understand the destructive effects of prejudice.

3. To identify the causes of prejudice.

4. To develop classroom techniques for eliminating prejudice.

RATIONALE FOR DOING THIS ACTIVITY:

363

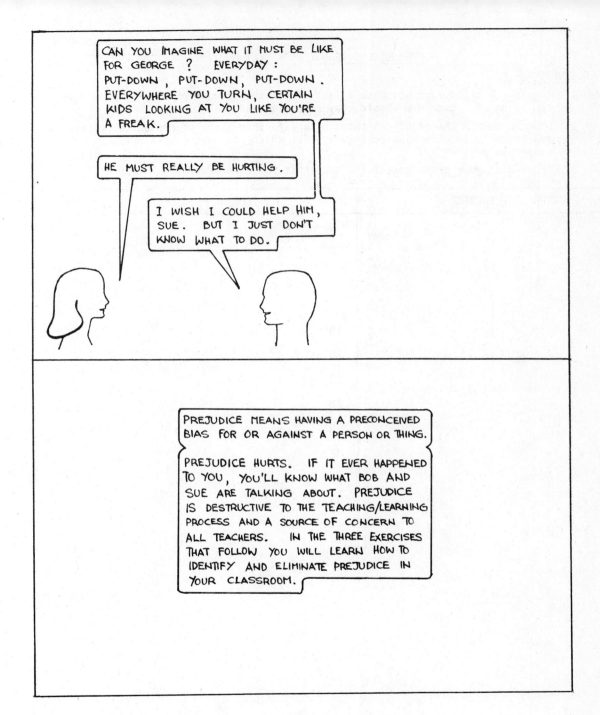

PREJUDICE CATEGORY WORKSHEET

INSTRUCTIONS:

1. Together with your group, make a list of all the categories of prejudice you can think of. Everyone should copy down the list.

2. When no one in the group can think of any further types of prejudice, circle all those types of prejudice in your list which you have experienced or witnessed personally.

3. Share with your group one of the incidents you experienced.

TYPE OF PREJUDICE	TYPE OF PREJUDICE
1.	21.
2.	22.
3.	23.
4.	24.
5.	25.
6.	26.
7.	27.
8.	28.
9.	29.
10.	30.
11.	31.
12.	32.
13.	33.
14.	34.
15.	35.
16.	36.
17.	37.
18.	38.
19.	39.
20.	40.

PREJUDICE ROLE PLAY WORKSHEET

1. Type of prejudice being role played: _____

2. Obtain group consensus on the specific situation to role play. (Start by trying to think of as many alternatives as you can, then narrow the list.) Decide on a subject for the role play (who, what, when, where), and decide on who will play what role. The space below can be used to write down simple dialogue and other ideas for the role play.

   WHO: _____

   WHAT: _____

   _____

   WHEN: _____

   WHERE: _____

SAMPLE DIALOGUE:

367

PREJUDICE ANALYSIS WORKSHEET

INSTRUCTIONS: On your own, make a list of all the causes and disadvantages of prejudice that you can think of, as they apply to society, to the prejudiced person, and to the person who is the target of prejudice.

CAUSES OF PREJUDICE	DISADVANTAGES OF PREJUDICE
1.	1.
2.	2.
3.	3.
4.	4.
5.	5.
6.	6.
7.	7.
8.	8.
9.	9.
10.	10.
11.	11.
12.	12.
13.	13.
14.	14.
15.	15.

PREJUDICE PROBLEM-SOLVING WORKSHEET

INSTRUCTIONS: One person should act as group secretary, and write down the group's consensus on the best ways to help Bob eliminate prejudice toward George in his classroom.

WAYS OF ELIMINATING PREJUDICE:

1.

2.

3.

4.

5.

6.

7.

8.

9.

10.

11.

RESEARCHING STUDENTS' SELF-IMAGE:

E

AN ASSIGNMENT FOR PRACTICUM

AIMS: 1. To develop and test hypotheses (guesses) about the effects of one of the variables--age, sex, achievement, misbehavior--on students' self-image drawings.

2. To develop an understanding of how students express their personalities in self-image drawings.

RATIONALE FOR DOING THIS ACTIVITY :

370

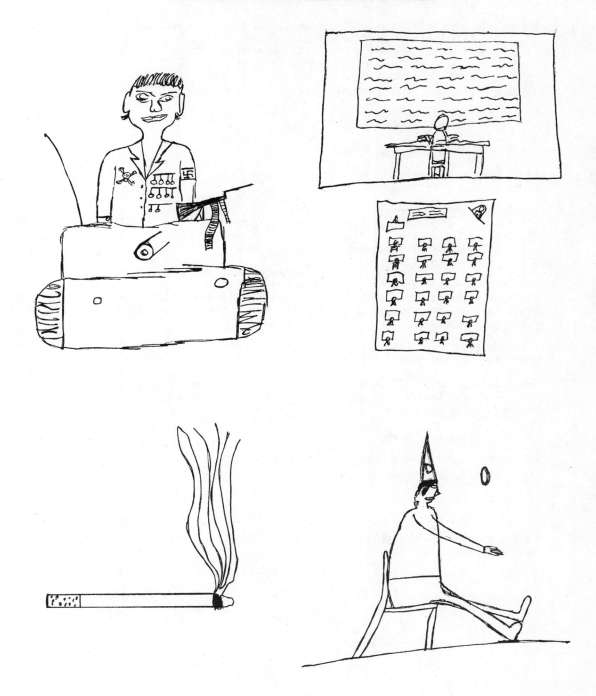

TIME REQUIRED FOR DOING THIS ACTIVITY:

> About 6 hours: 1 hour to think of hypotheses, make preparations for collecting data
> 1 hour to collect your data
> 3 hours to analyze and write up your results

> One 50 minute period following practicum

MATERIALS NEEDED:

> One or two classes of school students.
> Blank sheets of paper for each school student to draw on.

PROCEDURE: WHILE ON PRACTICUM (TO ACHIEVE AIM 1)

I. First, obtain the permission of your sponsor teacher to carry out this project.

II. Choose one of the four variables--
   1. Age (i.e. young students vs. older students).
   2. Sex (i.e. boys vs. girls).
   3. Achievement (i.e. students with good grades vs. students with poor grades.
   4. Conduct (i.e. students who are behavior problems vs. students who are well-behaved).
   and then formulate a hypothesis (or guess) about the effect that variable might have on the kinds of Self-Image Diagram your students will draw to represent themselves.

   For example: if you choose Age as the variable you wish to investigate, you make your hypothesis like this:

   Hypothesis 1: I predict that there will be a difference between the Self-Image Diagrams of older children and the Self-Image Diagrams of younger children. One difference I predict is......
   ....
   (Specify three differences you expect).

   The reason I feel there will be this difference is that........
   (Explain why you think each difference you predict will occur).

   Follow the four Guidelines for Formulating Hypotheses, presented on the next page.

   Write down your hypotheses on the Self-Image Worksheet provided.

GUIDELINES FOR FORMULATING HYPOTHESES

1. Each difference that you can predict represents a different hypothesis for investigation. Try to think of at least _three_ hypotheses to investigate.

2. _Remember:_ Think up your hypotheses and write them down _before_ you collect your data.

3. You will now be ready to gather some data in the form of Self-Image Diagrams in order to test your hypotheses. It is _not_ important that you formulate an hypothesis that is found to be correct. Accurate guesses will _not_ be marked higher than inaccurate guesses. What is important here is that you make some hypotheses before collecting your data.

4. In formulating your hypotheses, predict that there will be differences in the Self-Image Diagram in any of these areas:

   (a) in Diagram _content_ - the sorts of things used to represent the Self; e.g. animals, people, inanimate objects, etc.

   (b) in Diagram _size_ (large/small).

   (c) in Social values expressed - is the diagram of something that reflects a person with high or low self-esteem? e.g. a spider vs. a bird.

   (d) Anything else you can think of.

III. During practicum, have your students draw a Self-Image Diagram. Pick students in such a way that you have:

   A. two classes of different _age_ level (there should be at least 3 grade levels difference).

   e.g. grade 3 vs. 6
   grade 9 vs. 12

   B. The _boys_ in two classes vs. the _girls_ in the same classes. (sex variable)

   e.g. any two classes in the same grade - divide into boys vs. girls.

   C. two classes of different _achievement_ level (as measured by very high vs. very low marks).

   D. misbehaving students vs. well-behaved students.

GUIDELINES FOR WORKING WITH STUDENTS

To obtain a sample of students differing in achievement or in conduct, you can have your _sponsor teacher_ give you a list of such students, or, if you are familiar enough with the classes you are teaching, make up such a list yourself. Ideally, you will need a sample of at least _ten_ students in each category (e.g. misbehaving vs. well-behaved). Thus, it may be necessary to have two or more classes complete the Self-Image drawings to obtain an adequate sample. If you do need 2 or more classes, try to make them both of the same grade level, and have all of these students draw a Self-Image Diagram. After you have collected the drawings, you can then identify the ones that belong to the categories being investigated (e.g. high vs. low achievers). This procedure prevents students in the selected categories from being "singled out".

GUIDELINES FOR HAVING STUDENTS DRAW A SELF-IMAGE DIAGRAM

1. Give each child a blank sheet of paper, then say:

    "As part of my teacher training, I am making a collection of children's diagrams of how they see themselves. I want you to take your piece of paper and draw on it, using any kind of drawing you like, a drawing that represents you as you really feel you are."

    Stress to the students the fact that their self drawings don't have to be "mirror-like".

2. When the class members have finished their drawings, have them turn their sheets over and write on the opposite side:

    1. Their name;
    2. Their class and/or room number;
    3. Their age and sex;
    4. A brief verbal description of what it was they drew, e.g. "My picture is of a ...."
    5. The thing they like (a) best, and
                            (b) least, about what they drew.

3. Collect the Self-Image Diagrams.

N.B. Indicate that you will ensure confidentiality: The diagrams are for your private use and will not be shown to other students or teachers in the school.

IV. Write up your study using the Self-Image Worksheet provided.

SELF-IMAGE WORKSHEET

<u>INSTRUCTIONS</u>: Write up your Self-Image Project using the structured guidelines
shown below.

1. What variable (age, sex, achievement, conduct) did you choose to investigate?

2. State briefly your hypotheses and the reasons why you think your hypotheses may
be correct?

HYPOTHESIS ("One Difference I predict is....")	WHY DO YOU THINK YOUR HYPOTHESIS MIGHT BE CORRECT?
1.	
2.	
3.	

3. Describe the student sample (grade/age level, sex, ability, school, etc.) you used to test your hypotheses.

4. Analyze the diagrams you collected. <u>Examine</u> your diagrams using a simple numerical counting system to classify the diagrams. Try to see if there is a <u>pattern</u> in the diagrams that distinguishes one class (for example) from another. Do your results tend to support or to not support your hypotheses? Use the table below to show your findings.

HYPOTHESIS	WHAT EVIDENCE DID YOU FIND TO SUPPORT YOUR HYPOTHESIS?	ON THE WHOLE, IS YOUR HYPOTHESIS SUPPORTED (YES/NO)?
1.		
2.		
3.		

5. Use this page for any charts or graphs you wish to make of your results. (See your instructor for suggestions on how to do this).

6. If you found a pattern different to the one you hypothesized, <u>evaluate</u> why you think that pattern showed up.

7. If any of your results were inconclusive, indicate what you could do to clarify the problem.

CHAPTER 7

DEVELOPING SKILLS FOR MANAGING YOUR CLASSROOM ENVIRONMENT AND FOR DEVELOPING YOUR CLASSROOM PROGRAM

A COOPERATIVELY DESIGNING A VARIED CLASSROOM ENVIRONMENT

AIMS: 1. To design the internal aspects of a classroom so that it accomodates a variety of teaching/learning activities.

2. To identify advantages and disadvantages in four types of classroom design.

3. To identify problems each group experiences in co-operatively doing their design.

RATIONALE FOR DOING THIS ACTIVITY:

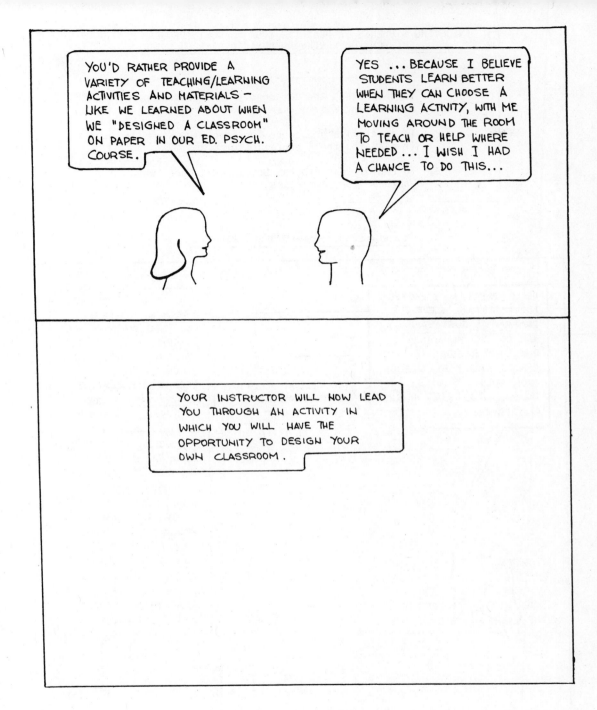

AIMS: 1. To understand the components in a Program
Development Model.

2. To identify a procedure for involving students
in planning their education program.

3. To employ this Program Development Model when
you have your own class.

RATIONALE FOR DOING THIS ACTIVITY:

WHAT IS THIS "PROGRAM DEVELOPMENT MODEL" YOU MENTIONED?

IT IS A THREE-STAGE PROCEDURE THROUGH WHICH TEACHERS CAN LEAD THEIR STUDENTS SO THAT EVERYONE IS ACTIVELY INVOLVED IN JOINTLY PLANNING THEIR PROGRAM OF STUDIES.

THE STEP-BY-STEP PROCEDURE PROVIDES THE NECESSARY STRUCTURE SO THAT BOTH TEACHERS AND STUDENTS KNOW
(a) WHERE THEY ARE GOING . . .
(b) HOW THEY ARE GOING TO GET THERE . . . AND (c) HOW THEY WILL KNOW IF THEY HAVE ARRIVED.

THIS STEP-BY-STEP PROCEDURE ALLOWS THE TEACHER TO REMAIN IN CONTROL OF THE SITUATION?

YES! THE STEP-BY-STEP PROCEDURE CONTROLS THE SITUATION FOR EVERYONE SO THAT EVERYONE KNOWS WHAT TO DO . . . AND THIS ENABLES THE TEACHER TO CONCENTRATE ON GETTING THE STUDENTS ACTIVELY INVOLVED IN PLANNING THEIR PROGRAM.

WHAT ARE THE THREE STAGES IN THIS "PROGRAM DEVELOPMENT MODEL"?

STAGE I INVOLVES IDENTIFYING AIMS . . .
STAGE II INVOLVES PROPOSING WAYS OF MEETING THE AIMS . . .
STAGE III INVOLVES EVALUATING WHETHER OR NOT STUDENTS HAVE MET OR ACHIEVED THE AIMS . . .
THERE ARE A TOTAL OF SIX STEPS INVOLVED, AS IS SHOWN IN THE "PROGRAM DEVELOPMENT MODEL" ILLUSTRATED ON THE NEXT PAGE.

THREE-STAGE "PROGRAM DEVELOPMENT MODEL" (CONSISTS OF SIX STEPS)

	STAGE I IDENTIFYING PROGRAM OBJECTIVES	STAGE II PROPOSING PROGRAM ACTIVITIES AND RESOURCES	STAGE III EVALUATING ATTAINMENT OF PROGRAM OBJECTIVES
PRODUCTION PHASE	1. Each student group brainstorms a set of possible program aims or topics to be studied and learned. These are listed on a large piece of paper and hung on the wall for all to see.	3. New student groups brainstorm a set of possible program activities and resources for achieving the program objectives identified in step 2. Hang written lists on the wall.	5. New student groups brainstorm a set of possible evaluation procedures for assessing student's attainment of the program objectives. Hang written lists on the wall.
SELECTION PHASE	2. Groups rate (1, 2, 3) each other's set of aims or topics, with the highest rated aims or topics being selected as "most important" for study. Written lists are again prepared by each group and hung on the wall.	4. Groups rate (1, 2, 3) each other's set of program activities and resources, with those receiving the highest rating being selected as the "best ones" to employ in order to achieve the program aims or topics already selected. Hang written lists on the wall.	6. Groups rate (1, 2, 3) each other's set of evaluation procedures, with those receiving highest rating being selected as the "best ones" to be used in the program. Hang written lists on the wall.

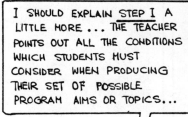

I SHOULD EXPLAIN <u>STEP I</u> A LITTLE MORE ... THE TEACHER POINTS OUT ALL THE CONDITIONS WHICH STUDENTS MUST CONSIDER WHEN PRODUCING THEIR SET OF POSSIBLE PROGRAM AIMS OR TOPICS...

CONDITIONS SUCH AS (1) THE COURSES FOR WHICH STUDENTS ARE RECEIVING CREDIT, (2) THE TIME AND RESOURCES AVAILABLE FOR ACHIEVING THE PROGRAM'S AIMS, AND (3) THE FACT THAT THE AIMS OR TOPICS FINALLY DECIDED UPON MUST REFLECT THE PREFERENCES OF ALL 55 STUDENTS AND TWO TEACHERS ABOUT WHAT "OUGHT" TO BE INCLUDED IN THE PROGRAM.

BY POINTING OUT THESE "LIMITING CONDITIONS", THE TEACHER IS PROVIDING NECESSARY GUIDANCE TO FURTHER STRUCTURE THIS GROUP DECISION-MAKING PROCEDURE ...

... AND, TO MAINTAIN CONTROL OF THE OVERALL SITUATION !

IT IS MOST IMPORTANT FOR THE TEACHER TO PROVIDE SUCH <u>HELPFUL GUIDANCE</u> — TO AVOID IMPOSING ON THE STUDENTS ONLY WHAT HE WANTS AND TO AVOID SIMPLY LETTING THE STUDENTS MAKE UNREALISTIC PROPOSALS ON THEIR OWN.

OH, I SEE ! THE TEACHER PROVIDES <u>DEMOCRATIC LEADERSHIP</u> INSTEAD OF "AUTHORITARIAN IMPOSITION" OR "LAISSEZ-FAIRE" NON-INTERVENTION !

385

386

FOUR-DAY RETREAT TO PLAN THE HUMANITIES II PROGRAM

I. **MONDAY, FEBRUARY 3, 1975**

   6:50 a.m. - Bus leaves School.

   9:30 a.m. - Group arrives at Camp, settles into cabins.

   10:30 a.m. - Meeting in Long House. Physical activities in and around the Camp. Search, scavenger hunt.

   12:30 p.m. - LUNCH!!

   1:30 p.m. - Introduction of teachers, resource and camp personnel. Explanation of what is going to happen at Camp.

   2:00 p.m. - Communications specialist leads everyone in exercises to develop communication skills.

   4:00 p.m. - Free time and possible Jog! Jog!

   5:00 p.m. - DINNER!!

   7:00 p.m. - Continuation of communication skill exercises.

   9:30 p.m. - Coffee and LIGHTS OUT!!

* *

II. **TUESDAY, FEBRUARY 4, 1975**

   7:00 a.m. - Rise and Shine!!

   8:30 a.m. - BREAKFAST!!

   9:15 a.m. - Explanation of the "Program Development Model" and how it will be used. Teachers point out conditions which will affect the decisions students are going to make. Divide students into groups of 6 each.

   9:30 a.m. - Each group discusses and makes a list of possible aims or topics they want to study in the program. Lists are displayed.

   10:15 a.m. - Each group clarifies for the other groups, any misunderstandings they might have about their set of aims or topics. (Lists displayed).

   10:30 a.m. - COFFEE BREAK and circulate studying the other groups' lists.

   11:00 a.m. - Re-convene in groups. Teachers present their views about possible program aims and topics. Each group rates each other group's list of aims or topics on a 1, 2, 3 point scale. Lists and ratings displayed.

   12:30 p.m. - LUNCH!!

   1:15 p.m. - Physical Activity

   2:30 p.m. - Aims and topics receiving a high consensus rating are discussed. New groups are formed to produce a list of possible program activities and resources to achieve selected aims and topics. Lists are displayed.

   5:00 p.m. - DINNER!!

   7:30 p.m. - Charlie Chaplin, Laurel and Hardy movies.

   9:30 p.m. - Coffee and LIGHTS OUT!!

III. WEDNESDAY, FEBRUARY 5, 1975

7:00 a.m. - Rise and Shine.

8:30 a.m. - BREAKFAST!!

9:15 a.m. - Re-convene into same groups. Teachers present their views about possible program activities and resources. Each group rates each other group's list of proposed program activities and resources on a 1, 2, 3-point scale. Lists and ratings are displayed.

9:45 a.m. - Teachers lead students in discussing the highest rated program activities and resources, which will become part of the program.

10:00 a.m. - Students are formed into new groups to generate a list of possible procedures for evaluation and a list of course requirements.

12:30 p.m. - LUNCH!!

1:30 p.m. - Physical Activity.

2:30 p.m. - Re-convene into same groups. Teachers present their views about proposed evaluation procedures and requirements. Each group rates each other group's list of proposed evaluation procedures and program requirements.

4:00 p.m. - Jobs that will need to be filled by student volunteers are outlined. Necessary program committees are formed.

5:00 p.m. - DINNER!!

8:00 p.m. - Wind-Up Group Activity: "TALENT NIGHT"

* *

IV. THURSDAY, FEBRUARY 6, 1975

7:00 a.m. - Rise and Shine.

8:30 a.m. - BREAKFAST!!

9:30 a.m. - Closing up of Camp.

1:30 p.m. - Arrive back at School.

* *

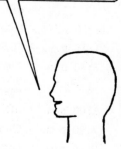

388

THE TEACHERS IN THE "HUMANITIES 11 PROGRAM" WERE ESPECIALLY PLEASED WITH THE HIGH QUALITY OF "PROGRAM REQUIREMENTS" AND "EVALUATION PROCEDURES" THEIR STUDENTS DECIDED UPON.

* *

TWELVE REQUIREMENTS DECIDED UPON DURING THE "RETREAT"

1. 80% participation at class activities (guest speakers, field trips, etc.)
2. 100% participation at P.E. activities.
3. 2 hours/week Community Involvement.
4. Compulsory attendance at teacher-run seminars.
5. Daily journal is maintained.
6. 3 Projects involving others — such as arranging speakers, field trips, seminars, etc.
7. 4 written projects — 3 showing valid research and 1 creative piece.
8. 1 non-written project.
9. 10 books read — a variety of fiction and non-fiction.
10. Presentation of their own Seminar on a topic of their choice.
11. Evaluate 5 other student's projects.
12. Final project presentation.

These minimum requirements are what is required of students to "complete" the Humanities 11 Program.

FOR EXAMPLE, IN ENGLISH AND SOCIAL STUDIES, STUDENTS AGREED TO BE EVALUATED IN EIGHT WAYS . . .

1. THEIR WRITTEN PROJECTS
2. THEIR JOURNAL
3. BOOKS READ ON READING LIST
4. A NON-WRITTEN PROJECT
5. OTHER STUDENTS' EVALUATION
6. THEIR SEMINAR PRESENTATION
7. OVERALL ATTENDANCE
8. OVERALL PARTICIPATION

BELOW IS AN EXAMPLE OF A TYPICAL WEEK'S SCHEDULE OF ACTIVITIES. EXCLUSIVE USE OF A CLASSROOM IS REQUIRED TO SCHEDULE SOME ACTIVITIES INTO LONGER-THAN-NORMAL BLOCKS OF TIME.

MONDAY	TUESDAY	WEDNESDAY	THURSDAY	FRIDAY
9:00 Hypnotist Speaker	Politics Workshop	Swimming at J.C.C.	Speakers from Jericho Hill School (for Deaf)	Large Group Accountability Session
10:00 Politics Workshop	Rabbi Hier	Student Seminar in English: "The Cinquain"	Student Seminar in Psychology: "Future Shock"	Candle Making Seminar
11:00 ↓	Karate Demonstration	↓	↓	↓
12:00				
1:00 Film & Speaker G. F. Strong Company	First Aid Speaker	Student Seminar in Social Studies: "Prejudice and You"	Law Seminar	Ice Skating
2:00 Slide Presentation on "Moulding Mankind"	"Dental Hygiene"	↓	Colour Developing: Williams Photo	Staff Meeting & Conferences With Individual Students
STUDENTS ALSO BLOCK IN 2 HOURS OF COMMUNITY INVOLVEMENT				

SUE, THIS REALLY LOOKS EXCITING — VARIED, INFORMATIVE, AND INTERESTING !! WHAT EVALUATION PROCEDURES ARE EMPLOYED ?

EVALUATION PROCEDURES

1. A weekly accountability session allows teachers and students to appraise the previous week's activities in terms of student input and participation.

2. Weekly Conferences with students on a rotating basis permits handling of individual problems and concerns.

3. Written projects receive a letter grade plus Comments from the teacher.

4. Seminar presentations are evaluated by teachers and peers after they are given.

5. Each student evaluates 5 other student projects.

6. Self-evaluations are done for each requirement.

7. Report card interviews are held between teachers and students to arrive at a "consensus grade" for each course.

THERE ARE CERTAINLY MORE FREQUENT AND MORE VARIED EVALUATION PROCEDURES USED IN THE "HUMANITIES 11 PROGRAM" THAN I'VE EVER SEEN IN ANY OTHER PROGRAM.

I CAN CERTAINLY SEE HOW THIS TYPE OF INTERDISCIPLINARY PROGRAM COULD BE COOPERATIVELY PLANNED WITH STUDENTS WHO ARE AT GRADE 4 OR 5 LEVEL UP... I'M GOING TO TRY IT WHEN I GET MY OWN CLASS BECAUSE I LIKE THE WAY STUDENTS BECOME MOTIVATED AND SELF-DISCIPLINED TO PURSUE THEIR OWN LEARNING, WITH THE TEACHER GUIDING THE WHOLE PROCESS.

YOU TOO CAN INVOLVE YOUR STUDENTS IN PLANNING THEIR EDUCATIONAL PROGRAM BY FOLLOWING THE GUIDELINES DISCUSSED ABOVE. TO HELP YOU RECALL THEM ALL, THESE GUIDELINES ARE LISTED BELOW IN OUTLINE FORM.

* *

GUIDELINES FOR INVOLVING YOUR STUDENTS IN PLANNING THEIR PROGRAM

1. Involve another teacher in the program — one with whom you can work harmoniously in this kind of program.

2. Advertise what your program will be like so that students who volunteer for it will know what they are committing themselves to (and so will their parents).

3. Involve everyone in planning the program during a tightly scheduled "retreat".

4. Prepare students for the planning task by having them (and you) develop better communication skills.

5. Follow the "Program Development Model" to provide structure for the planning task.

6. Secure a classroom for the program group's exclusive use.

7. Give students responsibility for preparing the weekly schedule of program activities.

8. Hold weekly accountability sessions to assess the program and students' contribution/participation.

9. Do not claim your program is "better than" other programs — other teachers resent this.

DEVELOPING A PROCESS-ORIENTED CURRICULUM UNIT: AN ASSIGNMENT FOR USE ON PRACTICUM

AIMS: 1. To identify the characteristics of a "process-oriented curriculum.

2. To develop a process-oriented curriculum unit for use on Practicum.

RATIONALE FOR DOING THIS ACTIVITY :

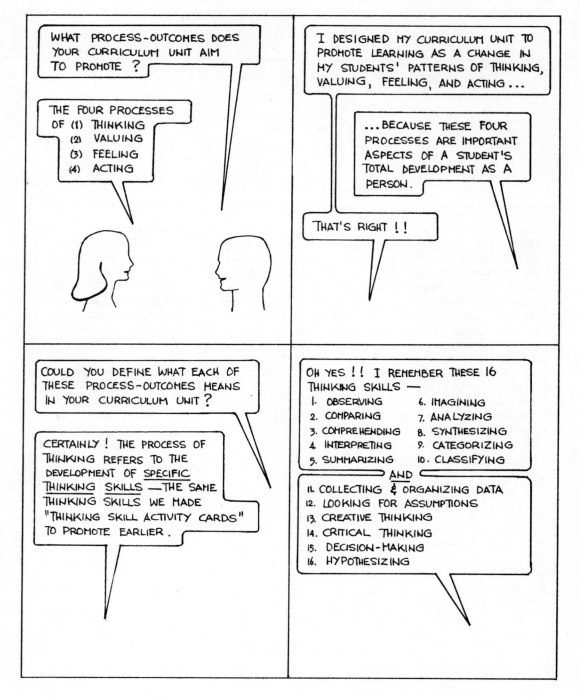

396

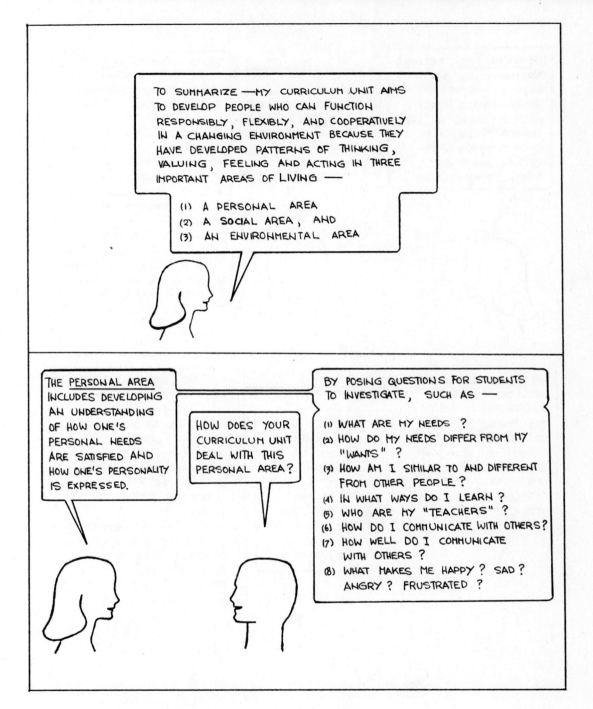

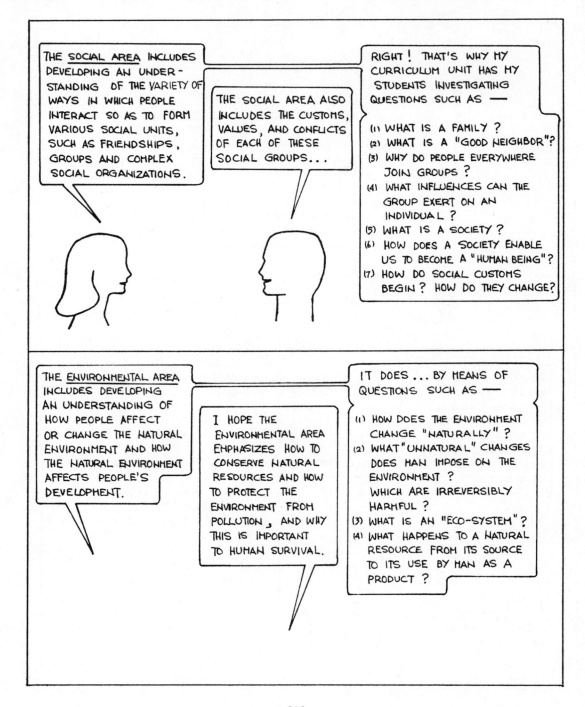

THE SOCIAL AREA INCLUDES DEVELOPING AN UNDERSTANDING OF THE VARIETY OF WAYS IN WHICH PEOPLE INTERACT SO AS TO FORM VARIOUS SOCIAL UNITS, SUCH AS FRIENDSHIPS, GROUPS AND COMPLEX SOCIAL ORGANIZATIONS.

THE SOCIAL AREA ALSO INCLUDES THE CUSTOMS, VALUES, AND CONFLICTS OF EACH OF THESE SOCIAL GROUPS...

RIGHT! THAT'S WHY MY CURRICULUM UNIT HAS MY STUDENTS INVESTIGATING QUESTIONS SUCH AS —

(1) WHAT IS A FAMILY?
(2) WHAT IS A "GOOD NEIGHBOR"?
(3) WHY DO PEOPLE EVERYWHERE JOIN GROUPS?
(4) WHAT INFLUENCES CAN THE GROUP EXERT ON AN INDIVIDUAL?
(5) WHAT IS A SOCIETY?
(6) HOW DOES A SOCIETY ENABLE US TO BECOME A "HUMAN BEING"?
(7) HOW DO SOCIAL CUSTOMS BEGIN? HOW DO THEY CHANGE?

THE ENVIRONMENTAL AREA INCLUDES DEVELOPING AN UNDERSTANDING OF HOW PEOPLE AFFECT OR CHANGE THE NATURAL ENVIRONMENT AND HOW THE NATURAL ENVIRONMENT AFFECTS PEOPLE'S DEVELOPMENT.

I HOPE THE ENVIRONMENTAL AREA EMPHASIZES HOW TO CONSERVE NATURAL RESOURCES AND HOW TO PROTECT THE ENVIRONMENT FROM POLLUTION, AND WHY THIS IS IMPORTANT TO HUMAN SURVIVAL.

IT DOES ... BY MEANS OF QUESTIONS SUCH AS —

(1) HOW DOES THE ENVIRONMENT CHANGE "NATURALLY"?
(2) WHAT "UNNATURAL" CHANGES DOES MAN IMPOSE ON THE ENVIRONMENT? WHICH ARE IRREVERSIBLY HARMFUL?
(3) WHAT IS AN "ECO-SYSTEM"?
(4) WHAT HAPPENS TO A NATURAL RESOURCE FROM ITS SOURCE TO ITS USE BY MAN AS A PRODUCT?

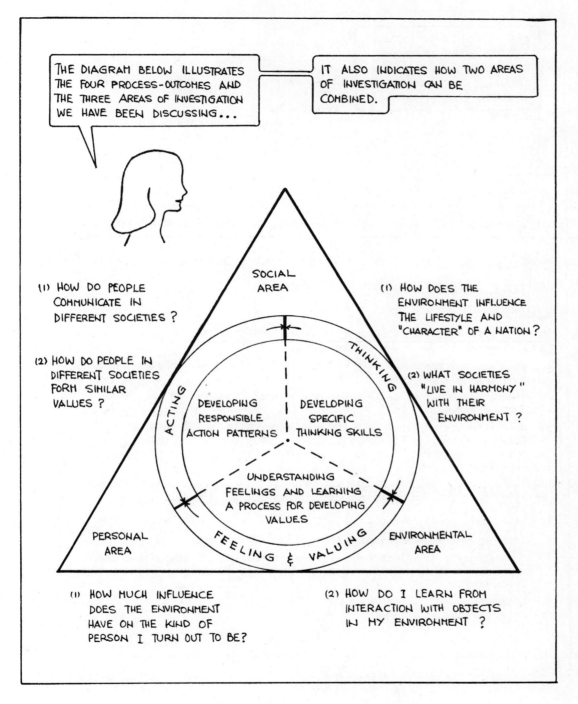

BOB, HERE IS THE OUTLINE FOR THE SEVEN-COMPONENT PROCEDURE I FOLLOWED IN PREPARING MY PROCESS-ORIENTED CURRICULUM UNIT

SEVEN COMPONENT PROCEDURE FOR PREPARING A PROCESS-ORIENTED CURRICULUM UNIT

I. BROAD FOCUS QUESTION: How and why did Canada's System of Law and Order Develop?

II. AREA(S) OF INVESTIGATION: SOCIAL/PERSONAL AREAS

III. DURATION OF UNIT: 6 weeks

IV. SPECIFIC QUESTIONS (AND TIME ALLOTTED FOR INVESTIGATION):
(Some examples for each day of the unit).

1. What law enforcement system existed before the Royal Canadian Mounted Police (RCMP) was formed? (Days 1 and 2).

2. What are the duties of the RCMP now? Then? Compared to policemen? (Days 3 and 4).

3. What were the original laws the RCMP were called on to enforce? (Days 5, 6, 7).

4. Etcetera

V. CORRESPONDING TEACHING/LEARNING ACTIVITIES AND RESOURCES:
(Employed to enable students to answer each Specific Question above).

1. Do a small group research project on Canada's law enforcement systems.

2. Visit a RCMP detachment post to find out RCMP duties.

3. Have students do silent role plays of the early RCMP stopping crimes against Canada's early laws and let the class identify which laws were being broken.

4. Etcetera

Continued

VI.   CORRESPONDING PROCESS-OUTCOMES: (Indicate the type: Thinking (T),
                                                Feeling (F), Valuing (V), and Acting (A))
      (Promoted by each Teaching/Learning Activity above).

      1. (a) Choosing appropriate research material and organizing the information
               it contains into a report (T).

          (b) Producing a report in which the group takes pride. (A & V).

          (c) Developing respect for each group member's contribution. (V).

      2. (a) Behaving responsibly while on a field trip. (A).

          (b) Developing a more positive view of the RCMP. (V).

          (c) Categorizing types of RCMP duties. (T).

      3. (a) Creatively portraying the breaking of early laws. (T & A).

          (b) Appreciating the need for law enforcement (V).

      4. Etcetera

VII. EVALUATION OF STUDENTS' LEARNING (i.e., attainment of process-oriented
                                              outcomes above)

      1. At the beginning of a unit —e.g. diagnostic test of student's knowledge
          of early laws and duties of RCMP, and survey of their attitudes
          towards the RCMP.

      2. During the unit —e.g. check on problems students have doing the
          research project and the role play.

      3. At the end of the unit —e.g. repeat test of students' knowledge of early
          laws and duties, and the survey of their attitudes towards the
          RCMP. (Differences Indicate the promotion of T/F/V/A outcomes in
          students).

NOTE: The number 1 in Component IV corresponds to the number 1 in
        Components V and VI. Similarly, the number 2 in Component IV
        corresponds to the number 2 in Components V and VI (likewise
        for number 3). This correspondence in these numbers reflects
        the correspondence between Process-Outcomes being promoted
        by particular Teaching/Learning Activities and Resources,
        which are related to a Specific Question being investigated
        in the Curriculum Unit.

THANK YOU, SUE, FOR EXPLAINING ALL SEVEN COMPONENTS IN YOUR PROCESS-ORIENTED CURRICULUM UNIT. YOUR EXAMPLE HAS GIVEN US AN EVEN CLEARER IDEA OF HOW A PROCESS-ORIENTED CURRICULUM UNIT DIFFERS FROM THE CONTENT-ORIENTED CURRICULUM UNITS WE ARE QUITE FAMILIAR WITH — BOTH AS STUDENTS, WHO HAVE HAD TO LEARN STRAIGHT SUBJECT MATTER CONTENT, AND AS TEACHERS, WHO HAVE TAUGHT IT.

NOW IT IS TIME FOR THE STUDENTS READING THIS TEXTBOOK TO PREPARE THEIR OWN PROCESS-ORIENTED CURRICULUM UNIT BY FOLLOWING YOUR SEVEN COMPONENT EXAMPLE ABOVE.

* *

TIME REQUIRED FOR DOING THIS ACTIVITY:

Varies depending on length and complexity of the unit. (If it is started during class time, the instructor or other students can provide assistance to enable you to complete it at home).

MATERIALS NEEDED:

Paper; Seven-Component Procedure For Preparing a Process-Oriented Curriculum Unit (in Rationale above).

PROCEDURE:

STUDENTS MIGHT WANT TO PREPARE
THEIR PROCESS-ORIENTED CURRICULUM
UNIT IN <u>PAIRS</u>. PREPARATION
SHOULD START <u>IN CLASS</u> SO THAT
THE INSTRUCTOR CAN PROVIDE ASSISTANCE.
A <u>BLANK</u> <u>WORKSHEET</u>, LIKE THE KIND
<u>SUE</u> USED, IS PROVIDED AFTER THE
PROCEDURE FOR STUDENTS TO USE AS
THEY FOLLOW EACH OF THE SEVEN STEPS
DESCRIBED BELOW.

I. <u>Pose a broadly stated question</u> to focus the topic to be investigated by your students.

II. <u>Identify the area(s) of investigation</u>: Personal, Social, Environmental (or combinations of two of them).

III. <u>State the anticipated length of time</u> required for students to do the unit.

IV. <u>Pose more specific questions</u> for student investigation. (These questions should be related to the Broad Focus Question). Indicate the number of class periods or days that will be available for students to investigate each question. (This is essential in <u>scheduling</u> the Teaching/Learning Activities and Resources to be employed).

V. <u>Specify the Teaching/Learning Activities and Resources</u> which must be employed to enable students to investigate <u>each</u> Specific Question. (This requires <u>relating</u> the Teaching/Learning Activities and Resources to the corresponding question in order that it can be investigated adequately).

VI. <u>Specify the Process-Outcomes</u> which will be promoted by each Teaching/Learning Activity and Resource. (Beside each Process-Outcome, indicate with the letters T, F, V, A, the <u>type</u> of Process-Outcome being promoted — i.e., Thinking, Feeling, Valuing, Acting).

VII. Indicate how you will assess your students' attainment or learning of each type of Process-Outcome identified in Step VI. (This assessment should be done <u>at the begining</u> of the unit to provide diagnostic information which enables you to plan how to start your unit and what T/F/V/A outcomes most need developing. Assessment <u>during the unit</u> will enable you to identify organizational and learning problems, which you can correct so that the unit can proceed and students can learn. Assessment <u>at the end</u> of the unit will enable you to determine how effectively the unit promoted the development of T/F/V/A outcomes specified in Step VI.

VIII. Another one or two class periods could be scheduled later for student teachers to describe (show) their process-oriented curriculum unit to the class and explain how it will be used by their students during practicum. This would also enable them to obtain feedback on ways of improving their unit or its use by students in school.

I. BROAD FOCUS QUESTION:

II. AREA(S) OF INVESTIGATION:

III. DURATION OF UNIT:

IV. SPECIFIC QUESTIONS (AND TIME ALLOTTED FOR INVESTIGATION):

V. CORRESPONDING TEACHING/LEARNING ACTIVITIES AND RESOURCES:

VI. <u>CORRESPONDING PROCESS-OUTCOMES</u>: (Indicate type - T/F/V/A - for each outcome)

VII. <u>EVALUATION OF STUDENTS' LEARNING</u>:

    1. <u>At the Beginning</u>:

    2. <u>During the Unit</u>:

    3. <u>At the End of the Unit</u>:

CHAPTER I: WHAT THIS BOOK IS ALL ABOUT

Coleman, J. S., Livingston, S. A., Fennessey, G. M., Edwards, K. J., and Kidder, S. J. The Hopkins Games Program: Conclusions From Seven Years of Research. Educational Researcher, Vol. 2, No. 8, August 1973, 3-7.

Good, T. L., Coop, R., Dembo, M., Denton, J. and Limbacher, P. How Teachers View Accountability. Phi Delta Kappan, Vol. LVI, No. 5., January 1975, 367-368.

Jenkins, Joseph R., and Bausell, R. Barker. How Teachers View The Effective Teacher: Student Learning Is Not The Top Criterion. Phi Delta Kappan, Vol. LV, No. 8, April 1974, 572-573.

Johnson, Henry C., Jr. Court, Craft and Competence: A Reexamination of "Teacher Evaluation" Procedures. Phi Delta Kappan, Vo. 57, No. 9, May 1976, 606-610.

Mitzell, Harold E. Teacher Effectiveness. In C. W. Harris (Ed.), Encyclopedia of Educational Research. New York: Macmillan, 1960 (Third Edition).

Sybonts, Ward. Performance-Based Teacher Education: Does It Make A Difference? Phi Delta Kappan, Vol. LIV, No. 5, January 1973, 303-304.

Westbrook, Douglas C. and Sandefur, Walter. Involvement of AACTE Institutions in CBTE Programs. Phi Delta Kappan, Vol. 57, No. 4, December 1975, 276-278.

CHAPTER II: DEVELOPING COMPETENCIES FOR COMMUNICATING MORE EFFECTIVELY

Counselor's Resource Book For Groups In Guidance, Grades 7-12. Winnipeg, Manitoba: Department of Education, Student Personnel Services, 1972.

Gazda, George M. Systematic Human Relations Training in Teacher Preparation and Inservice Education. Journal of Research and Development in Education, 4, No. 2 (1971), 47-51.

Gazda, George M. Human Relations Development: A Manual for Educators. Boston: Allyn and Bacon, Inc., 1975.

Gordon, Thomas. T.E.T.: Teacher Effectiveness Training. New York: Peter H. Wyden, 1974, (Chapters 1-5).

Hall, Jay. Decisions, Decisions, Decisions. Psychology Today, November 1971, 51-54f.

Hunter, Elizabeth. Encounter In The Classroom: New Ways of Teaching. New York: Holt, Rinehart and Winston, 1972.

Pfeiffer, J. W. and Jones, John E. A Handbook of Structured Experiences For Human Relations Training (Vol. I, II, III, IV). Lajolla, California: University Associates, 1969, 1970, 1971, 1972.

Pietsch, William V. Human BE-ing: How To Have a Creative Relationship Instead of a Power Struggle. New York: New American Library, 1974.

Purkey, W. W. The Task of the Teacher. In Altmann, H. (Ed.), Readings in Human Relationships. Berkeley: McCutchan, 1972, pp. 189-209.

CHAPTER III: DEVELOPING COMPETENCIES FOR MOTIVATING YOUR STUDENTS IN NEW WAYS

Glasser, William. _Schools Without Failure_. New York: Harper and Row, 1969

Glasser, William. _The Identity Society_. New York: Harper and Row, 1972.

Goldhammer, Robert. _Clinical Supervision: Special Methods for the Supervision of Teachers_. New York: Holt, Rinehart and Winston, 1969.

Maslow, Abraham H. _Motivation and Personality_. New York: Harper and Row, 1954.

CHAPTER IV: DEVELOPING COMPETENCIES FOR USING HUMANISTIC DISCIPLINE TECHNIQUES

Asselin, Cheryl, Nelson, Tom, and Platt, John. _Teacher Study Group Leader's Manual_. Chicago: Alfred Adler Institute of Chicago, 1975.

Dreikurs, Rudolf. _Psychology in the Classroom_. New York: Harper & Row, 1968.

Dreikurs, Rudolf and Cassel, Pearl. _Discipline Without Tears_. New York: Hawthorn Book, Inc., 1972.

Dreikurs, Rudolf, Grunwald, Bernice, and Pepper, Floy. _Maintaining Sanity in the Classroom_. New York: Harper & Row, 1971.

Glasser, William. _Reality Therapy: A New Approach to Psychiatry_. New York: Harper and Row, 1965.

Gordon, Thomas. _P.E.T.: Parent Effectiveness Training_. New York: Peter H. Wyden, 1970.

Gordon, Thomas. _T.E.T.: Teacher Effectiveness Training_. New York: Peter H. Wyden, 1974.

Madsen, C.K., and Madsen, C. H.   _Teaching/Discipline: Behavioral Principles Toward a Positive Approach_. Boston: Allyn and Bacon, 1970.

CHAPTER V: DEVELOPING COMPETENCIES FOR PROMOTING AND ASSESSING YOUR STUDENTS' LEARNING
AND COGNITIVE DEVELOPMENT

Adams, James. _Conceptual Blockbusting: A Guide To Better Ideas_. San Francisco: W. H. Freeman and Co., 1974.

Bigge, Morris L.   _Learning Theories For Teachers_. New York: Harper and Row, 1971, (Second Edition).

Bloom, B.S., Engelhart, M. D., Furst, E. J., Hill, W. H., and Krathwohl, D. R. _Taxonomy of Educational Objectives, Handbook I: Cognitive Domain_. New York: David McKay Company, 1956.

Glasser, Joyce. _The Elementary School Learning Center For Independent Study_. West Nyack, N.Y.: Parker Publishing Co., 1974.

Kirschenbaum, Howard, Simon, Sidney, and Napier, Rodney. _Wad-Ja-Get? The Grading Game in American Education_. New York: Hart, 1971.

CHAPTER V: Continued

CHAPTER V: DEVELOPING COMPETENCIES FOR PROMOTING AND ASSESSING YOUR STUDENTS' LEARNING
AND COGNITIVE DEVELOPMENT

Neisworth, John T.   The Educational Irrelevance of Intelligence. In R. M. Smith
(Ed.), Teacher Diagnosis of Educational Difficulties. Columbus, Ohio: Charles
E. Merrill Company, 1969. pp. 30-46.

Raths, L. E., Wasserman, S., Jonas, A., and Rothstein, A. M.   Teaching for Thinking:
Theory And Application. Columbus, Ohio: Charles E. Merrill Publishing Co.,
1967.

Rosenberg, Marshall B.   Diagnostic Teaching. Seattle, Washington: Special Child
Publications, 1968.

Spears, Harold. Kappans Ponder The Goals Of Education. Phi Delta Kappan, Vol. LV,
No. 1, September 1973, 29-32.

Tyler, Ralph W.   Basic Principles of Curriculum and Instruction. Chicago:
University of Chicago Press, 1949.

Voight, Ralph G.   Invitation to Learning: The Learning Center Handbook. Washington,
D. C.: Acropolis Books Ltd., 1971.

CHAPTER VI: DEVELOPING COMPETENCIES FOR PROMOTING YOUR STUDENTS' PERSONALITY AND
SOCIAL DEVELOPMENT

Berne, Eric. Games People Play. New York: Grove Press, Inc. 1964

Ernst, Ken. Games Students Play. Millbrae, California: Celestial Arts Publishing,
1972.

Freed, Alvyn M.   TA for Kids. Los Angeles: Jalmar Press, Inc., 1971.

Freed, Alvyn M.   TA for Tots. Los Angeles: Jalmar Press, Inc., 1973.

James, Muriel and Jongeward, Dorothy. Born to Win: Transactional Analysis with
Gestalt Experiements. Reading, Massachusetts: Addison-Wesley, 1973.

Harmin, M., Kirschenbaum, H., and Simon, S. B.   Clarifying Values Through Subject
Matter. Toronto: Holt, Rinehart and Winston of Canada, Ltd., 1973.

Mowren, O. H.   What is Normal Behavior? In Walter D. Nunokawa (Ed.), Human Values
and Abnormal Behavior. Glenview, Illinois: Scott, Foresman and Company,
1965, pp. 10-31.

Torrance, E. Paul. Mental Health and Constructive Behavior. Belmont, Calif.:
Wadsworth Publishing Co., 1965.

Simon, Sidney, Howe, Leland, and Kirschenbaum, Howard. Values Clarification: A
Handbook of Practical Strategies for Teachers and Students. New York: Hart,
1972.

Brissey, F. Lee, and Nagle, John M. The Consultants Manual For A Systematic
Approach to Joint Problem-Solving. Vancouver, B. C.: University of British
Columbia, Center for the Study of Educational Administration.

1975 Curriculum For Primary Schools: Social Studies Guidelines. Sydney,
Australia: New South Wales Department of Education, 1975.

Gordon, Thomas. T.E.T.: Teacher Effectiveness Training (Chapter VI). New York:
Peter H. Wyden Publisher, 1974.

Joyce, Bruce R.   Alternative Models of Elementary Education. Toronto: Blaisdell
Publishing Co., 1969.

WE RECOMMEND THESE REFERENCES BECAUSE WE HAVE FOUND THEM
TO BE ESPECIALLY USEFUL TO US — SOME ARE PRACTICAL AND
THUS HAVE HELPED US TO MAKE OUR TEACHING MORE PRACTICAL,
SOME ARE THEORETICAL AND HAVE HELPED US TO CONCEPTUALIZE
WHY WE TEACH AS WE DO.   WE HOPE YOU WILL FIND THEM
HELPFUL TO YOU IN YOUR TEACHING.